"One of the challenges of researching the cultural and creative industries is recognizing the relative newness of the fields of inquiry, while avoiding the traps of advocacy without rigor on the one hand, and critique without policy guidance on the other. With *Researching the Creative and Cultural Industries*, Simone Wesner has identified the ways in which theories, methods and practical skills can be combined in what is a burgeoning research field."

Terry Flew, *Professor of Digital Communication and Culture, The University of Sydney, Australia*

"This is a unique and comprehensive textbook on research practice in the field of creative and cultural industries. It sets out the entire spectrum of relevant methods and research procedures – from humanities and social science research, analysis and interpretation, to data collation and to ethics. It does this in as succinct and cohesive way as possible, making the book useful for a speedy consultation on a specific method, or as a general companion for professional research practice, essay or report writing, or project design – by student, consultant or academic professional. Its synthesis of a huge breadth of research practice contributes to the field-building of our unique and dynamic inter-disciplinary field, 'creative and cultural industries'. It will be a fundamental text for any course or professional project involving research."

Jonathan Vickery, *Associate Professor and Course Director, MA Arts Enterprise and Development, University of Warwick, UK*

RESEARCHING THE CREATIVE AND CULTURAL INDUSTRIES

Research into creative and cultural organisations has proliferated, benefitting from insights from a range of disciplinary perspectives. Starting a research journey can be daunting in such a diverse field. This book provides expert insights into research process and practice, with a qualitative focus.

The book helps readers to plan, execute, and analyse research, turning their work into data, results, and new knowledge. Taking an individual perspective, the author addresses a trio of paradigms, methodologies, and methods, and applies them to the whole research process, from start to finish. The book seamlessly links theoretical and conceptual aspects with best research practice along the way.

A book for researchers at all stages of their work, the resources are also valuable for students and reflective cultural practitioners who want to know how to plan, implement, and evaluate their research project.

Simone Wesner is Senior Lecturer in Cultural Policy and Arts Management at Birkbeck, University of London, UK.

ROUTLEDGE RESEARCH IN THE CREATIVE AND CULTURAL INDUSTRIES

This series brings together book-length original research in cultural and creative industries from a range of perspectives. Charting developments in contemporary cultural and creative industries thinking around the world, the series aims to shape the research agenda to reflect the expanding significance of the creative sector in a globalised world.

Creative Work
Conditions, Contexts and Practices
Edited by Erika Andersson Cederholm, Katja Lindqvist, Ida de Wit Sandström and Philip Warkander

Data-Driven Innovation in the Creative Industries
Edited by Melissa Terras, Vikki Jones, Nicola Osborne and Chris Speed

The Economics of Libraries
Marco Ferdinando Martorana and Ilde Rizzo

NFTs, Creativity and the Law
Within and Beyond Copyright
Edited by Enrico Bonadio and Caterina Sganga

Craft as a Creative Industry
Karen Patel

Researching the Creative and Cultural Industries
A Guide to Qualitative Research
Simone Wesner

For more information about this series, please visit: www.routledge.com/Routledge-Research-in-the-Creative-and-Cultural-Industries/book-series/RRCCI

RESEARCHING THE CREATIVE AND CULTURAL INDUSTRIES

A Guide to Qualitative Research

Simone Wesner

Routledge
Taylor & Francis Group

LONDON AND NEW YORK

Designed cover image: GabrielPevide / iStock/ Getty Images

First published 2025
by Routledge
4 Park Square, Milton Park, Abingdon, Oxon OX14 4RN

and by Routledge
605 Third Avenue, New York, NY 10158

Routledge is an imprint of the Taylor & Francis Group, an informa business

British Library Cataloguing-in-Publication Data
A catalogue record for this book is available from the British Library

Library of Congress Cataloging-in-Publication Data
Names: Wesner, Simone, author.
Title: Researching the creative and cultural industries : a guide to qualitative research / Simone Wesner.
Description: Abingdon, Oxon ; New York, NY : Routledge, 2025. |
Series: Routledge research in the creative and cultural industries | Includes bibliographical references and index.
Identifiers: LCCN 2024016113 (print) | LCCN 2024016114 (ebook) |
ISBN 9780367753061 (hardback) | ISBN 9780367753054 (paperback) |
ISBN 9781003161912 (ebook)
Subjects: LCSH: Cultural industries–Research–Methodology. | Qualitative research–Methodology.
Classification: LCC HD9999.C9472 W47 2025 (print) | LCC HD9999.C9472 (ebook) | DDC 338.4/77–dc23/eng/20240425
LC record available at https://lccn.loc.gov/2024016113
LC ebook record available at https://lccn.loc.gov/2024016114

ISBN: 978-0-367-75306-1 (hbk)
ISBN: 978-0-367-75305-4 (pbk)
ISBN: 978-1-003-16191-2 (ebk)

DOI: 10.4324/9781003161912

Typeset in Sabon
by Taylor & Francis Books

To Matthias and Ella

CONTENTS

FIGURES

TABLES

ABBREVIATIONS

ACE	Arts Council England
ACM	Association for Computing Machinery
AM	analytic memo
AR	action research
BBK	Birkbeck, University of London
C	coding
CA	content analysis
CAQDAS	computer-assisted qualitative data analysis software
CCI	creative and cultural industries
CDA	critical discourse analysis
CMC	computer-mediated communications
DA	discourse analysis
DM	data mining
DMP	Data Management Platform
DP	discursive psychology
EB	explanation building
ESRC	Economic and Social Research Council
EU	European Union
GDPR	General Data Protection Regulation
GT	grounded theory
IoT	Internet of Things
IRB	Institutional Review Board
LLM	large language model
NA	narrative analysis
NA	network analysis
OCM	outline of cultural materials
PA	pattern analysis

TA	thematic analysis
TEA	template analysis
UK	United Kingdom

ACKNOWLEDGMENTS

As a researcher, writing about research approaches and practices always feels like a collective effort of colleagues, students, and creative professionals who have shared their ideas, knowledge, and experiences over many years. This book has been made possible through their shared generosity and their passion for research, for which I am most grateful. All deserve to be mentioned but some need to be singled out as groups or individuals here.

Every year, I am fortunate to see students become absorbed in thinking about research. At first, they are astonished and puzzled about what research includes, as they unpack the complexities of their research experience. They go on to create research practices that sustain their careers beyond graduation, while helping the creative and cultural industries to have a sustainable future in many corners of the world. My gratitude and thanks go to all our students who questioned and discussed their research practices – and who keep on doing so in their careers.

A special thanks goes to Terry Clague at Routledge who encourage me with short, gentle, and kind messages to write about the research experiences of the creative and cultural industries community, no matter how long it might take.

Equally supportive and patient were my colleagues who politely guided me to submission while managing major changes in the college. An institutional thank you goes to Birkbeck for allowing me to spend time writing this book and for letting me reuse and rewrite some of the forms that are under development, which are part of Birkbeck's ethics practice.

I also thank Nick St Clair and Joshua Davis, who patiently proofread every chapter, dealing with my creative and not-so-rule-based interpretations of meanings and words.

Last but not least, thank you to my family, to Matthias and Ella, who allowed me to write, who care every day, and who tease out a smile when it is most needed. What would I be without you? This book belongs to you both.

1

INTRODUCTION

Asking Questions

As creative practitioners, we require research skills as part of our day-to-day activities and, as a result, it has become second nature that we consult the internet. We rely on it for instant access to information. We ask it direct questions, and the internet provides initial answers – a simple activity that we call *research*. But in scholarly research, we go beyond simply accumulating knowledge; we focus on the process, design, implementation, and evaluation of research. Janet Salmons (2019) argues that, while we are researching, we should stop and think about how to explain the nature of the problem we are investigating, how we know what we know, and what it is necessary to know in order to understand that problem. Asking questions provokes answers and research is about asking big questions. For example: What is real? What knowledge counts? How do we know what we know?

This book connects the big questions with the more nuanced practical approaches of carrying out research in creative and cultural industries (CCI). The aim is to weave together the theoretical discussions about paradigms and methodologies with the methods of collecting and analysing data.

Research is expected to feature prominently in creative and cultural industries programmes and courses. Developing a research practice is an ongoing theme of the learning process in higher education, with all the formative tests, exams, and assignments culminating in a research project and dissertation. Understanding the learner as practitioner and vice versa, the introductory discussion of research in this book is guided by the following questions:

1. Why do we keep researching?
2. What does it mean to be critical and reflective in a research context?

DOI: 10.4324/9781003161912-1

3. What is the scope of research in the creative and cultural industries (i.e. including fields, topics and subjects that embrace an interdisciplinary approach to understanding research)?

The way we carry out research depends on many aspects, such as education and training. For example, finding the right information in a university or college context is often the first hurdle that new researchers need to overcome. As an initial step, webinars can help explain how to find resources online and how to access resources in the library. But finding your personal approach to research may take longer, since it depends on your personal characteristics and your ability, which is expressed in curiosity or an inquisitive mind.

However, while understanding the need to further investigate what courts your interest in the first place can be motivating, it is not a prerequisite for delivering a sound piece of research. What is important is persistence, discipline, time management, and clarity, which are all learnable attributes. This book will guide you, the reader, through the research process from start to finish, providing you with a source of contextual knowledge, practical exercises, and templates, all while exploring best practice. I personally approach the research process as a holistic and all-encompassing activity. Simultaneously, with each chapter, I aim to build up your confidence in developing research practices that are clear and comprehensive yet remain flexible enough to be fit for purpose. In foregrounding the research process as seen through the CCI lens, the trio of *paradigms, methodology,* and *methods* will act as a guiding structure for your own research.

In practical terms, this book will help you to translate issues and problems encountered in the CCI into research questions that are answerable within the time constraints of your project. It will support you in choosing a methodology that is most closely linked to your own understanding and values, while explaining why it is important to get this right at the start of the research to avoid contradiction when the analysis is in full flow. At the conclusion of the book, you will be well equipped to match your individual research paradigm to your chosen methodology, as well as to suitable methods for data collection and analysis, thus completing the process of investigation as one complex and identifiable process.

The question of why we keep researching has engaged scholars and practitioners alike throughout history. Humans continue to endeavour to describe, explain, and analyse. The quest for further knowledge, for understanding human behaviour, and for innovations keeps many different types of exploration alive. For now, let us pause for a moment to consider why we want to carry out research. Remember, the role of research is to ask big question that stand apart from everyday routines but, nevertheless, remain connected to the problems and challenges creative practitioners face. There is a lot to be said about the usefulness of solution-based thinking in researching CCI and the satisfaction it brings when a problem has been resolved. Though, most of the big questions (e.g., What is reality?) are not meant to be answered definitively but are better approached as a process that opens further thoughts. Process-focused thinking connects to time and, in turn, the passing of time captures the development we crave both as individual researchers and collectively as human beings. Pausing for a moment gives us a chance to shift our definition and understanding of development away from a pragmatic focus, which may view research as something required for a degree or as part of a job description. The reasons for engaging in research are linked with the personal and societal aims that we set ourselves. Pausing enables us to relate the personal to the bigger questions. As a result, research can give a helping hand to define the places/spaces/ideas with which we wish to occupy ourselves.

Your reasons for carrying out research are likely to inform your understanding of another question that both researchers and students have asked in the past: What does it mean to be critical and reflective in a CCI research context? Both critical inquiry and deliberation are going to form the very foundations of this book. So, stopping to pause is good, but it is not enough. It is *thinking* that allows us to question our own assumptions and our ways of understanding the world, which opens new and different ways of thinking. Reflection allows us to question ourselves and, as a result, to be critical of the elements, processes, and practices that surround us. If you are keen to gain further knowledge about diversity in the CCI, you may want to start by asking yourself where this interest of yours originated. Have you or has somebody dear to you been treated unfairly in the workplace? Is your initial interest related to the Black Lives Matter or Me Too movements? Reflection can provide you with a starting point for further investigation. Abstraction and comparisons are other examples of thinking that could guide you to personalise informed opinions and share our intellectual endeavours with each other.

Creative and Cultural Industries

In doing so, we are fortunate that CCI provide plenty of scope and opportunity for research in many parts of the world. The two adjectives *creative* and *cultural* cover two sectors or industries that are in flux, with no clear boundaries between them. It all depends on the context the term CCI is used. The meaning and the wording varies in different geographical locations, states, nations, and regions. For example, in Japan the term creative industries is less common but is captured in the idea of "cool Japan" or *masukomi* (Oyama, 2015). In the United Kingdom the term *cultural industries* was replaced with *creative industries* in the 1990s. The term *cultural industries* was thought to be politically outdated and took on a slightly negative connotation. The government at the time wanted to present an optimistic outlook for those promising industries, deflecting from the negative implications that Adorno and Horkheimer introduced in the 1940s with their phrase "cultural industry" In the book *Dialectic of Enlightenment*, the authors interpreted cultural industries through their

personal experience of Broadway shows of the time as being of mainly enter-
tainment value that served the profit-generating machinery of late liberalism.
They questioned the educational and critical value of such shows, interpreting
them as examples of repetitive and damning (low) culture, which supported
uncritical views of society as a whole. Culture is mass-produced and perpetuated through all art fields, resulting in standardised production. More than
eighty years later, these remnants of such a negative understanding of cultural
industries has been overwritten.

The concept of cultural industries has developed to incorporate new ways of
creating, producing, and distributing products, which are related to advance-
ments in technology and the dominance of media in many societies. In the
United Kingdom and Australia, the term *creative industries* is now commonly
used and understood as being in close proximity to the term creative economy.
In business development, creativity is viewed as a competitive advantage that
can drive innovation. Emphasis is now placed "on industries which have their
origin in individual creativity, skills and talent which have the potential of job
and wealth creation through the exploitation of intellectual property" (DCMS,
2001 and 2022). This includes the cultural sector and in the United Kingdom
covers nine sectors: advertising and marketing; architecture; crafts; design; film,
TV and radio; IT, software and computer services; museums, galleries and
libraries; music, performing and visual arts; and publishing.

In other European countries, in Asia, and elsewhere, the two adjectives
creative and *cultural* sit comfortably in the one phrase, *creative and cultural
industries*, to include both the more narrowly defined cultural industries and the
industries that deal with creative approaches. Using the two adjectives of *cultural* and *creative*, values both sectors and is understood as going beyond the
normative approach to industries and reminds us, for example, of the philosophical dimension of culture as a wider societal good.

Today, the differences in usage of terms and their definition depend on a
variety of factors and are based on historical, creative, and cultural policy
developments that are in place at national, state, or local levels. In short, your
research could start by looking into which terms are in use and what approaches are applied in the countries and regions where you intend to carry out your
research.

At the same time, researching the CCI comes in many shapes and formats
and the multiple research approaches on offer can be confusing. The choices are
fed from different disciplines: sociology, psychology, political science, anthropology, feminism, cultural studies, and the arts, to name a few. Furthermore,
there are the ethical considerations that require thought when carrying out
research.

For example, arts management researcher and educator Constance DeVer-
eaux (2018) speaks about the dilemma that advocacy (policy-incentive driven)
research brings. Too often, advocacy for the arts masquerades as objective
inquiry – or, stated the other way, so-called objective inquiry is really arts

advocacy in disguise. CCI, cultural policy, and arts management are all relatively young disciplines, and researchers have been struggling to adapt their research intentions to capture and investigate the diverse practices. Caught in the middle between social research practices and the discourse-based approaches commonly used in the arts and in cultural studies, researchers have appropriated methodological frameworks as needed. Many have developed their own practice-based approaches, relying on what they recall from their time as students, paired with specific training for individual methodologies that are deemed most suitable for their specific research enquiries, which they rely on to build a research portfolio over time.

As an alternative, and this is often quoted as a way out of the dilemma faced when choosing fields, topics, and subjects, an interdisciplinary approach is embraced to understand the field. Taking advantage of a variety of approaches and mixing them may sound more appealing than it is. It presumes expert knowledge from different fields, and, as I will explain in later chapters, the theoretical frames of these different fields might be contradictory. Often, subjects focus on specific perspectives such as groups in sociology, institutions in political science, or the individual in psychology, that are difficult to address in a single piece of research. CCI research comes in many shapes and formats, and its multiple research approaches can be confusing, especially when a research approach is too closely coupled with the subject under investigation. For this reason, I will focus on the research process. I will guide you through disentangling it from the content. In this way, this book is designed to enhance the understanding of the initial stages of the research process, as woven into the agendas of CCI. The link between how to carry out research and the content of the research will not be lost. Instead, a wealth of examples and case studies will illustrate how both can live harmoniously together.

Please note that the book will focus mainly on qualitative research, disregarding the mechanics of analysing quantitative research methods. For this information, a book focused on quantitative analysis will better serve your interests. That said, some of the theoretical foundations of quantitative research are discussed in Chapter 2, but only to illustrate the opposing frames of qualitative and quantitative approaches of research.

Content of the Book

This book has been designed to provide you with a practical guide for undertaking research in CCI from the initial idea right through to writing up the research outcomes. For specific interests, the individual chapters stand on their own and allow for a targeted search.

This introductory chapter discusses the reasoning behind research as seen through a critical and reflective lens and introduces the scope of creative industries-related research. It provides an overview of the ten chapters and explains their common structure.

Chapter 2 focuses on the conceptual underpinning of research, introduced through the trio of paradigms, methodologies, and methods as the main explanatory frame in the first half. It discusses the function of research *paradigms* and explains positivism and interpretivism as schools of thought developed over time to guide and structure research practice.

The second half of Chapter 2 discusses specific contextual lenses that are commonly applied in CCI research. This ranges from experience-based phenomenology to language-driven hermeneutics and structuralism, to critical theory, pragmatism, critical realism, social constructivism, and postmodernism.

In Chapter 3 the paradigms are utilised to discuss *methodologies* as strategic implications that direct research practice and provide the lens through which analysis can be carried out. Following a similar structure to Chapter 2, Chapter 3 starts by discussing the meaning of methodologies, while locating methodologies in the trio as the intermediary between paradigms and methods. A selection of commonly used methodologies in CCI research follows on, ranging from different forms of ethnographic research (e.g., ethnography, netnography, autoethnography) to a discussion of how to choose the right case study, and how and why discourse analysis goes beyond textual interpretation. Turning to a focus on gathering experiences, grounded theory, phenomenology, and feminism are explained next, which provides the ground for introducing practice-based and action research as trendsetters in the CCI research environment.

Chapters 4 and 5 are dedicated to the data and tools called *methods* that aid the collection and analysis of the information that will ultimately answer research questions and discover new and original insights that we seek to set out in our work. Chapter 4 introduces methods as systematic procedures and techniques, while discussing what counts as data and detailing ways of collecting it. The focus is on approaches that support a variety of methodologies, including literature/systemic reviews, interviews and observations, case studies and surveys, as well as questionnaires.

Chapter 5 repeats the same pattern as Chapter 4 in providing an overview of the commonly used methods that help to analyse gathered data. It provides step-by-step guidance and suggests ways to get the most out of the collected data, aiding your research questions. It starts with thematic analysis (TA), a method that many people will be familiar with and therefore builds on prior experience. Braun and Clarke (2012) recommend six phases of TA practice that provide a frame from which researchers can develop their own version of thematic analysis. Content analysis works in a similar way, with the step-by-step guide understood to be a framework, as opposed to an instruction manual. Pattern and network analysis further advances comparative thinking and introduces coding as a means of breaking down data before reconstructing it in different ways. A selection and brief explanation of coding techniques is offered as a matter of choice, together with further complimentary methods, such as making sense of written notes in the form of analytic memos and discourse analysis methods. In the latter parts of the chapter, explanation building, template analysis, as well as narrative analysis are briefly discussed as alternative or complimentary methods.

With the trio set out in Chapter 2 (paradigms), Chapter 3 (methodology), and Chapters 4 and 5 (methods), Chapter 6 takes a closer look at formulating research questions. It takes readers on a journey and explains how to move from the initial idea, through locating the topic and subject, to identifying problems that then can be reformulated as research problems and rewritten into research questions that emerge over time. Explaining the different types of research questions that can be formulated while using explanatory, explorative, evaluative, and predictive approaches helps to connects the research question with the trio of paradigms, methodologies, and methods into a coherent design. In the last part of Chapter 6, I discuss four examples of how this is applied in CCI research.

With the research questions defined and the design set out, Chapter 7 focuses on how to implement the design and what it means to develop a research practice that offers ways of thinking and gaining skills that last beyond an initial piece of research. Objectives are discussed and the STARTER set is introduced to organise fieldwork and show how to use professional practices to mitigate common mistakes. This chapter concludes with a discussion of the turn to practice as an emerging popular option (e.g., for dissertation research), including practice-based and practice-led approaches.

Chapter 8 introduces critical evaluation tools to accommodate the validation and reflection of results and research practice. Discussing research limits, accidental turns, and bias, research is judged as success or failure. I understand both success and failure to be interdependent concepts foregrounding their relational character. In Chapter 9, attention is paid to ethical principles and practices. Understanding ethics has become a prime driver in research, informing ideas and concepts as well as their practical implementation. Ethics is discussed using scenarios that include choosing suitable locations, asking for consent, ensuring the rights and care of participants, and enabling compliance and data protection regulations that readers encounter in their research projects. The latter part of this chapter explains ethics in a university research context, in which even thought is specific in its institutional frame. Data management practices and the adjacent approval processes can be equally adopted in a CCI industry environment, including the challenges that artificial intelligence presents to the researcher.

The final chapter addresses how to present and write up research following multidisciplinary practices in CCI research, in the form of a methodology chapter for a dissertation or as a stand-alone research report. This chapter concludes the journey from conceptualising ideas and implementing research to disseminating research results and developing individual research practices.

All chapters open with a short introduction, defining what the reader can expect to learn in the chapter. They end with a summary of the key points. The introduction finishes with a set of guiding questions to kickstart a discussion, and Chapter 2 references learning objectives. In addition to the research topic, every chapter focuses on a relevant CCI thematic topic, highlighting the unique research challenges in CCI, and weaves examples into the chapters. For example, Chapter 2 introduces *intersectionality* interwoven with paradigms as theoretical frames, while Chapter 3 illustrates examples that investigate *cultural values*, and Chapter 4 focuses on *diversity*.

The book presents multiple forms of learning, highlighting different pedagogical features in the form of exercises, study questions, figures, and tools, as well as ready-made forms that help to put the research into action.

It is aimed at scholars, researchers, and students who navigate research within an academic setting, and aims to provide CCI practitioners with an understanding and critical approach to research that remains thought provoking and sustainable over time. The writing oscillates between an informal style that is based on experience and a formal way that contextualises research as knowledge provision.

QUESTIONS

- What does research mean to you?
- Why do you want to carry out research?
- What subjects, fields, and topics have you been researching before you acquired this book?
- What do you think the research process includes?

References

Braun, V., & Clarke, V. 2012. Thematic Analysis. In H. Cooper, P. M. Camic, D. L. Long, A. T. Panter, D. Rindskopf, & K. J. Sher (Ed.), *APA Handbook of Research Methods in Psychology, Vol. 2. Research Designs: Quantitative, Qualitative, Neuropsychological, and Biological* (pp. 57–71). American Psychological Association. doi:10.1037/13620-004.

Department for Digital, Culture, Media & Sport (DCMS)2001. *Creative Industries Mapping Document.* https://www.gov.uk/government/publications/creative-industries-mapping-documents-2001 (15 August 2023).

Department for Digital, Culture, Media & Sport (DCMS)2022. *DCMS Sector Economic Estimates Methodology.* https://www.gov.uk/government/publications/dcms-sectors-economic-estimates-methodology/dcms-sector-economic-estimates-methodology#definitions (15 August 2023).

De Vereaux, C. 2018. Cultural management research: Putting the cart and the tail in their proper places. In C. de Vereaux (Ed.), *Arts and Cultural Management* (pp. 91–107). Routledge.

Horkheimer, M. & Adorno, T. W. 2020. *Dialectic of Enlightenment.* Stanford University Press.

Oyama, S. 2015. Japanese creative industries in globalization. In Larissa Hjorth and Olivia Khoo (Ed.), *Routledge Handbook of New Media in Asia* (pp. 322–332). Routledge.

Salmons, J. E. 2019. *Find the Theory in Your Research: Little Quick Fix.* Sage.

2

THEORIES

Introduction

In this chapter, the theoretical or conceptual underpinnings of research are given prominence. Theories in cultural and creative industries (CCI), as in many other fields, are well-substantiated explanations that serve different functions. They could be seen as the gold standard for discourses to frame content alongside a variety of ideas, opinions, beliefs, and knowledge. As a scholar, I intend to compare theories against exemplar alternative concepts that for example, capture a situation, an experience, to the extent that I believe is correct and that it can be replicated as a thought, a model and as a process.

The casual use of the term *theory* implies an idea or an unproven hunch, but the meaning is different in academic studies. In research, we aim to develop theories and employ existing theories to question and justify the work we carry out, and we are bound by personal convictions and values that inform those research theories. In fact, we operate with multiple theories to develop and structure our ideas and findings in meaningful ways. This happens by questioning the theories and it is guided by our thoughts. In university assignments and dissertations, students are asked to discuss theories and apply a variety of theoretical frames to practice. For example, Bourdieu's classic concept (1986) that cultural knowledge serves as currency has been used to explain class divisions and inequality in CCI. He argued that exposure to cultural knowledge, which could be anything from a museum visit or ballet classes at preschool, alters experiences. This accumulated cultural knowledge promotes social mobility in a stratified society. In other words, it provides advantages to the people who have the means to access cultural knowledge and this impacts who will be working in CCI and consuming its products. Bourdieu developed his concept in the second half of the twentieth century, offering an explanation that

DOI: 10.4324/9781003161912-2

continues to be discussed today, but it is one way to explain the link between equality and knowledge. His approach is one among other theoretical frames that provide equally valued explanations, which are introduced later as specifically relevant CCI themes, and which run parallel to explanations about the research process. This chapter highlights *intersectionality* as a CCI thematic theory. As an example, it illustrates a more current theoretical frame covering questions of race, equity, equality, and class that envelopes the discussion as a content theme. I will come back to this later in the chapter, after I have laid out some foundations on which this book's understanding of theories is built.

Content and Methodology – Focused Theories

CCI thematic theories deal exclusively with specific content and are less focused on methodologies, but they include methodological thinking. However, the research process itself relies, uses, and can generate methodological related theoretical frames, so this chapter focuses on those and their relationship to the content. Research practice barely distinguishes between the two because, as I will elaborate later, they are closely interrelated. For the purpose of clarification, in this book I have divided theories into two strands: content (or thematic) theories and methodological theories. In both strands, ideas are developed and applied, but the focus or the viewpoint differs. As mentioned previously, a thematic approach foregrounds the development of the content, and in methodological theories it is the research process that becomes the content. The focus is switched from content to methodology. This relates mainly to how research is carried out: why we keep researching and what principles we apply when trying to find new understandings and insight into things, processes, and entities.

Abstract thinking about a phenomenon dominates in both strands, and it must be validated through evidence. In turn, evidence is produced and demonstrated through research. In this sense, the methodological strand of how we carry out research, focuses on itself, a kind of self-reflection as if it were a person. The choice to distinguish between content and methodological theories, at least momentarily, helps to untangle the complexities that the discussion of theories brings, but we should not forget that it remains an artificial division. As thinking about methodological theories makes up an essential part of the research process, locating or finding theories in research is trickier than first thought. Those methodological-focused theories are often neglected, underestimated, and underrepresented in research practice, because all eyes are on the outcome – that is, the content of the research rather than the theoretical research frames. Conceptual or theoretical frames allow researchers to distinguish between scholarly or academic research, advocacy research, and other types of research that are commonly in use in CCI. This chapter focuses on the different schools of thought that inform our understanding of knowledge and its interpretations. It asks fundamental questions of how we know what we know, what is reality, and what is real about a problem. Also, what assumptions do we make when defining research questions, how theories impact the formulation of research questions, and how theories guide the research process.

A case study will conclude this chapter. Drawing on my own research experiences, as well as those of my students, this case study will explore ways to test assumptions and explain and challenge different schools of thought against our own personal beliefs and convictions.

Paradigms – The First Trio Encounter

Janet Salmons (2019) argues that research is about asking big questions and that paradigms are the key that enables us to question the world. Paradigms as distinct sets of concepts inform the choices we make when selecting methodologies. In turn, the methodology guides what methods for data collection and data analysis are most appropriate and suitable for application. As laid out in the introductory chapter, there is no rank order between the trio of paradigms, methodology, and methods to tell us where to start. The three parts are linked though the research process and depend on each other to the extent that a research project cannot be complete if any part of the trio has not been considered.

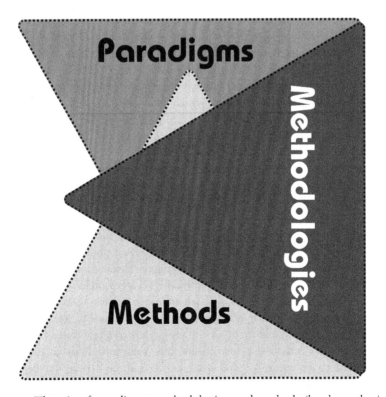

FIGURE 2.1 The trio of paradigms, methodologies, and methods (by the author)

The paradigm, as the most theory- and individual-focused part of the trio, will be explained and analysed in this section of the chapter. The word *paradigm* can mean different things, but in a research context it mostly refers to a distinct set of concepts – the philosophical underpinnings – that are in use. Paradigms are abstract and theory-driven concepts, but they are by no means distant because they relate to combined and collective experiences. Paradigms are all around us and, for us as individuals, they relate to the set of experiences, beliefs, and values that affect the way we perceive reality and respond to that perception of reality.

Personally, when confronted by perceptions that go against my own convictions, I tend to respond with scepticism and disbelief. For example, people sometimes argue that the arts, as an inclusive component of CCI, do not require public support and that the market will provide sufficient income for artists instead. In this instance, I would defend my personal view using a phrase such as, "it is hard to believe that the value of the arts has not been translated into sufficient support programmes that would allow artists to create/practice without financial constraints". Based on my personal experience, I value the arts highly and perhaps this is related to my experience of working in the arts for over thirty years. At a personal level, I find it difficult to accept that people put commercial interests above the intrinsic value of the arts. I understand the arts to be an essential and unique condition that should be supported as a societal good and should not be left to market forces. My passion for the arts seems to override other values that would provide a more measured and tolerant approach. Instead, my response is formulated as an opinion, showing limited respect to the other worldviews, which in this instance presents the market-driven approach as opposed to a welfare-support model. As an art activist, I am not alone with my passion-driven approach, but as an individual I present my own view, which illustrates just one opinion among many. Importantly, views and opinions are guided and informed by personal experiences, the environment, cultural, and economic factors that let me develop those beliefs, convictions, and values.

The emotional attachment that is demonstrated in expressions of passion about the arts adds another layer of complexity that needs to be noted. At the same time, as a researcher, I thrive on the multiplicity of values and opinions and defend this as an important cornerstone of democratic life. I understand that multiple socially constructed realities exist. Instead of focusing on reality as the one and only proof, I believe that different and varied perceptions guide our understanding of what is real. Having said this, I often find myself quoting the throw away phrase "in reality or in the real world", referring to a commonly accepted understanding of a phenomenon. This phrase implies a collective approach neglecting individual perceptions as real references. It brings to light the power relations we operate in, but it does not capture the experience of all and only refers to a few instead.

In research, we have the choice to embrace the multiplicity of experiences, but we need to be aware of and account for our own personal beliefs and values, which we bring to the research practice. Be it a conviction of the intrinsic value of art, as in my case, or the market-driven approach that others share. Applying a reflective approach is part of qualitative research practices because it raises awareness of the position of the researcher, thereby helping to identify where personal beliefs and values resonate with other worldviews, like those I share with many researchers and colleagues. In a more abstract way, paradigms are understood as shared worldviews representing beliefs, commitments, outlooks, and values in a discipline. They provide a guide as to how problems are understood and solved. In other words, paradigms represent a disciplinary matrix that provides a philosophical underpinning of science (Schwandt, 1989 and 1994). Therefore, developing a self-reflective approach from the start of the research will contribute to an understanding of your own views and the assumptions of the people who participate in the research studies. Students will be presented with a variety of paradigms gained from their studies, and which are informed by their personal worldviews. As paradigms come in different forms, and are further divided into subfields and splinter groups, I discuss a selection of paradigms that are present in researching CCI. Students encounter different world views in the varied bodies of literature (e.g., academic books, journal articles, blogs) that represent specific understandings of how to view the world in terms of truth and knowledge.

Distinguishing between the different schools of thought remains complex, without clearly defined parameters and fluent interpretations. Taking a historical view, like most concepts, paradigms are unstable. They could be abandoned and can become outdated. Paradigms shift when current theories cannot explain a new phenomenon, and a new theory becomes widely accepted in the field. For example, the feminist movement, which is now in its fourth generation, has maintained the questioning of male dominance in positions of power, but the argumentation has changed, and new positions have gained attention in society as a whole, not just in the arts or the CCI. Until the middle of the twentieth century, writing about diversity broadly covered one aspect. It was either race, gender, or class that was presented as the social category that caused disadvantage and discrimination among people, groups, and societies. Today, we argue for the *intersectionality* of these categories, the interconnected nature of social categories, which create overlapping and interdependent systems of discrimination or disadvantage (see case study at the end of this chapter).

Until now, I have explained what paradigms are and talked around and about paradigms as intellectual frameworks that make research possible. In the following section, I discuss what paradigms consists of, and what they contain, by looking at the inner lives or the core ideas that paradigms hold. The term was first coined in Thomas Kuhn's book *The Structure of Scientific Revolution* (1962). As a physics graduate at Harvard University, Kuhn was asked to teach a science course for humanities students through historical case studies. He read Aristotle and concluded that his work on motion was full of errors of logic and observation. But it is well known that Aristotle's ideas in general have influenced many subsequent thinkers, and he is still considered one of the greatest thinkers in politics, psychology, and ethics. Kuhn concluded that to appreciate

Aristotle's thinking, one must be aware of scientific conventions, intellectual options, and strategies that are available to people at a given time. Studying these conventions shows how communities of researchers cluster around ways of thinking, beliefs, and conventions, which he called *paradigms*.

The core of a paradigm is divided into three parts: **epistemology, axiology,** and **ontology**. Each captures specific aspects of how we make sense of the world. Questions about the idea of knowledge are asked in **epistemology**. For example: What is possible for us to know and how do we obtain knowledge? What are ways of knowing and how do we know what we know? What are the sources of knowledge? How reliable are the sources? What can we know? Thinking through these questions comes with its own philosophical assumptions about the nature of social reality. I mentioned the casual use of the word *real* in relation to what is happening in the real world. For many it remains a throwaway comment, but it applies an understanding that what is real is also the truth. The questions raised here are: What can we know is real? And what do we know exists? In scientific terms, this is known as **ontology**. This covers, for example, our understanding of reality. Do we believe in one verifiable reality, or do we think the world contains multiple socially constructed realities? The third part is known as **axiology** and covers our ideas related to ethics and value, which guide our judgements about what is true or untrue.

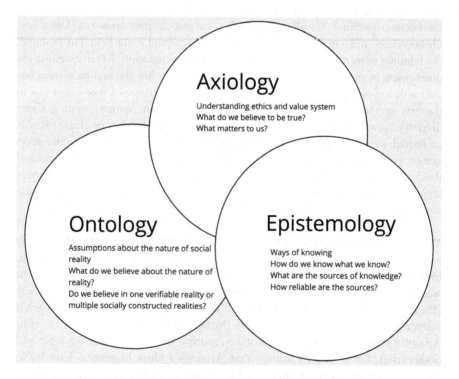

FIGURE 2.2 The core components of a paradigm (by the author)

Presenting the three components separately from each other may give the impression that they are separate entities. In fact, they all make up what we know today as a paradigm. As mentioned earlier, the parts are distinct because they present different aspects: epistemology deals with our knowledge, ontology covers how we understand reality, and axiology asks questions about truth. Importantly, when we talk about paradigms, we emphasise the links between the three concepts. For example, if you believe that there is one verifiable reality as a researcher, you will set out to find uncovered laws. You might envisage developing a model that aims to evaluate cultural organisations, following the same format, which can then be used to compare cultural organisations. Meaning is understood to be created by uncovering something that has not been known or has not been evidenced before. In ontological terms, this approach assumes a given reality and the knowledge that is produced while doing so. But the two ontological and epistemological qualities are useless if we are not convinced that they are the truth. This evaluation model might work in one set of circumstances, but we are less certain about the general applicability. The Cultural Count evaluation (Phiddian et al., 2017) was developed in Australia, and partly adopted through the United Kingdom's arts councils, but many cultural organisations remained sceptical that it would work in a UK context.[1] One plausible explanation was that the model did not correspond with arts managers' beliefs that an Australian evaluation tool would sufficiently capture their practise in the UK. Some managers opposed the idea that a one-size-fits-all approach would work, and questioned the idea of a unified approach, understanding arts and culture as a nonmeasurable entity. Setting this nonmeasurable approach of multiple practices of truth or multiple truth, against a unified or one truth approach as the evaluation model intended, is bound to create tensions. Disentangling conflicting paradigms from the start, in the developmental phase of the research design, takes some time. But it helps to propel the research process forward later because, if not discussed initially, those discrepancies will appear in later research stages, hindering the process and carrying the potential to devalue the research.

Applying the view that multiple realities exist to paradigms allows us to understand that paradigms are incommensurable. There is no common measure to evaluate or judge them against each other. No overall model will capture all paradigms with their associated ideas, so no metatheory will emerge. Instead, paradigms remain fragmented and changeable. They follow different methodologies or methods and, as I mentioned previously, there are many to choose from. Covering all of these goes beyond the remit of this book, so I mention the two most commonly used paradigms in CCI: positivism and interpretivism (along with some of their many subgroups and variations). As distinctive as paradigms are, researchers have been engaged in disciplinary conversations, drawing from a variety of fields and disciplines. CCI is no exception, borrowing theoretical frames from sociology, psychology, business studies, media, and cultural studies. Each of these could be traced back to positivism, interpretivism, or both. Researchers move between the two, sit between them, or develop their own approaches in reaction to another. On a personal level, we might be doing the same, switching from a positivistic view in managing our everyday life to an interpretivist view when conducting research.

Positivism

In positivism, the research goal is to provide objective knowledge and develop general principles to explain phenomena. Etymologically, positivism has roots in the verb "to posit" or to put forward, to suggest critical scrutiny, which is rather the opposite meaning of the common understanding of being positive, as most self-help literature misleadingly implies. The underlying philosophical principal dates to early Plato and Pythagoras, Athenian philosophers in Ancient Greece, who favoured the idea of that our world is perfectly ordered, even when we are unable (or not yet able) to discover the structures in the world that await verification. Pythagoras argued that mathematical structures are superior to aesthetic judgments. Kuhn judges Aristotle's thinking as lacking stringent logic. Exercising reason became the guiding principle for the enlightenment thinkers in the seventeenth and eighteenth centuries in Europe to oppose superstition, dogma, religion, or metaphysical beliefs. Auguste Comte's (1798–1857) interest lay in applying reason to solve social (cultural) problems. He argued that at first, we seek theological explanations but will in the end settle for logic and reasoning mainly through observation, experiments, and comparison, when researching social phenomenon (Comte, 1855). Today, we speak of assumptions instead of superstition, but the quest for evidence remained ongoing throughout the centuries. Closer to our time, the philosopher Karl Popper (1902–1992) argued for formal theories, or thinking in hypotheses that can be tested, resulting in either proof or disproof, and in this way learning through mistakes. Popper defended the objectivity of scientific knowledge and in later years argued for an understanding of knowledge as being free from all psychological constraints. He affirmed that objectivity, as a concept, does not require the notion of a subjective mental state. In evolutionary terms, knowledge develops through interactions with the environment, as for example the hives built by bees and the dams by beavers. He argues that humans develop intellectual products that shape the environment. Therefore, he concluded that growth in human knowledge is an evolutionary process (evolutionary epistemology) that includes the development of problem-solving theories, which in turn are challenged through criticism, modification, and replacement (Popper, 1979 286–287). Absolute knowledge does not exist, and we must work step by step in order to uncover better ways of coming to understand the world. Again, this refers to the notion that with new discoveries, paradigms shift. In this case, this is not a shift in the fundamental principles, but a further development that is based on the ideas of what we know today as logical empiricism.

Historically, we can stay in Vienna and meet some of Popper's con-temporaries, the members of the Ernst Mach Society (1926–1936). Moritz Schlick, Hans Hahn, Philipp Frank, and the Neuraths started as an academic reading group at the University of Vienna and later became known as the Vienna Circle. They advocated logic as the main concept for investigating the world. The use of deduction (from the general to the specific), induction (from specific to general), as well as direct observational experience were discussed as the dominant methods of reasoning. Ludwig Wittgenstein's early thoughts about the verification of meaning, which is often attributed to him as the "ver-ifiability principle", states that something is meaningful only if it can be empirically verified.

Today, applications of this kind are commonly in use as evidence-based research. In CCI, we are familiar with the quest for and the belief in evidence. Arts organisations are asked to provide evidence, which is in turn accepted as proof, as for example when funders ask grant recipients to demonstrate that their funds were spent appropriately or that the anticipated goals were achieved. As with the phrase "seeing is believing", in everyday life, visual evi-dence is convincing, which underlines the call for empirical proof to generate meaning. Many research studies in CCI, including in arts management and cultural policy, follow these principles. Over the years, *impact studies* often prove with numbers how well the arts are doing, creating evidence that con-vinces by means of figures. Measurability is a key indicator, and it was con-verted into a familiar government cultural policy tool in the 1990s and early 2000s in many Western countries, most notably in the UK, Australia, and the USA. It is therefore not surprising that some subfields, such as audience studies and arts marketing, are keen subscribers to positivistic thinking. Social media studies, as part of the digital turn in CCI, relies largely on evidence given in numbers generated from large data sets. Numbers and size matter when it comes to counting internet audiences, or views and clicks. Closer to home, and in addition to statistics and numbers, are the discussions in the classroom and in assignments where evidence and proof are vigorously defended. For example, students' essays could be well written, but without proof or evidence the argu-ment remains an assumption, and therefore carries less weight than when it is evidenced correctly.

No matter how common and useful positivism has been, as a theoretical frame, in developing CCI as a field of study, there are several restrictive condi-tions that question such a mechanistic worldview of reality. I struggle less with the notion of causality and the idea of learning through mistakes. It is the single objective view of reality (ontological position), which is thought to exist inde-pendently of individual perception, that I cannot relate to in my research, because I focus on people's multiple perceptions of the world.

Interpretivism

Developed in opposition to the positivistic approach, interpretivism offers an alternative approach to research. It focuses on our experiences in the social world and concentrates on making sense of the world with the thinking, meanings, and intentions of people. An interpretivist approach problematises positivist ideas of truth correspondence, objectivity, generalization, and linear processes of research. Interpretivist research approaches do not negate reality, but reality is understood as an expression or sign of deeper-lying processes. In this sense it is much more about discovering an agent's experience, working with the duality of explaining and understanding meaning, which for example is cocreated in the social interactions of people. As a result, we speak of multiple realities that are relative to the time, situations, values, and context. The role of the researcher is embedded in the process and an objective view is not envisaged. The meaning of the verb *interpret* is twofold, focusing both on understanding and explaining. Providing an explanation requires prior understanding. The term *interpretation* emphasises that there are multiple ways of understanding and explaining an idea or a phenomenon, and this includes research outcomes. This contrasts with the objectivity that is implied in some positivistic approaches. Having said this, interpretivism and positivism are the opposing ends of the paradigm spectrum, with a variety of theories falling somewhere between the two, along the spectrum that defines the environment of the nonlinear spectra.

Interpretivism itself is an umbrella term, housing multiple theoretical frames that unite in the centrality, characteristics, and intelligibility of meaning, but disagree about the different ways questions can be asked and answered when researching meaning, experience, and perceptions. Some researchers renounce methodological foundations of objectification and validation, staying completely focussed on the multiplicity of discourses that generate value through diversity and difference, while avoiding any form of generalisation. Other researchers attach meanings to the social structures, understanding them as reflections of the lifeworld and intersubjectivity. Developing their own validations, such researchers allow for some generalisations (e.g., referring to the dominant power structures, as we see in decolonial research approaches). As a result, marginalised voices are recognised, hidden variations are unveiled, and alternative research content highlighted. These advances have been adopted in many fields and disciplines. In CCI research, we have seen the development of a range of areas that tackle issues of precarity, white privilege, equity, and diversity, which have been prevalent for a long time but are now part of mainstream research agendas.

When designing a research project, thinking about paradigms helps us to understand the directions of travel. Even so, paradigms are never straightforward. They are full of paradoxes. They are difficult to figure out and often appear entangled with each other, but perseverance in exploring ontological, epistemological, and axial meanings pays off. You will be rewarded with an informed understanding of the research content. An initial step to untangling the paradoxes is to study the use of some of the key terminology that is applied by scholars and researchers alike. One of those key notions is the role of *empirical evidence* generated through research, as explained above. Another key term is *human experience*, which leads to the subfield of phenomenology, which allows us to take a deeper look into the first of various theoretical frames that the paradigm of interpretivism includes.

Phenomenology

In phenomenology or in phenomenological studies, as the name states, the phenomena as they exist in our experience are the centre of attention. We are familiar with natural phenomena such as tides, gravity, and photosynthesis that relate to observable situations. Contemporary cultural phenomena such as the ice bucket challenge, flash mobs, and diets are more commonly known as the bandwagon effect, when individuals copy the behaviours of others. But in academic terms a phenomenon is anything that can be experienced, and the emphasis is on the experience and how this is perceived, interpreted, and analysed as a concept, as people, as organisations, and as value.

Experience is understood, from the first person's point of view, to include perception, thought, memory, imagination, emotion, desire, and volition. It also includes bodily awareness, embodied action, and social activity. All are understood as critical reflections upon our conscious experience. German philosopher Edmund Husserl (1859–1938) referred to *intentionality* as a directed mental experience that might not need a physical target but, as an experience, it exists in the form of concepts, ideas, thoughts, and images, which are collected and structured as part of the experience (Smith, 2018). While experiencing, we can reflect, but we hardly characterise the experience straight away. Rather, we do so later after we have first established that we lived through it. We will look for familiarity in the experience by comparing it with previous experiences, such as whether we played a similar game before or whether a piece of music sounds familiar (Husserl, 2001). This comparison with this type of experience allows us to characterise music when listening at another time.

Phenomenology, as the study of experience, covers a wide range of fields and can be considered both a paradigm and a methodology. The term *phenomenology* is a discipline within philosophy and a movement in the history of philosophy. In CCI, we study the experiences of people and their practices (e.g., how arts managers run organisations). We investigate how creative artists work and what ideas and concepts creative workers develop in order to sustain their careers and what they contribute to organisations and to society. We investigate how audiences experience cultural productions and how creative worker perform as professionals over time. It covers the meaning we assign to objects and to the flow of time. Within this stream-of-conscious experience, phenomenology accounts for a range of complex studies that relate to our awareness of space and time, both of other people and ourselves, as thinkers and actors. In short, we engage in studying the lifeworld of culture. Historically, phenomenology developed as a philosophical discipline around the first half of the twentieth century with Edmund Husserl (as mentioned above), his student Martin Heidegger, and the Frenchmen Maurice Merleau-Ponty and Jean-Paul Sartre, as well-known prodigies of phenomenological discussions in the early stages. As phenomenologists, all worked through characterisations of experiences, but they focused on different points. Heidegger (1982) emphasised that we are "being in the world", immersed in the world, and as a consequence of this immersion, committed to understanding. Therefore, any investigation will start with us as a part of the being of the world. He argued that we relate to things through practice. Sartre (1956) focused on freedom of choice and on the experience of phenomena as the central aspect of consciousness, which laid the foundations for existentialism. Merleau-Ponty (2012) emphasised the role of the body in this experience of phenomena.

Hermeneutics

Staying within the interpretivist paradigm, hermeneutics is perhaps the most obvious subparadigm. The adjective *hermeneutic* originated in ancient Greek from ἑρμηνεύς (*hermeneus*) meaning to interpret or to translate, and the noun *hermeneutics* stood for the art or the study of interpretation. As phenomenology promotes the interpretation of experiences, hermeneutics specialises in the interpretation of the meaning of human interactions with the written word, with text. It is based on an understanding that meaningful activity can be interpreted in the same way as a text is interpreted. To use the ontological dimension, which defines the perception of reality, hermeneutics captures the textual, discursive, and linguistic nature of reality. Hermeneutics lets us see the world in many ways, but it is not arbitrary in the sense that we can make things up. Instead, we can understand things through personal involvement.

What is investigated in hermeneutics is the interpretation of meaning that forms the backdrop and understanding of language and actions, including intuition, for example. Heidegger, who brings his phenomenological understanding to the interpretation of texts, understood that "*Dasein* (being in the world) projects its *Being upon possibilities*" (1962 189) and that working out the possibilities of interpretations is projected to understanding. As a research activity, hermeneutics describes any efforts to understand both written and oral communication by establishing rules for interpretation. For example, tradition is not seen as being in opposition to critical thinking, but rather as a useful starting point for how the world has been understood so far. In understanding, we fuse other viewpoints with our own, and by doing so we transform tradition. Language plays an important role as the medium in which thoughts take shape through symbols and concepts. Understanding is context dependent, and this is explained through the *hermeneutic circle*, a tool that is commonly applied to critical reading. For example, while you are reading this text (1 in Figure 2.3), you compare what you

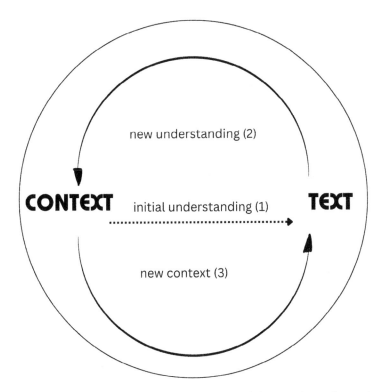

FIGURE 2.3 The Hermeneutic Circle redrawn (original drawing by DukeLondon)

have read to previous interpretations, as well as existing understandings, beliefs, and expectations. As a result, new understandings develop (2 in Figure 2.3) that will inform the context in which it is applied, which will impact how we understand the text and the context (3 in Figure 2.3). For example, reading the same text twice often reveals new understandings that went unnoticed in the first reading.

Early hermeneutics had two strands. Both sought a text's underlying meaning, but in different ways. In objectivist hermeneutics, meaning-making is understood as a re-enactment of the meaning. This is an important reference for studies of intuition, or "gut feeling". In alethic (uncover) hermeneutics, truth is understood as an act of disclosure between object and subject, and between understanding and explanation (Heidegger, 1962). Here, recontextualisation is stressed as opposed to re-enactment.

Structuralism

In structuralism, language and the spoken and written words are similar to hermeneutics' main tools of interpretation. However, structuralism has a special interest in finding meaning in hidden structures. Claude Levi Strauss (1908–2009), one of the most well-known structuralists, set out to uncover the underlying structures of a texts, stories, or fairy tales. For him, structures were invariable relations that link different content. In structuralism, cultures are viewed as carrying structural elements that could be discovered, which reveal specific information about how cultures are organised. For example, Strauss is known for an investigation of kinship systems. He was influential in France at the time and in his book *Tristes Tropiques* (1955) he reflects on meaning-making in relation to these structures by investigating (in)dependent community cultures in India, Africa, and South America. Today, we regard this as a restricted, male-dominated western view, but I think that if Strauss were alive today, he would probably agree. He was not the first to focus on structural thinking. At the turn of the twentieth century, the Swiss philosopher Ferdinand de Saussure (1957–1913) created linguistics as a new theory for understanding how semiotics influences our thinking. He noted that the meaning of words depends on structure more than on the objects it describes. Towards the end of the twentieth century, in 1984, feminist theorist Alison Assiter summarised the various forms of structuralism, highlighting that a structure determines the position of each element of a whole. Assiter argued that every system has a structure and that structural laws deal with coexistence rather than change (Assiter, 1984). Researching structures in CCI is often used as a first step to understanding system-based investigation. For example, CCI managers need to know how funding structures work, or how staff and human resources are organised within a company. Often a simple organisation chart gives an orientation of how information and money flows through an organisation. This initial gathering of information can be extended to the study of the underlying structures that correspond to complex systems, such as formal and informal power arrangements, which will impact how CCI work is organised.

Critical Theory

As Assiter highlighted, structuralism as a theory is limited when investigating change, but many researchers are interested in capturing and implementing change in CCI. Famously, the members of Frankfurt school in the 1920s developed another theoretical frame, known as *critical theory*. As the name suggests, it aims to critique and change society. The purpose of critical theory is to capture and explain the assumptions that prevent people from having a full and true understanding of how the world works. It is a theory influenced by Karl Marx's critiques of the economy and society. As a research strand, it is motivated by emancipation, in the sense that the individual needs to be liberated from social oppression. Members of the Frankfurt school in the 1920s and 30s were deeply concerned about the inequalities that existed in society, which continue today. Critical theory proved to be highly relevant in explaining labour conditions in the creative industries. The Frankfurt School initiated what later became CCI labour studies. Specifically, Theodor Adorno and Max

Horkheimer's work, *Dialectic of Enlightenment*, was the first to address changes in the cultural industries (see also the Introduction). The authors explained that culture-industrial hyper-commercialisation evidences a fateful shift in the structure of all commodities, and therefore in the structure of capitalism itself. When the emphasis is on marketability, the culture industry dispenses entirely with the "purposelessness" that was central to art's autonomy. Horkheimer and Adorno (2020) analysed and highlighted the consequences that an already occurring societal shift will have on art and cultural productions. Critiquing societal development and discussing consequences drives this form of research. Today, this critical perspective, as well as its description of its future developments, anticipated CCI research. Many scholars are motivated by criticality, and it has become a common and general expression in many academic settings. Some of the fundamental understandings in CCI can be traced back to the application of critical theory. For example, Jim McGuigan's lifelong work of exposing the consequences of neoliberalism and later neoconservatism for CCI provided a stark warning for future generations, based on a rigorous critical societal view (McGuigan, 2016). Currently, we see this discussion invigorated in our determination to understand cultural value and what role arts, and what role *cultural* and *creative* play, as adjectives, when framing and developing an industry (Wesner, 2022).

Critical theory is easily misunderstood as focusing on negativity, pointing out the ills in society and not developing a forward-looking perspective. On the contrary, the aim of the societal critique has been to better society by pointing out the pitfalls and dangers that are hidden or not instantly obvious. Part of the process involves highlighting ideas that might hinder development or blind our understanding in discovering new explanations. Walter Benjamin, an associate of the Frankfurt school, wrote about the loss of the aura in the reproductions of artworks as an opportunity to revolutionise "the whole social function of art. Instead of being founded on ritual, it is based on a different practice: politics" (Benjamin, 1969 6). He moved attention away from the overtly aesthetic function of art and toward the people who practice art, while promoting the investigation of politics. For example, this includes researching power relations and how power is generated and enacted.

In the second half of the twentieth century, Jürgen Habermas, a German philosopher and student of Adorno's and Horkheimer's, looked at how people communicate and how a mutual understanding can be achieved through dialogue. He argued that a society that focuses on instrumental rationality as expressed, for example, in the profit maximising rule of markets, suppresses communicative competences of the lifeworld in favour of the logic of the system (Habermas, 1984).

Habermas was also involved in what is known today as the positivism dispute, which developed among German sociologists in the 1960s and that summarised some of the fundamental differences between positivism and interpretivism within the field of sociology, even till today. Interestingly, the positivism dispute originated from a discussion of the status of values in the social sciences, a dispute that started at a conference about methodologies. Researchers defending positivism argued that scientific approaches must be applied in sociology, while Adorno, Horkheimer, and Habermas, the critical theorists of the Frankfurt school, argued that empirical questions are rooted in philosophical issues and that scientific methods, such as observation, are influenced by the researcher's social existence. Both camps agreed that value judgements influence the findings of research, but in science this is judged as a limitation, while for the interpretivist it is a valuable expression of the societal environment. In CCI research, we are familiar with a similar distinction between science and art (or humanities) that is also based on value judgement. C. P. Snow discussed "the two cultures" in his Reith lecture of 1959, tracing the history and distinctions of the split in societal life (Snow, 2012). Even contemporary thinking judges science to be essential, a necessity, while art and humanities are valued as a nice addition to our life. The underlying principle is that science is valued above the arts, and that investigations in sociology should be purely scientific – as, for example, discussions about STEM subject preference in schools, which has been highlighted recently. Distinctions are less exclusive, and opinions are represented as laying on a spectrum rather than contradictions, but those differences are not dissolved.

Pragmatism

Leaving the idea of values and value judgement to one side, pragmatism focuses on the outputs, on solving problems. If the solutions work in practice, then there are no further questions asked. Pragmatism is a welcome strand in CCI research. The down-to-earth attitude, the focus on consequences, is mirrored in day-to-day CCI management that is based on the same problem-solving ideas.

William James (1842–1910) developed pragmatism as a philosophical outlook while at the University of California, Berkeley in the early twentieth century. At the University of Chicago, John Dewey (1859–1952) shared James's viewpoints. He also understood theories as tools or instruments for coping with reality. The problem-solving capacity enables theories to be applied repeatedly, with the option of replacement when they become out of touch with practice. This view allowed for an understanding of culture as ongoing communication, as ever changing, and in contemporary understandings it has given rise to practice-based and process-focused thinking. Knowledge is understood as a product of inquiry gained through experience, in which we change and alter our views of the world. In this sense, knowing has agency while exploring the world. Consequently, observation is thereby seen as a selection process and not as independently discovered data or facts.

Pierre Bourdieu (1930–2002), a well-known and regularly quoted author in CCI research, showed familiarity with pragmatism in his later years, with his work on habitus and field, giving us further insights on how to research cultural practices. With the concept of *habitus*, he positions the individual within "a system of durable, transposable dispositions that are regular, but not regulated, and adapted to goals, but without being predetermined" (1977 72). Bourdieu saw habitus as "practical sense", which might be organised through structure, regularity, or improvisation. He understood habitus as an internalisation of social order that is dependent on time and place. The second concept that he called *field* is simply expressions of social life in which habitus becomes practical. While the field relates to historical and objectified relations as expressed in the form of power or capital, in *habitus* the relations are internalised as perceptions, appreciations, and actions. In the *field*, competition is a driving force and through constant comparison, participants try to gain advantage or maintain advantage to set the rules and behaviours. Bourdieu introduced cultural, social, economic, and symbolic capital as forms through which the competitive struggles are played out in field. All forms of capital take time to accumulate and have "the capacity to produce profit and to reproduce itself in identical or expanded form". He continues to describe *capital* "as a force that is inscribed into the objectivity of things, representing the imminent structure of the social world, determining the chances of success for practices" (Bourdieu, 1986 241). The most straightforward form is economic capital, which covers everything that is directly convertible into money. Cultural capital is gained through educational qualifications, and social capital is expressed in connections or institutionalised forms, such as titles and honours. Symbolic capital is the result of the transformed economic, cultural, and social capital. CCI studies such as those focusing on art education have been applying the cultural capital frame to explain access/engagement, and the lack of it, with cultural organisations since the 1980s. The idea of habitus has influenced understandings of the democratisation of culture as an embodied experience of art and culture. Bourdieu might not be recognised as a pragmatist in the first instance, but he shares with James the same interest in patterns of embodied dispositions that explain individual relationships to the social environment. Bourdieu's work features social structures and uncovers hierarchies of domination. In this respect, he goes beyond the focus on practice, but shares the pragmatist belief in a unified notion of continuous change. This form of change is gained through experience and action. Explaining the essence becomes unimportant in favour of investigating the function of things. In doing so, established norms of social science dualism of theory/practice and objectivity/subjectivity are broken down for good.

Critical Realism

Advocates of critical realism also abandoned the binary of objectivity versus subjectivity when applying a different view. They emphasise that we are unable to see the world objectively. Our worldview, as expressed in concepts and biases, guides what we see. This understanding shares with positivism an interest in the objective world but recognizes the relationship between reality and its perception (i.e., there is a true reality, which is measured imperfectly). As a new paradigm, critical realism marries positivist and interpretivist thinking, thereby addressing the issue of ontology. What is there? How does knowledge exist? Critical realists argue that we need to distinguish between the real, actual, and empirical. The real is understood as structures, which have properties that empower other structures (causal mechanism). The actual is envisaged in events that are generated by the activation of the causal mechanism, while the empirical as domain covers the events that can be observed or experienced.

In CCI study, this relates to many pertinent questions of access and evaluation. For example, a right to culture, education, and health exists in many democratic countries but not all people are aware of it. In CCI research, nonattenders of cultural events were omitted from the research agenda for many years. The ever-increasing thirst for growing attendance numbers triggered a shift in research agendas. The resultant investigation into why people don't attend, showed previously unseen causal links to social stratification, gender, and inequality, which were highlighted as barriers to attendance. As a result, the real (access for all) was set in conflict to the actual (not all use the access) and the empirical (talking to non-attenders) highlighted the barriers to access that are equally perceived as real.

Social Constructionism

This frame carries the meaning in the words. Its name gives an accurate description of its qualities. Knowledge is constructed through interaction or human activity, and individuals create meaning through interactions. Social constructionism builds on the ontological understanding that reality is not naturally driven. In terms of research, we should focus on investigating how social reality is constructed and how knowledge arises from studying the processes that are related to ideology, interest, and power, for example.

In an organisational context, we could investigate how people identify with institutions. The phrase "I have been institutionalised" is not uncommon in academic circles. People sometimes refer to the dichotomy of feeling comfortable in an institutional setting but regretting their inability to escape the institution's narrowmindedness and barriers. It emphasises that being inside or outside of an institutional setting gives us a specific view and informs our understanding of the processes that are conducted. I am sure you are familiar that knowledge is never abstract, but is local and embedded in a community. Arts education has applied social constructionism in projects that are of a collaborative nature. Learning is achieved, for example, though the development of scenarios or through reconstruction and play, paying attention, respecting, and integrating the cultural and social context of interactions in the research settings. Team problem solving is equally seen as a learning method in social constructionistic settings.

Postmodernism

All previously mentioned paradigmatic frames developed within the context of modernism, which is a constructed and questioned concept that might be better described as a societal and cultural movement, which has undergone many kinds of transformation, but nevertheless loosely frames a large collection of ideas. As an art movement, modernism included several subgroups, such as symbolism, futurism, cubism, formalism, and absurdity, all of which sought to develop new forms of expression and break with old, outlived norms, and cultural traditions. Modernism served as a friction or counterpoint to postmodernism, which remains influential in the discussion of contemporary paradigms. Postmodernism, as an umbrella paradigm, claimed to turn modernism on its head. It did not just question but rejected reason, deep structures, or underlaying patterns, and sought to replace them with a fixation on surface and depthlessness. The author is dead, or as the French philosopher Michael Foucault declared, the author is a hinderance because of the single voice that declares all authority stifling to the free composition of fiction. Art was co-opted as brand, serving capitalism. Reality is a mental construct. The way out was postmodernism, "a giddy, joyful liberation movement" (Byrne, in Jeffries 7), against functional style as oppressive modernism celebrating antihierarchal, fun-loving, and exuberant liberation. Postmodernists applied broad scepticism, subjectivism, or relativism in favour of a free-for-all philosophy.

However, the role of ideology in asserting and maintaining political and economic power remains part of many discussions. For example, in the arts we see how creativity utilising technology has shifted from traditional forms of art and culture to the likes of social media influencers. In their quest to celebrate free choice and buying power, they summarise and pair differentiated consumerism with individual libertarianism as a winning formula. The consequences for us as researchers are multiple. Apart from becoming online savvy, our private/public binary thinking requires adjustment. What is happening to our critical thinking when it is exposed as corrupted by binaries? How can we capture ideas when an anything-goes philosophy dominates? Can we design entertaining and fun-loving questionnaires or surveys to follow the postmodern turn? Should we focus on ambivalent knowledge and forget about the underlying pattern? Not all people agree, and the philosopher Daniel Dennett summarised that this no-truth-and-only-interpretation paradigm has rendered conversations "in which nobody is wrong and nothing can be confirmed, only asserted" as meaningless (quoted in Jeffries 15). He argues that the relationship to truth, evidence, and science, is lost. This takes us back to the opposing idea of what I argued in the beginning, under the positivistic paradigm, which emphasises evidence and reason as their main principle for research. Matthew D'Ancona (2017) argued in *Post-Truth: The New War on Truth and How to Fight Back* that postmodernist approaches were less helpful to confront the wave of fake news that propels with ease through social media platforms. In short, only focusing on power and interest, while leaving objectivity and truth aside, requires timely revisions. But through and with research, it is achievable.

Conclusion

This chapter captures a selection of theoretical frames that have been applied in CCI research, both by researchers and students. I have introduced a variety of paradigms that all developed and carried forward specific ideas or focus, but all relate to epistemological, ontological, or axiological understandings of our world.

As researchers, it is important to find out if the concepts and ideas resonate with our personal understanding of how to perceive knowledge, reality, and beliefs. Understanding matters in research, whatever paradigm you adopt. Paradigms do not judge, but they carry convictions and values that we might or might not share. Being aware of what paradigms hold together, how they change and transform, feeds research curiosity. It helps us to stay truthful to our convictions, as expressed in the variety of paradigms. Additionally, paradigms question our worldview and raise personal awareness of how and why we think in certain ways as individual researchers. Paradigms enable us to challenge presumed ideas and reveal unfamiliar ways of thinking. Paradigms offer a spectrum of alignments for our thinking, but equally enable us to question our convictions as we think critically about our values, how we perceive reality, and how we understand the knowledge that is generated.

In research, working against personal convictions needs to be a conscious choice that is informed by rationales. Naturally, we choose what is familiar and align with what makes us feel comfortable, but the challenge is to raise personal awareness to the point that it enables us to make a choice.

Paradigm Exercise

In this exercise you are asked to think through and investigate the personal assumptions, convictions, and values that have and will shape the way you understand paradigms.

1. Start by writing down the values you treasure and believe in. For example: humanity, freedom, locality, security, love, creativity, diversity.
2. Answer the following questions:

   a How do you think knowledge is generated, produced, and understood (for example, through research, studying, practice, experience, etc.)?
   b What is your understanding of truth? Do you believe in an absolute, variable, diverse, objective, or subjective notion of truth?

   c   How do you define reality? Is there one verifiable reality or is reality socially constructed and interpreted? Is reality how things exist, as represented in their essence?

3.   Set your answers from section two in relation to your beliefs and values from section one. Do you think that all knowledge needs to be objectively verified and/or subjectively interpreted? Do you understand research to be the process of finding out the truth?

4.   Check your answer from section two against the description of the above-mentioned paradigms. Do you see some of your answers match, align with, or oppose those theories? Could you recognise some of the ideas mentioned earlier, which describe your perception of the world?

5.   Find out more about the paradigms that have the strongest alignment with or opposition to your perspectives by using your library.

THEMATIC HIGHLIGHT: INTERSECTIONALITY

Race, gender, class, and disability have all been studied extensively in CCI and many inconsistencies and inequalities have been highlighted by research. For example, discourses addressed repressive behaviours towards women as separate categories, focusing on gendered pay, career inhibition, and sexual exploitation. Working class actors cannot rely on extensive networks to propel their careers in the same way that their middle- and upperclass counterparts can. Coloured skin remained a hindrance in ballet education until very recently. While critical research has addressed the ills of each of these categories, Kimberlé Crenshaw applied a different perspective. She went one step further by demonstrating the interconnected nature of these categories, while highlighting the areas of overlap and interdependencies betweeen social categories. Intersectionality captures the different modes and identities that result in discrimination and privilege. Crenshaw (2017) acknowledged that a single categorisation does not account for the accumulation of privilege and discrimination that is practised when class, gender, and race come together as one personal or collective identity. Instead, she argued that social identities are multiple and intersecting. The critical step is recognising that systems of oppression as practiced at the macrolevel of society, which result in multiple social inequalities and equities at the personal or individual experience. Intersectionality provides a framework for understanding and thinking through these identity-focused links.

In this section I reflect on my personal understanding of intersectionality, working though some of the big questions asked in this chapter, while applying and identifying some of the frameworks that foreground intersectionality linked to critical theory. I will use three questions as a starting point. How do I think? What are my cultural values? Who am I as a researcher?

Being trained in the German and British Higher Education system of the 1990s and early 2000s, I absorbed theories of the Frankfurt school and felt that a general critique of society is a welcoming framework. Improving society through research motivates my work today. My interest in cultural values is equally defined through my understanding of the importance of values as underlying principles that shape human behaviour in the long term. My previous background as cultural producer instilled an appreciation of the arts and of culture as an intrinsic good. So, it is no surprise that this has translated into my understanding of how I approach research. My focus is on understanding experiences and how people interact with cultural goods. Intersectionality is embedded in all cultural activities and, as a researcher, I benefited from privileges of education and cultural upbringing, which are reflected in attitudes of curiosity towards knowledge and imprinted in cultural capital. However, this is just one part of the multiplicity that helps shape my identity as researcher. I grew up in the former German Democratic Republic (GDR) where school education focused on rationality. The oppressive ideology favoured values such as obedience, discipline, and self-censorship. Through curiosity, personal freedom, and rebellion, after German unification, I learned to appreciate, scrutinising the limits of neoliberal and neoconservative frameworks as a student and as a lecturer. I experienced *otherness*, as nonbelonging in Western Germany and the UK and learnt to understand individualism and competition as a capitalist motivational trait.

Alongside these developments, the power of interpretation remained a defining force and for me there is no absolute truth, merely multiple perceptions. When analysing data, I acknowledge that truth is a human-made concept that comes in multiple forms and shapes, as brilliantly diverse as people are. In this respect, I am cautious about objectifying evidence-based cultural policies research. I argue for a proximity to the subject and understand that my own convictions need to be scrutinised through reflection, as a continuing process in all research phases. Martin Heidegger captured this moment in the phrase *being in the world* (1962), an understanding that includes being close to the human subject and that locates the researcher as part of the investigative environment or context. Investigation of culture as a human-made concept requires a mindful and open approach that accepts interpretation at its core. Having said this, I can indulge in pattern, minimalistic design and I cherish clarity. All these attributes have become hallmarks of my professional identity and might equally be seen as suitable in positivistic frames and theories. Finally, I find postmodern thoughts challenging and intriguing in their rigorous approach to critiquing, not just structures or patterns, but the complete makeup of all thinking, so far as it is expressed in Francis Fukuyama's statement "the end of history?" (Fukuyama, 1989). I am curious to look beyond the remits for an example of nonhierarchical depthlessness or surface surfing, but so far, I am holding on to explanations that are guided by experience and a combination of rational logic and emotional depth.

LEARNING OBJECTIVES

- To understand the meaning of paradigms
- To develop awareness of different strands and field-specific thinking, as explained through the theoretical lenses of paradigms
- To distinguish between the different schools of thought

Note

1 Culture Count (https://culturecounts.cc) operates as an evaluation service provider, for example, accessing cultural value for cultural organizations in different parts of the world. It developed a sector-led, matrix- evaluation platform and since 2013 has been operating as independent company.

References

Assiter, A. 1984. Althusser and structuralism . *British Journal of Sociology*, 35(2): 272–296.

Benjamin, W. 1969. The work of art in the age of mechanical reproduction. In H. Zohn (Trans.) & H. Arendt (Ed.) *Illuminations*. Schocken Books.

Bourdieu, P. 1986. The forms of capital. In J. Richardson (Ed.), *Handbook of Theory and Research for the Sociology of Education* (pp. 241–258). Greenwood.

Comte, A. 1855. *The Positive Philosophy of Auguste Comte*. C. Blanchard.

Comte, A. 1975. *Auguste Comte and Positivism: The Essential Writings*. Transaction Publishers.

Crenshaw, K. W. 2017. *On Intersectionality: Essential Writings*. The New Press.

d'Ancona, M. 2017. *Post-Truth: The New War on Truth and How to Fight Back*. Random House.

Fukuyama, F. 1989. The end of history? *The National Interest*, 16: 3–18.

Habermas J. 1984. *The Theory of Communicative Action*. Beacon.

Heidegger, M. 1962. *Being and Time* (J. Macquarrie and E. Robinson, Trans.). Harper & Row.

Heidegger, M. 1982. *The Basic Problems of Phenomenology* (A. Hofstadter, Trans). Indiana University Press.

Horkheimer, M. & Adorno, T. W. 2020. *Dialectic of Enlightenment*. Stanford University Press.

Husserl, E. 2001. *Logical Investigations: Vols. One and Two* (J. N. Findlay, Trans.) Routledge.

Jeffries, S. 2022. *Everything, All the Time, Everywhere: How We Became Postmodern*. Verso Books.

Kuhn, T. 2021 [1962]. *The Structure of Scientific Revolutions*. Princeton University Press.

McGuigan, J. 2016. *Neoliberal Culture*. Palgrave Macmillan.

Merleau-Ponty, M. 2012. *Phenomenology of Perception* (D. A. Landes, Trans). Routledge.

Phiddian, R., Meyrick, J., Barnett, T., & Maltby, R. 2017. Counting culture to death: an Australian perspective on culture counts and quality metrics. *Cultural Trends*, 26(2): 174–180.

Popper, K. 1979 [2007]. *Die Beiden Grundprobleme der Erkenntnistheorie*, Tübingen: Routledge. Translated as *The Two Fundamental Problems of the Theory of Knowledge* (A. Pickel, Trans., T. E. Hansen, Ed.). Routledge.

Salmons, J. 2019. *Find the Theory in Your Research: Little Quick Fix* (pp. 1–120). SAGE.

Sartre, J.-P. 1956. *Being and Nothingness* (H. Barnes, Trans.). Washington Square Press.

Schwandt, T. A. 1989. Solutions to the paradigm conflict: Coping with uncertainty. *Journal of Contemporary Ethnography*, 17(4): 379–407.

Schwandt, T. A. 1994. Constructivist, interpretivist approaches to human inquiry. In N. K. Denzin, & Y. S. Lincoln (Ed.), *Handbook of Qualitative Research* (pp. 118–137). Sage.

Smith, D. W. 2018. Phenomenology. *The Stanford Encyclopedia of Philosophy.* https://plato.stanford.edu/archives/sum2018/entries/phenomenology/.

Snow, C. P. 2012. *The Two Cultures.* Cambridge University Press.

Wesner, S. 2022. Cultural values as policy directives: Techniques, technologies and symbolic work. *International Journal of Cultural Policy*, 28(7): 858–874. doi:10.1080/10286632.2022.2137153.

3

METHODOLOGIES

Introduction

In this chapter, the emphasis shifts from paradigms to methodologies in CCI research. Methodologies sit between paradigms and methods, occupying the middle ground, the in-between that negotiates, guides, and connects, creating the trio of research. Paradigms explain the ways we think in abstract and theoretical terms by providing underlying concepts and theories. Methodologies apply these theoretical frames, breaking them down in specific and focused approaches. Methodologies help guide us when choosing suitable research tools and methods that can be applied in formulating rationales for our research approach. Methodology provides the lens through which our analysis occurs. The methods we select are prompted and validated by the methodology. In short, in terms of functionality we understand methodologies as the go-between paradigms and methods, but the meaning and usage of the term is wrapped in ambiguity. Often, *methodology* is used as a more sophisticated word for *methods*, but the terms are not synonymous in any way. The same meaning, but applied in reverse, is often used when *methodology* is confused with *paradigms*. In this case, epistemological and ontological questions are bundled together with methodology, under an overall investigation of concepts and reasonings. In this book, I understand paradigms to be the theoretical frames and methodology to be the strategy that is applied to CCI research. The previous chapter focused on paradigms. In this chapter, our attention moves to methodology and methods, which are explained in depth in the following two chapters, which are divided into methods of data collection and data analysis. This table of content follows a logic that starts with broad concepts of paradigms before becoming more specific and individualised with methodologies and methods in later chapters.

DOI: 10.4324/9781003161912-3

This chapter is organised into two parts. In the first, after I explain the meaning of methodology and its role of as part of the trio, in the same manner as I introduced paradigms in the previous chapter, I introduce a selection of common methodologies used in CCI research. But this time, intersectionality is exchanged with the concept of *cultural values* as a content-specific example.

Meanings of Methodology

Moses and Knutsen (2019) introduced the analogy of a well-stocked toolbox, to explain the difference between method and methodology. As a hobby weaver, I prefer to refer to a sewing box, but the analogy is the same. Methods can be viewed as tools (or threads, needles, buttons, and yarns) and the methodology represents the ensemble of tools in the box, together with the ideas, narratives, and memories that we connect with the items in the box. Methodologies tell us what we can do with the tools, but they are much more; they carry memories that can be called up by the button that came off a favourite dress, or the leftover name tag from a school uniform. Methodology refers to how you have arranged items in the box (all threads together, buttons bundled by size, shape and colour), and the different purposes (tailoring, sewing, crocheting, mending things) that you apply to the items and the people who use the sewing box (including different generations of sewing bees). The items in the box, the methods on their own, are useless without an assigned meaning, without a plan or methodology that guides us how to use them. Box users will pick out the items that best suit the purpose, by relying on experience, using the knowledge acquired that they have memorised on how to use the items.

Creswell calls methodologies "a strategy or plan of action that links methods to outcomes" (2003 5). I argue that methodologies give strategic guidance to how we could find out what we want to find out, even when we cannot achieve specific outcomes. Said in a more formal way: a methodology describes the "general research strategy that outlines the way in which research is to be undertaken" (Howell, 2012 ix). Methodologies tell us how to design and conduct research. For example, you can ask prompting questions about what it is that interests you. Are you going to focus on the experience of people as explained in actions, or do you want to focus on the text of how the experiences are expressed in writing?

In practical terms, with a dissertation or a major project, you will have a dedicated section often called "methodology". Here you are asked to explain how you have conducted your research, together with an explanation of your paradigms and methods for data collection and analysis. This chapter or section will provide an indication of your study's overall validity and reliability.

Methodologies

Discovering the variety of thinking with and through methodological frames enriches our knowledge base, and discussing methodologies helps to negotiate the process of researching. There are many different methodologies to choose from, when it comes to the diversity and variety of methodologies, I recommend that novice researchers skim as many methodologies as possible, in the first instance, with the aim of selecting a few for further study. An old-fashioned visit to the library and scanning the general methodology section will help you to gain an overview. Do not allow yourself to be overwhelmed by the number of books on display. If you do find navigating the diversity of the methodology landscape overwhelming, focus on specific subjects (sociology, cultural studies, philosophy, policy studies). This section is organised in a similar way. I will discuss a selection of methodologies that are commonly used in our field of study, which students have used in the past. These are: ethnography, case studies, discourse analysis, grounded theory, phenomenology, feminism, practice-based research, and action research. These methodologies serve many fields, such as social science, cultural studies, cultural policy, and arts management. Specific readings are available, and at your disposal as a researcher, through your resource centres, including the online provisions of libraries. Importantly, this section introduces methodologies, but further in-depth information awaits your exploration and detailed study. I have focused on the main aspects of the eight methodologies and how we can distinguish these from one another. Which methodology you will choose for your studies depends on what you want to investigate and what values, convictions, and ideas you bring with you, which you have already explored in your thinking about paradigms in the prior chapter. Like paradigms, methodologies are not fixed. They are discussed, disputed, and extended in their own discourses, and we can trace their development over time. They provide you with parameters for your investigation and make sure your research is valid and reliable. Every researcher or group of researchers brings their personal understandings and interpretations, resulting in an array of applications that are unique. Your approach, too, will evolve, be changed, and adapt over time.

Ethnography

Starting with a student favourite, ethnography is often described as the in-depth or holistic study of people, cultures, habits, and their mutual differences. Ethnography is the practice of verbal description. It gives accounts of other people's lives and cultures, and is delivered as finished pieces of work, most commonly in writing, but it can take other formats, like a documentary or a video essay. Ethnographers understand that human behaviour is a complicated phenomenon, composed of and influenced by a multitude of factors. They set out to capture the interplay of complexities in a location, region, or place. Often this is done with in situ research that focusses on groups of people. There are numerous accounts that describe cultural dimensions, shared practices, and belief systems. Famously, Margaret Mead (1901–1978), whom you might have encountered in previous studies, was a well-known social anthropologist (a different name for ethnographers in the USA) whose work covering South

Pacific and Southeast Asian traditional cultures in the 1920s influenced the 1960s sexual revolution in the USA. Her interpretations of sexual freedom in premarital relations as woven into Samoa's communities, sparked a great deal of interest. But it was not as directly related to the her topic, as I had initially expected. Instead, Mead's research practices were questioned. Derek Freeman (1916–2001) contested her work about adolescents' sexual behaviour in Samoa on the grounds of reliability and neutrality. Today, this is known as the Mead-Freemann controversy. Freemann argued, using a positivist paradigm, that all research, if repeated by another researcher, should yield the same result and must not be biased by the researcher's personal and political commitments. Mead's studies were considered biased and unrepeatable (Shankman, 2009). Today, we speak of multiple validities, and it seems hard to comprehend that an objectified view of reality is applicable in contemporary ethnography. In natural sciences, the repeatability of experiments remains respected, but the role of humans and human behaviour is also recognized and that recognition is not limited to matters of potential bias. In social science, there is praise for the various outcomes of human research and researchers are asked to reflect on consensus and imbedding environment as part of the research design. By viewing realities as multiple and complex, we accept that there is more than one way of making sense of the world, as opposed to a universal interpretation that covers all eventualities.

Before introducing digital ethnography for social media, which is another student favourite when carrying out CCI research, let me first argue for a differentiated and informed use of the terminology. Initially, it can be confusing that *anthropology* is the preferred term in the USA and that European countries have a history of referring to the same field as *ethnography*, but geographical specificity is not the exclusive reason for the different usage. Therefore, please note that *ethnography* and *anthropology* are not interchangeable terms and, like many other terms we apply, you are asked to investigate in which context the usage occurs. The idea of the *field* or *going into the field* is also a contested term in anthropology, which relates to the usage of both terms. Commonly, ethnography is associated with fieldwork. Anthropology tends to apply to an all-inclusive approach, with fieldwork and other aspects of analysis, like the writing up of fieldwork, seen as components of an holistic investigation (Ingold, 2008). I suggest defining your frames of reference from the start to avoid any misunderstandings.

Netnography

Adding to the context of ethnographic terminology in the 1990s, the new name *netnography* emerged in relation to the internet and was later applied to social media research. Kozinets (1998) introduced *netnography* as a methodology that investigates the specific instance in which community is produced through computer-mediated communications (CMC) (Kozinets, 1998). At the time, it resembled a combination of ethnography and network theory, and it stressed that, in addition to procedural steps, human connection and personal presence online are important identifiers. So, is netnography ethnographic research that takes place online? Yes, netnography adapts the ethnographic research methodology to the study of online communities in order to discover the natural behavioural patterns of internet users. But other names have been circulating, for example, "virtual ethnography" (Hine, 2000), which was later rephrased as "ethnography for the internet" (Hine, 2015); "cyber-ethnography" (Ward, 1999); and "connective ethnography" (Dirksen, Huizing, & Smit, 2010). The terms aimed to capture research carried out either exclusively online or in combination of on- and offline variations. As a methodology, netnography began to focus on what was going on exclusively online, and adapted research investigations to newer forms of communication, moving from static webpages to Web 2.0 and to Web 3.0 approaches, which include tweeting, podcasting, social networking, and virtual environments. Kozinets (2010) argued that netnography stands out from the other ethnographic investigations with its systematic, step-by-step approach that addresses ethical, procedural, and methodological concerns. In an earlier paper, Kozinets (2002) noticed six steps: namely research planning, entrée, data collection, data analysis, ethical standards, and research representation, which are specific to online research. These are not so far removed from the steps that I recommend in this book for best practice for research. The increased use of automated social media responses and, on a broader scale, our constant exposure to digital technologies through the Internet of Things, challenges the distinction between online and offline research. More recently, Kozinets (2015) defined netnography as a "more human-centred, participative, personally, socially and emotionally engaged vector" (p. 96), including the study of emerging or now widely adopted technologies such as AI.

In CCI research, netnography is applied in various forms and circumstances that require anonymity. It allows for unobtrusive and noninfluencing monitoring of communication behaviour when, for example, studying cultural wars or other politically sensitive topics. Netnography could be a choice for any online issues that may be stigmatized and difficult to study in face-to-face situations. Netnography offers a place from which to study emerging data, as well as to support research about marginalised groups, feeding into issues about access to culture in CCI research. De Valck et al. (2009) point towards cost-effective and rapid data collection as an advantage to researchers, which should not be interpreted to mean that those studies are carried out quickly and without costs. Kurikko and Tuominen (2012) argued that immersive depth, researchers' prolonged engagement, and persistent conversations are quality standards of netnography. Costello et al. (2012) identified value creation, through cocreation among online groups and members, as another benefit of this methodology. Culture is constructed among the members who communicate, participate, and develop the online spaces, just as it is with offline spaces. As cocreators, both participants and researchers gain agency, which defines alternative power relations, as we have seen in social media communities, such as the #MeToo movement that impacted our cultural identities both on- and offline. Netnography is based on ethnographic elements, and as Kozinets (2010) argues, Gertz's "thick description" (1973) has its place, being able to focus on the common, as well as on the unique and novel. For example, we can gain insight through rich data by studying the word-of-mouth processes of the online communities. In terms of scale of studies and the numbers of communities that are investigated, it depends on the study design, but no limitations are given, apart from those of the analysing capacities of the researchers. Students often ask how many communities should be investigated. Netnography is suitable for the in-depth study of a single community or to compare multiple groups.

Lorenz (2017) provides an example of choosing a single community in her study of the working lives of freelance female musicians. She used netnography as her methodology. Lui et al (2022) studied online reviews posted on Google and TripAdvisor from tourists that visited four anime tourist destinations in Japan, comparing Eastern and Western tourism experiences as an example for analysing multiple communities. The active or passive involvement of the researcher highlights a further consideration when considering this methodology. An active stance involves participation with or being a member of the community, while the passive or nonparticipatory role leaves the researcher monitoring communities without any direct communication. Loanzon et al. (2013 1576) described this as a specialised type of lurking that focuses on observation. Netnography provides different rationales as to why hanging around and lurking in the communities, without participation, captures the community in its "natural state", minimising biased behaviour and researcher interventions. This argument is not without controversy since the announcement of an online researcher lurking and observing the community might trigger a change in members' behaviour from the start. A different case could be made if the material is analysed retrospectively (e.g., in an archival setting, as a historical study, after active involvement has ceased to be possible). The discussion about the role of the researcher, in both the active and passive setting, is furthered through the perception of the researcher's vision, as it is applied to the community, which the community members may not share.

The researcher remains a crucial part in every methodology. In netnography, the degree of self-reflection, as described in this chapter in autoethnographic studies, gives an indication of what roles and functions might be beneficial for advancing the overall aim of the study. This can range from being part of a community (e.g., a fan in an online fan club, discussing fan practices) to organising online focus groups or interviews that act as a springboard for further online participation. In Kozinets' (2010) step-by-step guide, he mentions ethical responsibilities that are entangled with the role of the researcher (see Chapter 9). A self-reflective approach helps to facilitate and assist communities in cocreation through sharing the process of design, data collection, and analysis with the community, as long as it remains within privacy guidelines. These can be simple tools (e.g., sharing a research diary or regular feedback session). To conclude, netnography is an adaptable methodology focused on online communications, offering both passive and active involvement. It can be a stand-alone methodology or be part of a mixed-methods approach. It utilises various resources, ranging from text, video, images, and sound and can be combined with other digital resources.

Autoethnography

To utilise and analyse your own professional experience, a self-reflexive or autoethnographic approach places you as a practitioner at the very centre of the study. Instead of focusing on the experiences of groups or people –as the words *self* and *auto* indicate – you investigate your position and experience in relation to the topic, theme, or people. The aim is to observe or recall your own practices and to analyse behaviours, actions, and situations. Auto-ethnography acknowledges that subjectivity and emotions are a valuable part of the investigation. You learn with and through reflection. This methodology has been applied to successfully instigate change and sustainability in CCI leadership management.

You do not have to be in a senior management role to employ an auto-ethnographic approach. It works for all levels of professional experience if you are investigating your experience. With the disappearing distinction between private and working life this can be difficult, but it can be rewarding to recognise the complexities of personality and character that are interwoven with one's cultural context. We learn best through failure and mistakes, and those experiences are waiting to be critically analysed. But autoethnography is not a self-help methodology. It has the potential to clarify positions and roles for yourself, but the emphasis remains on researching the field, the environment, and the context of which you are an integral part. The focus is on under-standing cultural experience through the analysis of personal experience. This includes paying attention to the process and product of the research, recognising how the personal experience of the researcher influences the research design, implementation, and results.

Ellis et al. (2011) points out that autoethnography recognises a multitude of ways of thinking, speaking, valuing, believing, and analysing, and as a result expands the understanding of what kind of people we are or claim to be. In a similar way to ethnography, autoethnography provides a handy set of descriptive and analytical tools to be used as a methodology in their own right and along with other methodologies (see grounded theory section). As a process, autoethnography focuses on your past experiences, which you selectively assemble using hindsight, while consulting a combination of text, oral, and visual experiences. For example, when investigating life trajectories, self-claimed transformative, special moments, or epiphanies, are often remembered.

On their own, they may not have a significant impact, but they have been known to act as triggers or starting points for studies. The effect of those intense situations lingers as images, feelings, and memories, which can frame the overall storytelling that sits at the heart of the writing-up process. Applying conventions of storytelling (character, scene, and plot development) requires writing skills that are evocative and, as with all ethnography, provide "the thick description of culture" (Geertz, 1973 10).

Autoethnography can take different shapes and forms. It depends on the emphasis that is placed on the role of the researcher, the interactions with others (i.e., community, co-constructed, collaborative autoethnography), and the space that is given to academic literature (i.e., traditional analysis). Every year, I see students excel in applying an autoethnographic approach, growing as researchers and creative professionals. But when you choose this methodology, you must pay attention to the ethical implications (see Chapter 9), both for yourself and for others. Importantly, ethics apply in all stages of the research, including taking care of yourself and of anybody else that is involved in your analysis. Self-analysis can trigger past experiences that evoke traumatic or painful memories, so knowing where you can seek help is important when choosing to analyse personal experiences.

Case Studies

The real-life context makes case studies one of the most attractive methodologies that can be used inside and outside an academic assessment frame. Most methodologies investigate real-life context, but case studies have claimed it as their prime appeal. Adding the attraction of providing an in-depth explanation of social and cultural behaviour, it is understandable why case studies are so popular in CCI. However, the widespread use of case studies can be misleading. Case studies often serve as illustrations and are confused with examples. In some reports (including annual reports from arts organisations), case studies are used as what Yin (2009) calls popular case studies, which differ from research case studies. When case study methodology is used as research, this goes beyond presenting an example or an illustration of a specific point. The main difference is the comprehensive approach of using a variety of quantitative and qualitative methods (see Chapters 4 and 5) to collect as much data as possible. Case studies build up and capture complexity and, in this respect, they elevate a view of life that opposes studying broken-down and small-sized chunks (Thomas, 2021). Ultimately, multiple sources of evidence help to create holistic research that brings together context and phenomenon in a single investigation. Most research methodologies are linked to content-specific theoretical frames, but in case studies this remains decisive. The difficulty lies in bringing the multiple sources of evidence under a unifying theoretical roof.

When unsure if case studies will work for a study, then the following three questions can be employed. They will provide an indication if this methodology is suitable for a research study:

1.   Is a contemporary phenomenon in the here and now being investigated?
2.   Are *how* and *why* questions being asked?
3.   Is a real-life situation to be studied, where the researcher's control is limited?

If the answer to all these questions is *yes*, you are good to develop your case study design. As a next step, you might want to think about numbers. How many case studies will you choose? The number of cases to study depends on the topic, in the first instance, but also on the type of case study you choose. In short, the type of case study you select will determine how many cases you will explore. For example, a single case is suitable if a specific theory is to be tested or if the case is unique or stands out in its characteristics and therefore can justifiably stand on its own. It could be a previously inaccessible phenomenon that can now be studied.

Multiple case studies are used to develop a theoretical framework that is built on replication, so you can predict similarities or contradictions amongst the cases. The different types of research case studies all carry a clue to their intent in their name. They can focus on an explanation (explanatory) that is often related to a presumed causal relationship. For example, if you are interested in studying gender imbalance within an art organisation, you could analyse wages and recruitment practices, to explain how differences or similarities affect the overall picture. Choosing the exploratory case study type works well when there is little known about the phenomenon, and you are interested in employing an in-depth approach to find out as much as possible about this case. For example, if you wish to explore the communication practices of art collectives in less-connected environments.

The descriptive case study focuses on documenting a phenomenon in a real-life context, asking how, what, and where questions. The overall aim of this type is to deliver a complete description, including statistics, web-based information, and locally sourced information. Most researchers collect information as a starting point and as a way into the research context, regardless of what methodology is used. A descriptive case study expands and perfects this exercise. The archetypical case study represents the dominant practice and exemplifies a trend or a moment in time. In terms of practice, it leads the way and embodies issues/themes and problems that are relevant to the wider field. The composite case study maps the field and highlights different approaches and positions. It demonstrates the flexibility of a theory and suggests the complexity of a cultural category, for example. This type brings together the unique or archetypical with the exceptional approach, which results in challenges to existing assumptions and creates complex conclusions. The pragmatic case study relies on the opportunity for information and access, making the most of an opportunity to carry out research. Many researchers cannot help but be in research mode all the time, and especially when they come across a phenomenon or issue that corresponds with their research interests. In my experience, holidays often turn into information-gathering exercises when visiting cultural sites, with some even developing into research studies. Reflecting about the place and position of the researcher is required for all methodologies, but with the pragmatic case study the sense of opportunity will need to be worked into the research design. Ideally, this goes beyond the simple notion of declaring an interest in reflecting about the meaning of the choice of place and situation in the researcher's own life.

Other forms of case studies are simply defined though another adjective in front of the noun. Hence, you might have come across descriptive case studies where the main function is to document and describe the phenomenon in question. Collective case studies focus on the broader appreciation that the study of multiple cases simultaneously or sequentially have to offer. Intrinsic case studies log the uniqueness of a case, asking how and why this example is unlike anything else and why it comes across as remarkable or unusual when compared to others. Instrumental case studies could be atypical to other cases. But emphasising a particular aspect, which might be a theory or a phenomenon that is captured in the case study, and therefore instrumentalising it for this purpose, makes the case study secondary, a helping tool to get the message across.

My favourite approach in case study research is to use the intrinsic case study model to understand something that is unique. At the same time, this unique aspect is used to provide knowledge that is then applied to other cases and contexts. Generally, I recommend Yin's excellent book (2009) on case study research to anyone who wants to engage further with this approach. It has a chapter about research case studies as methodology and applies case study methods using multiple cases.

Discourse Analysis (DA)

If there were a historical social media competition about which methodology gets the most likes, discourse analysis (DA) would most likely come out as the favourite for one simple reason: it has been used extensively. DA is widely applied in the humanities, arts, and cultural studies, including CCI research. If you have written essays in previous studies, you will be familiar with the concept of examining text as your main object of analysis. Text is understood as a window into broader social and cultural processes and Williams (1977) described DA as a moment of the material social process. The emphasis is on the conversations, the verbal, written, and semiosis (including body language) communications, that people have with each other or have encountered in letters, books, and blog posts. In fact, DA focuses on any communication that pays attention to the meaning of language and the context of its production and recognition. DA originates from the ethnomethodological tradition. It makes sense of the world around us, and in this case makes sense of the text that is presented. But it is not just the text; equal emphasis is also placed on the surroundings or the environment in which the text was produced. Many disciplines have developed their variations of discourse analysis and apply different theoretical traditions, focusing on slightly different aspects, such as language or structure. What most have in common is the focus on text or, indeed, anything that can be studied as text, and therefore written down. An interview transcript is a text, as are blogs and expressions on social media. In comparison to content analysis, DA asks for the meaning of the language and the words in use. It can focus on structure, sound, or grammar, and not just the meaning of content.

As with many methodologies, DA has developed variations and subgroups. But all subforms aim to provide a framework of how to approach text to be inclusive of the meaning of the content, and the surroundings (i.e., authors, location of publication, social and historical, context, as well as timings) applying accompanying views to the text. Often, it is a collection of discussions that forms a discourse. In essays, we tend to practice DA in presenting collections of discussions that other authors have previously been paying attention to, by adding our take on, and critical understanding of, what has been discussed.

Critical discourse analysis (CDA) foregrounds criticality as the main value that guides analysis, by examining how people interpret the text as part of their cultural resources. For example, Stephanie Taylor (2022), is a psychologist who is interested in common sense and how people integrate established ways of doing things into their understanding of the meaning of text. She argued that when operating from given perspectives, we follow, take for granted, or contradict ideas that provide starting points for our understanding. We then use this understanding to negotiate who the writers and speakers are, and what we understand they want to achieve with the text. While this provides us with the opportunity for a shared understanding (e.g., how common sense develops), it allows us to untangle and analyse the multiple associations that come with the relatively simple meaning of common sense (Wesner & Woddis, 2022 13).

Fairclough (2013) has written extensively about the social function of communication and how he captured those moments of practice with CDA. His theory is inclusive of all elements of practice, including cultural values, consciousness, means of production, identities, and semiosis. He is especially interested in the relationships between the different elements and how these relations are shaped and change over time within networks of practice. For example, the changing character of the language of the Arts Council of England from administration to management and from arts to culture, emphasises directions of change and takes account of representations of changing practices. Art organisations pushed the agendas of wellbeing and resilience during the COVID-19 pandemic lockdowns to aid survival. With CDA, we have a framework that enables us to critically research these changes in language, capturing the meaning of social practice in words in, for example, arts organisations. This could be through studying meeting notes, policies, people's conversations, and self-evaluations of work and practice. This information evidences the discourses of social life, representing different social actors, and how they are positioned within their environment. Class divisions are expressed in language through, for example, the use or non-use of accents. Having a strong accent can result in discrimination and inequality for their users when away from the accent's home environment, and they can equally act as identity markers. Semiotic difference can indicate dominance and social ordering, which can be exposed through research applying CDA. For example, investigating the cultural access policies of organisations founded by the Arts Council England, could indicate the different types and ways of interpreting access, and could also indicate the dominant form that represents cultural access. A common sense of how access is understood and practiced among arts organisations, may or may not convey the *access for all* policy of the Arts Council England and help perpetuate dominant meanings of access and enforcing hegemony.

This ongoing relationship between activities, practice, and text has been expressed in CDA as interdiscursivity, which foregrounds that texts are made from other texts, which harbours other discourses, styles, and genres. As a result, specific articulations prevail that CDA analysis helps to unravel. Fairclough based his framework on Roy Bhaskar's concept of "explanatory critique" (2013), combining relational and dialectical elements that offered a way to discuss problems, seeing positive and negative critique as illuminating the problem and contributing resources to overcome the problem. The similarities to action research are striking. Both methodologies explore the structure and action of problems. The difference is that CDA focusses on structuring the order of discourses, while action research emphasises action before structure.

The practical step-by-step guide of how to analyse texts is explained in detail in the methods chapter. To sum up, using DA comes in many shapes and forms, but it will always discuss a variety of opinions and facts. It also summarises a collection of spoken and written words as text, focussing on language, and cultural, political and historical context that is set in relation to their environment. It is less structured than content analysis but applies comparative elements while interpreting collections of communications.

Grounded Theory (GT)

In the first instance, the name *grounded theory* seems to suggest that this is a theory not a methodology. The adjective *grounded* gives little indication what grounded stands for, or what being grounded in theory means in this context. In this case, the answer is simple: *grounded* refers to being on the ground, or in a real-world scenario. Today, the classification of *real* or *grounded* references hierarchies within the binaries. For example, *real* and *unreal* carries a judgment that researchers will consider when developing their research design. As explained in Chapter 2, paradigms reference different understandings of *real*, and the idea of doing research in the real world follows the same understanding. Research of this kind is based on the ground and relates to us humans and our relationships, activities, and behaviours.

As with many methodologies, GT develops over time, and adapts to change as much as it tries to capture change. GT methodology has been applied to many disciplines and in reference to the name, it is better to read it as a compound word to understand why it is called grounded theory. It means that a theory is not applied at the beginning, as is the case for other disciplines. For example, when developing a hypothesis that is based on a theoretical framework, we are seeking to prove or disapprove the theory. Instead, the understanding of theory in GT refers to the theory being built on the behaviour, words, and actions of those being studied. As a result, a new theory is being generated from the data, not an already existing one applied to the data. This has consequences as to how we understand the people we study, including ourselves. The role of the researcher is embedded in the process of research.

Glaser and Strauss developed GT in the 1960s, both being rooted in symbolic interactionism and ethnography in their thinking. What ethnography and GT have in common is the embeddedness or the holistic approach. For both, meaning is culturally created, mediated, and takes roots in communities (Glaser & Strauss, 2017). Having applied GT in my own research, it helped me to understand how artists create cultural policy in the form of their behaviour, their interpretation of the world, and how they communicate with each other and society as a whole (Wesner, 2018). Cultural policy is created through a variety of functions and roles that artists inhabit throughout their career. Artists are not just artists, they are parents, citizens, lovers, carers, and activists. They perform multiple roles, which develop through interactions, and GT foregrounds this. In this way, it provides a methodology that allows us to investigate, capture, and analyse change, although it cannot predict change as a research result. As with many other methodologies, researchers need to have an open mind, because they will not know what they might find until the data is analysed. For example, in the Artists' Voices Cohort Study, memory, myth, and identity emerged as the key categories that dominated the result. Yet memory was a concept that I had not come across before in relation to artists' policies.

As a methodology, GT prescribes a set of steps to undertake during the research (as outlined in detail in Chapter 4). These can be time consuming and go into as much detail as possible when analysing (e.g., interview transcripts involving several stages of coding that apply summative and axial coding methods). In short, GT analysis can take several months to understand and gain an overview of the data collected, such as in the interviews. Therefore, in an MA dissertation setting this needs to be factored into the time planning. Commonly, MA students might apply an abridged version of GT methodology and limit the number of field resources (e.g., interviews, focus groups, and observations) to single digit numbers and run reduced coding circles.

Having said this, as a researcher I regard GT as one of the most rewarding methodologies. It takes you on a journey of discoveries with an abundance of research surprises that are dressed in originality about all the people involved. Another way to see if GT is a suitable methodology for your research project depends on how you direct your research questions. Questions that enquire about perceptions of experience work well, asking, for example: How are creative practitioners experiencing cultural policy related workload allocations models? or What drives female leaders to develop their career? As you can see, questions tend to be broad and open-ended, but you can add clarity in terms of location, place, and subject. The idea is not to avoid assumptive interpretations, but to acknowledge them, by allowing for description and analysis or interpretation to develop gradually and staying close to what people expressed in the first instance, without losing sight of clarity and focus.

Phenomenology

Discussing phenomenology foregrounds experience. In this methodology the perspective of the experience is the key to the investigation. Being familiar with the term from Chapter 2, which covered phenomenology as a paradigm, in this section, I am highlighting the methodological aspects. In practice, the distinction between phenomenology as a paradigm and as a methodology remains artificial, but while developing a research design the distinction adds clarity of how to do what and when. The methodology involves exploring the subjective experience of the individual in order to gain insight into their world. Frechette et al. (2020) argued that the core of phenomenology aims to highlight what we usually take for granted and this could mean studying moments and situations that we do automatically, such as swiping the surface of a smartphone. It is not giving them additional meaning, instead it is the recognition that it is what we do that is contributing to what Martin Heidegger (1927) called "being in the world". The Greek word phenomenon means appearance, and phenomenology is about capturing and describing experience within a specific context and environment. For many years, phenomenology was seen less as a structure to fully capture experience, and so it avoided developing a set of methods that would help carry out phenomenology research. In a post-postmodern world, phenomenology represents a more flexible methodology that points towards an understanding that is less concerned with a fixed understanding of essence (Vagle, 2018).

Like many adjacent methodologies that qualify rather than quantify data, phenomenology uses reflexivity as a tool to guide the researcher in the process of researching. In the early days of phenomenology, the researcher was assumed to be literally put in brackets, by removing the researcher from the findings. Researcher's assumptions had to be fenced off to avoid interrupting or influencing the description of the phenomena as forms of experiences, as opposed to raising awareness of the researcher's own performative actions. However, revisiting Edmund Husserl's (1859–1938) original idea of bracketing brought to light that he wanted to overcome objectivism by recognising subjectivity as a part of the research process. Husserl's intention was that the researcher refrains from judgment by focusing on the sensations, feelings, impressions, and emotions of all participants, including the researcher. After this initial stage of bracketing, two further stages direct attention to interpretation or analysis of what Polanyi referred to as "indwelling" (cited in Dörfler & Stierand, 2021), utilising the researcher's knowledge and experience to be applied to the subject. In recent years, bracketing acknowledges the researcher's reflexivity as a component, which describes the relationship between experience and phenomena. Dörfler and Stierand (2021 11) argued that "bracketing is more about making conscious what is happening anyway, whether we like it or not", which introduced transpersonal reflexivity. Referencing interview situations, I argue that we can extend this idea because the dialogue between the participant and the researcher shows that bracketing as a dual practice that is negotiated and not something that can be foregrounded by the research team alone.

To sum up, phenomenology demonstrates that the researcher's awareness goes beyond the object/subject relationship. It refers to experience in multiple forms, covering the part of lived experience that cannot be put into words, including the gut feeling and the butterflies in the stomach when excitement strikes. Despite having a long tradition of being applied as positivist paradigms, the dominant forms of phenomenology today are variants of interpretivism, which have adopted subjectivity to different degrees. When phenomenology is applied as a methodology, researchers are required to find their own approach through lived experience that are linked to the context of the participant's experience. The concepts of *Dasein* (existence or being-there) and *Lebenswelt* (life-world) are merged and phenomenology is not about untangling them, but understanding and discussing this relationship.

Feminism

Feminism aims to understand the impact of gender on all aspects of life, including perceptions, experiences, and perspectives. It rightly questions traditional assumptions, which have suppressed women and marginalised groups of women, excluding them from participating on equal terms with men. Specifically, feminism challenges the dynamics of power structures, asserts the rights and civil rights of women and other marginalised groups, with the aim of bringing about social change and changing the mainstream discourse. As a methodology, feminists follow this agenda, creating the space for underrepresented voices and participants to speak out and rectify the unequal and equity-based advantages and privileges of men and other groups that dominate and supress people (e.g., through the male gaze) (Sampson et al., 2008). Compared to other methodologies, feminism advantages the marginalised by following a set agenda.

Historically, you might have heard about the four distinct waves of feminism, which argued for different aspects of women's equality. Exploring rights and civil rights in the first two waves, feminism adopted an intersectional approach in the third wave by becoming more inclusive and open to the different ideas of feminism, acknowledging and investigating gender oppression as related to, for example, racism and class struggles (Dicker & Piepmeier, 2016). In the early 2000s, we see studies on and investigations about many interwoven practices of oppression. The lack of countable results is addressed in the fourth wave, which focused on taking action and developing women's activism as a social movement that spans all continents, starting from the Woman's March to the #MeToo movement, addressing gender-based violence, reproductive rights, and online harassment. It extended and made use of on- and offline activism, recognising the power of individual and collective voices in the struggle for equality.

In methodological terms, the overall focus, or the agenda setting, has not changed. The fight for women's equality remains, but attention has moved to foster permanent change in all societies. Feminist methodology uses standpoint theory, which acknowledges the position of the oppressed and underprivileged participants. It is based on the understanding that knowledge and experience are situated within a specific standpoint that shapes a person's understanding of the world and their ability to act on it. Women in marginalised social positions, who for example experienced precarity and poverty, are in a better position to understand their social world than people in power and with privilege. Standpoint theory emphasises the role of research as a starting point for social change. In this sense, feminism has grown out of its methodological remit. Having said this, it explains why, unlike other methodologies where there is a step-by-step strategic guide, feminism doesn't have a one-size-fits-all model of how to best engage in feminist or gender-focused research. This methodology covers all subject fields and feels equally at home in the social sciences as it does in the humanities and art-based critical approaches. Feminism has stayed close to the critical theory that utilises the fundamental wrongs of society. It incorporates activism into methodologies such as discourse analysis, phenomenology, and action research. Flexibility and openness are demonstrated in feminist research practice and have challenged conventional approaches (e.g., opposing single authorship and instead collectively writing up research results). A general sense of experimentation and questioning that feminism brings through their philosophical underpinning, has been translated into research practices that are transparent, rigorous, and sometimes unconventional (Wigginton & Lafrance, 2019).

Feminist methodology shares a deep interest in the process of how the research is carried out and understands methods as tools that help to achieve and document the process. For example, a research journal can illustrate the researcher's self-reflection and discusses situations covering the research process. It compares with the memo book in grounded theory methodology that acts in the same way as the research journal, as an anchor point to reflect and discuss existential questions, such as to whom we are accountable, linking the feminist philosophical approach with research practice. As a result, oppressive research practices are questioned and actively resisted.

To sum up: feminist research methodology strives to create a more equitable research process through a combination of listening and reflecting on the researcher's privileges in relation to power and power dynamics that are upheld in unequal positionings. It is a social agenda- driven methodology aimed at social change.

Practice-Based Research

As we explored with feminist research methodology in the last section, most methodologies are developed through practice and are motivated by exploring practice to improve societies. So, when most research is based on practice, why is there a need for a special section on practice-based research? In short, the focus on practice as a kind of theoretical base has intensified alongside similar etymological discourses that interpret and discuss questions of practice as their main research focus. In recent years, practice-based research has been developing into a stand-alone subfield and CCI researchers have been keen to explore this methodology, especially by linking their own creative practice to scholarly research.

Locating what is at the core of this methodology remains a challenge because there is no unified body of knowledge that would allow exploring it under this name. Instead, this methodology has many names, covering different aspects and covering different aspects of foregrounding practice: practice-and-research, practice-as-research, practice-centred, arts/practice-led, and studio-based research. Some of the names make direct links to art by referencing artistic practice, which deemphasise the research aspects of the activities and align with the notion of a craft or artist-in-residence in academic departments. Skains (2018) argues that the term "practice-led research" is most commonly used, suggesting that creative practice takes precedent over the communication of academic or scholarly ideas of knowledge and analysis.

However, the many shades and forms of practices in CCI apply and define terminology according to their research needs, so I will use examples to explain some of the variations. *Practice-and-research* distinguishes between the creative output and scholarly analysis. Let us meet Helen: She has produced several screenplays and uses her practice to analyse the work of other screenwriters in her MA dissertation. In her case, research is informed by her practice of writing crime screenplays, but the research topic (i.e., the role of emotions in crime dramas, as investigated though other crime screenplays) is different from her own practice. Most researchers will use previous research experience to improve research skills over time. The difference here is that the professional knowledge and the research skills are directly acknowledged and linked, in much the same way as transferable professional skills might be used. But the focus here is on transferable research knowledge and skills. In Helen's case, her MA dissertation is the scholarly output, and the creative output of her own crime screenplays are independent outputs, which are not part of the MA dissertation. But she could not have written the dissertation without drawing on her screenwriting expertise.

In *practice as research* the weighting between scholarly and creative output matters less. This is because of the understanding that creative practice produces research knowledge in its own right, and this knowledge is rooted in creative practice that can be shared and discussed. There is no value distinction between creative and scholarly knowledge or between creative and scholarly research. Instead, creative practice is seen as a form of research and not just as a means of producing a piece of art and culture. Creative subjects and disciplines (e.g., theatre, art, design, music, film) have been developing this approach and it is becoming more and more common in other fields, such as health and education. Being seen as an active form of enquiry and exploration, the emphasis is placed on developing new ways of looking at topics, contexts, and experiences. The context and process of learning from each other and from your own work foregrounds reflection and experimentation. In Helen's case, she wrote a screenplay that reflected on her own practice, while letting her creative characters play with analytical skills and understandings. As a result, creative and scholarly analyses are woven into each other. In her case, the reflective action becomes accessible to a wider community of interested people, helping to distribute her work beyond the academic community.

Practice as research opens the remit of research and is often applied to gain new insights into specific problems and issues that arise, such as in communities. The actions and the process of researching together with participants and communities can provide tailored solutions that are more effective and efficient than those that have been generated in a purely academic environment.

Practice-centred research is another term that aims to position practice as the dominant force or main influence in the relationship between practice and research. Like practice as research, the focus is on the day-to-day practice, such as how practitioners work with each other and how different practices shape their interactions and the outcomes of their work. Since the focus is on specific practices that are tied to professions, this type of research is often used to gain a greater understanding of the profession in order to inform decision making and improving the practice. We hardly ever speak of creative industries managers in a general sense. Instead, many of us work with a specific artist or within a cultural field, whereby a field-specific practice is generated that combines knowledge and experience.

Helen's friend, Martina, is a screen production manager keen to make further efficiency savings in her small-scale production company. Over coffee, they discuss how they go about researching how these changes can be implemented. They develop a research plan that involves creative interventions in which they both take on the job of the other for half a day. Helen will attend the board meeting of the company instead of Martina and Martina is set to write a one-thousand-word character layout for Helen's latest screenplay. Both reflect on their experience in an open discussion, involving all members of the company. As a result, both worked through their respective practices, highlighting not only efficiency savings, but gaining an awareness of what is involved in these processes. Based on this understanding, the company team could work out that to make efficiency savings an integral part of the process they could focus on activities that could be acquired. So, they started to develop a storyline with Helen's characters that enabled them to act out efficiency saving in a fictitious company.

In some artistic-focused academic environments, Helen and Martina's approach might be called *arts/practice-led*, because knowledge is acquired through the practice of an art form, in this case screenwriting. Individual researchers often apply a two-step process: firstly, artworks are produced to understand a specific issue or topic; secondly, the meanings and implications of the work are explored through reflection. When based in a studio or craft workshop, thinking about practice might also be called *studio-led research*. This form emphasises the impact that the environment or the confinement to a specific location might have on researching. The studio or laboratory is understood as a primary research context, that highlights experimentation, creativity, and exploration that is compounded by a controlled environment.

Sullivan (2009) developed four types of *practice-led research* that all pay specific attention to various roles and forms, either during or while in the process of developing projects and ideas. The four types covered are: theoretical (i.e., developing a methodology theory out of the practice); conceptual (i.e., studying the artefacts and creating outputs that demonstrate better understanding of creative work as part of the research process); dialectical (i.e., focusing on the relationship between materials, objects and humans and how meaning can be conveyed through this relationship); contextual (i.e., paying attention to the social implication and actions for change). This division helps to clarify the methodological focus when creative practice is woven into research.

As a novice researcher, it can be challenging to distinguish between the different forms, roles, and functions of practice. But it is important to note that these various forms will create different outputs and focus attention on different areas of research in terms of design and process. Most universities offer a range of forms to choose from in creative subjects and it has become increasingly common in the CCI to acknowledge the role creativity plays in our daily work. Aligning creative investigations with scholarly knowledge is more than a trend; it demonstrates how thinking about research cannot be separated from how we manage and approach work in general. Therefore, if you are interested in incorporating practice as a fundamental part of your research methodology and advance your studies in this field, a wealth of materials exists to choose from. Articles from Nicolini et al. (2016) and Candy and Edmonds (2018) provide useful starting points.

Action Research (AR)

In the final methodology explored in this chapter, we stay with practice as a main component. Action research is embedded and comes out of a practice like practice-based research. But it is exclusively focused on the outcome, achieving results, solving problems, and providing solutions to a specific issue or problem that has been identified as part of the research design, or that has been given to the researcher to address in advance. As with phenomenology, experience is at the core of this approach, but the focus in action research is on achieving a specific solution and improving a situation. In short, to make improvements, or to initiate or maintain positive change. Actions are the key to demonstrate and work through the solutions (Stringer & Aragon, 2020). It depends on how invested the researcher is in the research environment, and in order for action research to work best, the researcher is often part of a working team. For example, student professionals who continue to work while studying choose this methodology to address problems and issues that occur in their workplace (Coghlan, 2019). It enables them to research content that directly feeds into their day-to-day work practices and to continue to collaborate with colleagues while researching.

Imagine the scenario of Amber, who studies art management in the evening and works in the stage production team at her local theatre. The issues that she chooses to address in her research project for the dissertation relate directly to the lack of teamwork at her workplace. The work gets done so senior management is not concerned, and it seems that everyone buckles down and gets on with their work as always. Communication is limited to the most essential exchange of information. Aiming to improve the way colleagues relate to each other, Amber starts her research by interviewing colleagues to discover what motivates them in the workplace. In the second step, after analysing the interview data, she compares the motivating factors, identifies commonalities, and then discuss her results with the group. From there, further actions are taken to bring people together in the form of regular team meetings.

Action research can involve multiple cycles of collecting information and as a result can be very time consuming. This informal discussion with participants and the recycling of ideas before a solution can emerge is not always considered to be scientifically rigorous and instead is often dismissed as being anecdotal and subjective. However, this is partly offset through the collectively achieved solution that is supported by many, if not all the people involved in the action research project. Amber's task is to document and reflect on this process in her dissertation. This way she can ensure that her academic studies are informed through her practice in the workplace, while her colleagues gain an insight into research through their participation. The team benefits from a better understanding of each other, enriching the work environment, and perhaps becoming more efficient and creative as a group. They might apply this methodology again when other issues or problems need to be addressed. It will be a different process. The analysis and actions are unique and cannot be replicated in the same way as is the case with other methodologies, but the collective experience will act as a motivating factor, even for people who have not been involved in previous action research projects. Occasionally, the lack of generalisations has been critiqued in AR, but with good documentation researchers can stand their ground and so should you, if you decided to use this methodology for your project.

Conclusion

The selection of methodologies that are presented here correspond with their frequent use and the familiarity that the creative industries research community has demonstrated over several years. But there is much more to explore, and methodologies continue to develop. This chapter should give you an introduction, and whatever methodology you favour, make sure that it is suited to your ideas as expressed in the paradigms (i.e., etymological, ontological, and axials ways of thinking) and that it offers you a strategy to explore exactly what you are seeking to investigate. All the methodologies mentioned offer opportunities to discover and enhance your research. Which one to choose should be guided by the topic, the research question, and the research context, all of which are informed through paradigm thinking. Remember, when your ways of thinking align or match with theoretical frames that are applied in the different methodologies, you are advancing your research design.

In the introduction to this book, I mentioned the trio of paradigm, methodology, and methods that complement each other. Using the analogy of building a house, the foundations and the structure are now solid (paradigm) and fully constructed. The house amenities have also been installed and are in working order (methodology). The next step will be to think about how to furnish the rooms, deciding what goes where (methods) and the colour schemes, but you are not yet ready to move in because you do not have any furniture. There are the odd pieces that you have acquired from friends and family, but nothing seems to work together. The next chapter will help you to find suitable methods for data collection and for data analysis. In short, it will guide you in designing the rooms and how to paint and furnish them, so that you can finally move in. There is still work to do, but while setting a date for the housewarming party might be premature, you may start thinking about who you would like to invite.

References

Bhaskar, R. 2013. *A Realist Theory of Science*. Routledge.

Candy, L. and Edmonds, E. 2018. Practice-based research in the creative arts: Foundations and futures from the front line. *Leonardo*, 51(1): 63–69.

Coghlan, D. 2019. *Doing Action Research in Your Own Organization* (pp. 1–240). Sage.

Costello L., Witney C., Green L., & Bradshaw V. 2012. Self-revelation in an online health community: Exploring issues around co-presence for vulnerable members. In *Proceedings of Australian and New Zealand Communication Association (ANZCA) Conference* (pp. 1–12). http://ro.ecu.edu.au/ecuworks2012/179/.

Costello, L., McDermott, M.-L., & Wallace, R. 2017. Netnography: Range of practices, misperceptions, and missed opportunities. *International Journal of Qualitative Methods*, 16(1). https://doi.org/10.1177/1609406917700647.

De Valck, K., van Bruggen, G., & Wierenga, B. 2009. Virtual communities: A marketing perspective. *Decision Support Systems,* 47: 185–203. doi:10.1016/j.dss.2009.02.008.

Dicker, R. & Piepmeier, A. (Ed.) 2016. *Catching a Wave: Reclaiming Feminism for the 21st Century*. Northeastern University Press.

Dirksen, V., Huizing, A., & Smit, B. 2010. "Piling on layers of understanding": The use of connective ethnography for the study of (online) work practices. *New Media & Society*, 12: 1045–1063. doi:10.1177/1461444809341437.

Dörfler, V., & Stierand, M. 2021. Bracketing: A phenomenological theory applied through transpersonal reflexivity. *Journal of Organizational Change Management.* doi:10.1108/JOCM-12-2019-0393.

Ellis, C., Adams, T. E., & Bochner, A. P. 2011. Autoethnography: An Overview. *Historical social research/Historische Sozialforschung*, 12(1): 273–290.

Fairclough, N. 2013. *Critical Discourse Analysis: The Critical Study of Language.* Routledge.

Frechette, J., Bitzas, V., Aubry, M., Kilpatrick, K., & Lavoie-Tremblay, M. 2020. Capturing lived experience: Methodological considerations for interpretive phenomenological inquiry. *International Journal of Qualitative Methods*, 19: 1609406920907254.

Geertz, C. 1973. *The Interpretation of Cultures.* Basic Books.

Glaser, B. & Strauss, A. 2017. *Discovery of Grounded Theory: Strategies for Qualitative Research.* Routledge.

Heidegger, M. 1962. *Being and Time.* (J. Macquarrie & E. Robinson, Trans.). Harper & Row.

Hine, C. 2000. *Virtual Ethnography.* Sage. doi:10.4135/9780857020277.

Hine, C. 2015. *Ethnography for the Internet: Embedded, Embodied and Everyday.* Bloomsbury Academic.

Howell, K. E. 2012. Preface. In Kerry Howell (Ed.), *An Introduction to the Philosophy of Methodology.* Sage. doi:10.4135/9781473957633.

Husserl, E. 1999. *The Essential Husserl: Basic Writings in Transcendental Phenomenology.* Indiana University Press.

Ingold, T. 2008. Anthropology is not ethnography. *Proceedings of the British Academy*, 154(January): 69–92.

Kozinets, R. 1998. On Netnography: Initial Reflections on Consumer Research Investigations of Cyberculture. In J. W. Alba & J. Wesley Hutchinson (Ed.), *NA – Advances in Consumer Research*, 25 (pp. 366–371). Association for Consumer Research.

Kozinets, R. 2010. *Netnography: Doing Ethnographic Research Online.* Sage.

Kozinets, R. 2015. *Netnography: Redefined.* Sage.

Kurikko, H. & Tuominen, P. 2012. Collective value creation and empowerment in an online brand community: A netnographic study on LEGO builders. *Technology Innovation Management Review*, 2: 12–17.

Liu, T., Liu, S., & Rahman, I. 2022. International anime tourists' experiences: a netnography of popular Japanese anime tourism destinations. *Asia Pacific Journal of Tourism Research*, 27(2): 135–156.

Loanzon, E., Provenzola, J., Sirriwannangkul, B., & Al Mallak, M. 2013. Netnography: Evolution, trends, and implications as a fuzzy front-end tool. In *2013 Proceedings of PICMET'13: Technology Management in the IT-Driven Services (PICMET)* (pp. 1572–1593). http://ieeexplore.ieee.org/document/6641649/.

Lorenz, U. 2017. *The working lives of freelance female musicians in the United States music industry: A netnography* (Doctoral dissertation, Northcentral University).

Moses, J. W. & Knutsen, T. L. 2019. *Ways of Knowing: Competing Methodologies in Social and Political Research.* Bloomsbury Publishing.

Sampson, H., Bloor, M., & Fincham, B. 2008. A price worth paying? Considering the cost of reflexive research methods and the influence of feminist ways of doing. *Sociology*, 42(5): 919–933.

Shankman, P. 2009. *The Trashing of Margaret Mead: Anatomy of an Anthropological Controversy*. University of Wisconsin Press.

Skains, R. L. 2018. Creative practice as research: Discourse on methodology. *Media Practice and Education*, 19(1): 82–97.

Stringer, E. T. & Aragón, A. O. 2020. *Action Research*. Sage Publications.

Sullivan, G. 2009. *Making Space: The Purpose and Place of Practice-led Research*. In H. Smith & R. T. Dean (Ed.), *Practice-Led Research, Research-Led Practice in the Creative Arts* (pp. 41–56).

Thomas, G. 2021. *How To Do Your Case Study*. Sage.

Vagle, M. D. 2011. *Post-intentional Phenomenology and the egocentric predicament in qualitative research*. Paper Presented at the Seventh Annual Congress of Qualitative Inquiry, Champaign, IL.

Vagle, M. D. 2018. *Crafting Phenomenological Research*. Routledge.

Ward, K. 1999. Cyber-ethnography and the emergence of the virtually new community. *Journal of Information Technology*, 14: 95–105. doi:10.1080/026839699344773.

Wesner, S. 2018. *Artists' Voices in Cultural Policy*. Springer.

Wesner, S. & Woddis, J. 2022. Artists and cultural workers in cultural policy and creative practice: from the big break narrative to mutual aid and collective care. *Journal of Cultural Management and Cultural Policy*, 8(2): 11–29.

Williams, R. 1977. *Marxism and Literature*. Oxford Paperbacks.

Yin, R. K. 2009. How to do better case studies. In Leonard Bickman & Debra J. Rog (Ed.), *The Sage Handbook of Applied Social Research Methods* (pp. 254–282). Sage.

4

DATA COLLECTION METHODS

Introduction

In everyday life, we are surrounded by data. Many of us will start the day with music selected from a pool of music data stored on streaming devices. Downloading a new app on your phone prompts messages about data collection, asking for permission to collect data that we generate through our behaviour, tastes, and habits. Spending a day without social media seems unthinkable and when services are interrupted on the main platforms, we realise how much we depend on data-generating technologies. As much as we generate data for others and for ourselves through and with electronic means, we use and handle data to locate, manage, and aid work practices in both the public and private spheres. In doing so, the distinction between public and private disappears, so that data generation and collection is woven into technological advancement.

However, data collection is by no means bound to technology alone, as historically we can trace data collection back to ancient civilisations. For example, population data in the form of the census have been accepted as the basis for informed government decision-making for millennia. At the operational level, ancient theatres collected figures about audience behaviour to determine the popularity of plays, just as current theatres harvest demographic data and ticket sales to inform programming decisions. The interest in data collection or information gathering has not changed, but the amount of data that is generated has exceeded expectations many times over. Today, data is collected in increasing quantities, with or without a specific purpose. The internet as we know it is one example, while the increasing connectivity between devices through the Internet of Things (IoT) will continue to grow at a rapid pace.

This wealth of data provides a welcoming arena for research, but it can equally be challenging to select from the pool of increasing amounts of data.

DOI: 10.4324/9781003161912-4

Researchers decide to make use of existing data or to collect their own primary data. This decision is informed and guided by a selection process related to the type of data (e.g., facts, figures, information, experience) and in what form the data is generated. You will have come across the qualitative or quantitative division of data. Quantitative data is number-focused and is in many cases intended to plot and to measure. Here, a positivist or postpositivist paradigm is often the theoretical frame, while qualitative data refers to humanistic, interactive, and interpretative methods. The combined use of quantitative and qualitative data clarifies a situational setting. When the research design refers to triangulation, it tests data from one method against data collected with another method. Using qualitative data to test results from quantitative data, or vice versa, is common in larger studies. For example, *the taking part survey* (DCMS 2023), a longitudinal audience study in the UK, collects quantitative attendance data in the form of statistics. At the same time, it collects data through participant interviews providing more nuanced and detailed information in the form of narrated text.

What counts as data varies a lot. When we think of quantitative data we may think of numbers in the form of statistics, but this is just one small segment of the data that can be collected. Quoting from a text or direct speech generates information that in a social science context can be read as data. Summaries in reports often deliver useful background information and count as data in similar manner as informal comments do. Discussions with colleagues, in the field, or in public debate generates data. Information gathered via observation, describing how events unfolded or how people reacted in an experimental setting provide a variety of different data. Images (visuals) are data. Imagine the photographs you took of your friends to record moments of your shared life for sentimental analysis. You might not regard these records as data, but they could be understood as data when compared with other photographs in a research project.

The adjacent field of data visualisation including showcasing big data is another example of using images, but applies a different meaning. Data is already collected and with the help of visual tools such as graphs, diagrams, and drawings, and the meaning of the data is broken down into familiar forms and shapes. However, data visualisation forms part of data analysis, which is the aim of Chapter 5. Here, in Chapter 4, the focus remains on the various forms of data collection.

CCI researchers use all forms of data, including the broader distinction of qualitative and quantitative forms, either in combination or as stand-alone data collection, depending on the research question and the research design, which references paradigms (Chapter 2) and methodologies (Chapter 3). The use of data raises ethical questions in relation to consent, unauthorised access, copyright, and ownership. As a result, the handling of data requires careful consideration, which are discussed in detail in Chapter 9.

In this chapter, I discuss data collection methods that relate to the paradigms and methodologies that researchers have used in the past and that have complimented their research design. Applying the trio of paradigm, methodology, and methods, we are nearing completion regarding the metaphor of building a house. Paradigms hold the most abstract ideas about the meaning of knowledge and the values that are generated through and with research, building the fundamentals (i.e., the purpose of the house and the basic structure, walls, and the roof). Methodologies focus on the process of how to carry out research and offer strategic direction as to where the research is going. It deals with how the house is built and fosters all the arrangements for the house (e.g., rooms, amenities, etc.) Methods, the third category in the trio, deals with all the data practicalities that enable you to use the house as your home.

Methods stand for the most practical and hands-on part and are associated with systematic procedures and techniques. The idea is to standardise processes as much as possible to enable repetition of procedures that aid comparisons. In practical terms, methods can tell us how to collect data. Methods provide guidelines that alert us to possible challenges and help to direct and raise awareness of potential pitfalls. Thinking through methods in advance of the research will help to raise awareness of what can be achieved.

The separation of data collection from data analysis in two different chapters in this book is artificial according to the logic of the process, which has data collected first and analysed afterwards. While discussing specific data collection methods, I follow the same logic: starting with methods that are commonly and frequently used in student coursework and assignments throughout their studies. Covering a wide range of methods means that they cannot all be discussed in detail, so the overview provided aims to help you choose a suitable method that complements your methodology and paradigm. For a more detailed approach, please consult specialist literature of which hallmark studies and textbooks are good starting points. Most methods match several methodologies and can deliver data for analysis, but distinctions are made in the detailed approaches. For example, interviews are carried out to collect data in ethnography, action research, grounded theory, phenomenology, case studies, and practice-based research. However, the type of interview (i.e., ranging from structured to narrative forms) and the way interviews (i.e., online, in-person, via email) are conducted differs depending on the research design. The practicalities of the research environment also matter, and they stay foregrounded in our initial approach to the topic. For example, questions about access must be addressed. Are you able to secure an interview with a celebrity in the given timeframe? Bechhofer and Paterson (2012) suggested that securing the overall principles of the research design has priority over practicalities. But for many of us, research needs to fit into our busy lives, which are full of multiple responsibilities that we must juggle through a continual process of compromise.

Literature Reviews

Since first learning to read, we have been communicating about literature. Everyone has their own anecdotes about trying to convince a friend to read a favourite book, simultaneously describing its content, analysing the characters, the plot, and anything else that will help convince them to pick it up. In a nutshell, the literature review is the same in written form, but covers the entire debate as opposed to a single book. It tries to capture the various opinions and explanations, while summarising discussions that are of interest to the chosen topic. Literature reviews provide a critical overview of where things stand in current discourse(s). As a single review, it forms the basis for your own argument, from which you either formulate new opinions or discuss existing ones. While assessing academic sources such as books, journals, or reports, the aim is to summarise, structure, classify and evaluate when synthesising existing research.

In the literature review you deploy and develop your theoretical frameworks. A theoretical frame contains other people's ideas that you could use for further analysis and discussion. For example, Foucault's notion of power; Bourdieu's ideas of habitus, fields, and capital; or Arendt's understanding of work are all familiar concepts to CCI researchers and could help to evaluate and develop your own ideas. For the reader, it provides all the background information they need to be able to follow the argument.

Literature reviews can take many different forms (e.g., a stand-alone piece of work or coursework and assignments in student modules). Academic essays are structured like mini literature reviews, following the same idea of using literature to provide a summary of what has been written before by others regarding your case. The result remains like other forms of literature review, which is to inform practice and to develop a comprehensive understanding of your chosen topic and approach. Dissertations contain a more comprehensive literature review, covering what bodies of literature are in the public domain that may contribute to and help you develop your topic. This includes discussing the broader frame of your study, but also homing in on a detailed analysis of some of the theoretical concepts that you choose to advance the discussion and develop your argument. In this sense, the literature review lends a helping hand to provide the frameworks that, in the case of a larger study (e.g., a dissertation), delivers enough ideas and material to allow you to pursue the answers to your research questions. The ability to analyse includes judging the quality of the existing research, while also identifying and weighing conflicting evidence. It could mean a simple strengths and weaknesses approach, but going beyond dualities or binaries requires you to determine what has not been studied and would need further research, which you aim to provide with your study. Depending on the methodology, it could provide the link between your findings and the analysis that you will discuss in subsequent chapters, following the literature review. In the case of discourse analysis, literature reviews act as the main data collection, and instead of pointing to the gap in the literature at the end, the implications for research are discussed throughout.

Assessing or making quality judgments requires comparing information and knowledge. Reading is the first step, but selecting, extracting, and handling information remains key for understanding. Questions to be asked while collecting data could be:

- What was the intention of the study?
- What is presented in the research?
- When and who carried out the study?

Working with the different viewpoints, opinions, models, and theories that are discussed in the literature requires a systematic approach. This can mean simply synthesising discussions while advancing your argument and opinion.

Research sources can be divided into primary data (i.e., collected by you) and secondary data (i.e., collected by others). For the literature review, secondary sources are mainly studied and compared to other studies, their authors, and their environments. Some of these studies will present and analyse primary data, providing the opportunity to scrutinise their findings, thereby applying a form of secondary approach, and justifying the epithet of secondary data.

However, the division between primary and secondary has become opaque and blurred due to ephemeral works such as reports, policy papers, working papers, and documentations that provide the analytical frameworks for the literature reviews. In CCI research, multimodality is a common feature that brings together semiotics (i.e., communication through sign and symbols) and the dissemination of messages through media in the form of podcasts, videos, and films. These resources represent the many culturally embedded and not strictly text-bound modes that have been contained in literature reviews.

In the past, students asked what type of approach or format a literature review can take and how best to select from multiple choices. As with previous questions, there is no clear answer, but Onwuegbuzie and Frels (2016) provide a starting point by presenting two main branches of literature reviews: (1) the narrative type that can be historical, theoretical, or methodological; (2) the systematic review including meta-analysis, a summary, meta-synthesis, and rapid reviews. The integrative review combines both types, consisting of the narrative and systematic elements. All reviews aim to discuss academic literature in the broadest possible sense, but the way in which they involve the reader in the selection process differs. The narrative review offers a broad overview of a given topic without providing details of how the literature has been selected. The systematic branch makes the selection criteria explicit and provides a transparent search strategy that analyses the studies that were included in the search. Depending on the topic and subject, dissertations could accommodate any of the reviews, but the specific application might be best discussed with colleagues, supervisors, and tutors. For an initial approach, in the past a historical or theoretical overview helped students to start writing. But depending on the topic, a systematic approach requires advanced decision making of how to structure the review, by discussing the classifications and characteristics of the selections. To recap, literature reviews provide a critical assessment and an overview of existing research through summarising theoretical arguments, synthesising evidence, and evaluating their relevance in relation to the research question.

Interviews

As reading is a prerequisite tool for the literature review, talking or conversing allows us to relate to the interview, one of the most popular methods in research. All methodologies that are discussed in Chapter 3 use interviews in order to collect data. Interviews are the most ancient form of obtaining knowledge. They are deliberately initiated and controlled exchanges that collect insights into the thoughts, opinions, and experiences of people. In everyday life, interviews take on a variety of forms, shapes, and sizes, such as job interviews that can range from a polite conversation to serious questioning. Media talks and questioning can involve extremely heated exchanges, such as in the BBC's interview series *Hardtalk*, in which the interviewer deliberately provokes and challenges the opinions of the interviewee. These interviews differ from research interviews, even though they can be carried out using the same format as face-to-face or as IT-assisted online interactions. Research questions that are designed to capture perceptions of a phenomena or an experience, often use interviews as a suitable method for collecting data. Research interviews, like other methods, aim to gather information for a research study, but depending on the choice of methodology the type of information that is deemed relevant for the analysis differs. Content analysis focusses on the spoken language information from the interview, while other techniques such as narrative interviews include syntax, grammar, and sound analysis.

Qualitative interviews can also be divided into different types. Brinkmann (2007) offered a useful distinction between the doxastic interview that aims to understand interviewee's experiences and behaviours and the epistemic interview that focusses on co-constructing the knowledge between interviewer and interviewee (Berner-Rodoreda et al., 2020 and Brinkmann & Kvale, 2018). Both interview types are on a spectrum, and most interviews will occupy a space somewhere in between. In recent years, the focus has shifted toward more neutral encounters, fostering dialogue and deliberation instead of capturing experience, especially in some areas of social science research. This enables the researcher to question the imprinted power relationship between the interviewer and interviewee that positions them as unequal partners, away from establishing a neutral relationship and moving towards an understanding of a partnership, while focusing on the co-construction of knowledge. On the experience side of the spectrum, the most formal types follow a clear, predefined structure, comprising a questionnaire-type set of questions and an interview schedule that sets out exactly the time frame and the sequence of questions. Every interviewee is asked the same questions without deviation. Semi-structured interviews allow a bit more flexibility, by still following an interview guide with topics and questions, although with this type of interviews you can use more open-ended questions, as you would in a conversation. The least formal approach is practiced through in-depth or narrative interviews, with the premise of allowing the interviewee to talk. There might be some questions, but they are meant to seek out further detail without interrupting the flow of the story being told by the interviewee.

After deciding on the structure of the interview, we have some idea about the format of the questions. Yet all interviews require careful advance planning to ensure that the data can be collected as smoothly as possible. In many research settings, interviewees volunteer their time, expertise, and experience. In my opinion, researchers therefore have a moral obligation to come as prepared as possible to honour the commitment of the interviewees.

Preparing questions or using the slightly looser form of an interview guide both follow the same principles of any conversation: introduction, main interview section, and concluding remarks.

An introductory question invites the interviewee to talk freely, such as "Can you tell me how you got involved in playing mahjong?" Alternatively, you could start by asking the interviewee to describe a specific detail or a process. One question could be, "Can you describe in as much detail as possible how you prepare and set up for a game of mahjong?" To maintain the flow of the information, follow up questions or encouraging verbal acknowledgements or gestures could help to indicate a curious, interested attitude. Or, probing questions will enable you to delve deeper into a specific matter or behaviour. Examples of this are, "Can you tell me something more about that?" and "Do you have further examples of this?" In this way, you create a conversational flow moving swiftly from the introduction to collecting detailed information about your topic in the main section of the interview. A slight change in direction, but still focused on detail, could be achieved by asking questions like, "What did you think? or "Have you experienced this yourself?"

Asking direct and indirect questions depends very much on the cultural context in which the questions are asked. For example, direct questions, like "Have you received prizes for your work?", could imply that the interviewee has never received a prize. I would ask direct questions only if I am sure that the interviewee is used to direct questioning, which depends on the cultural context. In some regions or countries, like Germany, direct questions are a common part of conversations. No offence is taken when asking people directly, for example, how old they are. In the UK, this might be perceived as rude or insensitive. Alternatively, indirect questions – "How do you think other artists regard prizes in the arts?" – work better because of the indirect cultural approach that is practiced in the UK context. While I am mindful of my own stereotypical assumptions of different cultural landscapes, it illustrates how important it is to realise that paying attention to the diversity of cultural contexts is a researcher's responsibility.

Duty of care includes a legal responsibility to ensure the safety of people we are working with when undertaking the research process. The interview, as a method and process, is an integral part of the researcher's ethical responsibilities. It covers physical and psychological care prior to, during, and after an interview. Good research practice involves minimising risk for the participants. The researcher is responsible for providing a secure and safe environment so that the participants are not exposed to harm. It starts with the interview questions, extends to the interview environment, and to the safe storage of the data collected. Part of the interview preparation involves setting out the frame in which the interview is set, which includes an up-front briefing to discuss and obtain consent from the interviewee. Participants need to be aware of their rights and the processes that enforce this right (e.g., to stop recording at any point during the interview or to withdraw data after its conclusion). The researcher must ensure that interviewees are by no means coerced or manipulated into participating. In the past, students asked if they could interview friends and relatives since they are easy to access, often supportive, and willing to help. Depending on the questions, personal contacts can be a rich source of information. But you would need to consider their willingness to help and take this into account in the subsequent dialogue. Furthermore, you must still carry out your duty of care as a researcher and ensure that this responsibility is not transferred to the interviewee.

Higher education organisations have developed ethics policies and researchers, including all students, are required to follow a due process to gain ethics approval. In short, this means that you should not interview anyone without ethical approval from your supervisor in the case of a dissertation. For coursework, students need to consult the module convenor for up-to-date ethics procedures. This will usually involve completing an ethics form, which is designed to help you think through your research interviews and to follow best ethical practice. In Chapter 9, further details are provided to raise awareness to help you navigate how to think ethically and gain ethical approval for your project.

During the interview, as with any other situation, the first five minutes are decisive. Interviewees need to establish trust from the very start, to reassure the interviewees that they have signed up to a worthwhile undertaking. The interviewer's first port of call is to listen attentively, to demonstrate, through listening, that they are interested in and respect the interviewee. For novice interviewers, this can be a big ask in the first five minutes, while you are introducing yourself and your project. Interviews tend to improve with training, and I recommend that you practice your interview technique in advance. Self-interviews or practice interviews of your friends and family can help you gain confidence in multitasking and navigating the interview situation.

It is essential to recall the reasons for interviewing participants in the first place. Your interviewees are experts who can provide rich, specific, and relevant answers. Best practice shows that your questions should be short, with the answers extensive and informative. Providing a good balance between questions that ask for meaning and clarity as well as follow-up questions will ensure that your interviewee is engaged until the very end. I would also advise that, if you are unsure about any aspect of what was said, then verify your interpretation of the interviewee's answers by summarising and repeating it back, in order to confirm what you have heard. Often, interviewees will ask questions, and this is a good reminder that the interview process is a conversation. Rounding off the interview should be signalled through a summary of the main content, followed by a big thank you, and information on what will happen next with the interview (next steps). To sum up the interviewer's qualities: preparation is essential and remember a good interviewer is knowledgeable, can structure well, is clear, gentle, sensitive, and open. Having defined the theme and topic, prepared questions that are aligned with the associated documentation, conducted the interview, and recorded it, about one-third of the work is completed.

I am often asked about interview numbers (i.e., how many interviews are required for a piece of work?). Methodology, the research question, and the paradigm act as approximate indicators, not in terms of actual numbers, but in relation to the depth and amount of information that the research study needs to cover. Phenomenology and grounded theory work with saturation points, interviewing as many people as required to reach the point that no new information can be collected. Interviews can vary greatly in length. Narrative interviews can take as long as the story is told, while in structured interviews a time limit is established in advance. Best practice dictates that the interviewee is informed at first contact about the approximate time commitment, and this acts as an agreement that researchers should follow. Experience is paramount here, and for your dissertation you should draw upon the experience of your supervisor. Pragmatically oriented research, such as the first cycle of interviews in action research, might define the number of interviews from the outset. In any case, you should develop selection criteria that again would need to match your research design, which might refer to demographics, time, and location. You may be required to approach more interviewees than you need to account for those people who cancel at the last minute. When you approach people for an interview, allow them to suggest a date and location, while ensuring your personal safety. This is often a case of negotiating what is right for both the interviewee and the researcher. A café has a lot of background noise, so you could suggest a quiet place and bring a coffee/tea for the interviewee instead. Many interviewees would like to see either the transcript (see Chapter 5), the finished work, or even both. This is regulated by the consent form before the interview takes place, but it is good practice to share the fruits of your work with your interviewees on completion.

Observation

Acquiring information from a primary source through observation is also one of the oldest forms of collecting data and has been used for centuries across many disciplines and fields. In general, observation refers to the activity of watching, listening, touching, and documenting the processes, people, and animals, which includes living and non-living activities, materials, and objects. In CCI research, observation is a common method and can be applied to both qualitative and quantitative data collection. But it is most often used in applying a qualitative lens to study behaviour, feelings, thoughts, and opinions in natural, social, and cultural settings, or environments in real time.

While interviewing always involves a direct exchange between two or more people, when we observe someone, the focus is on being as unobtrusive as possible. Observation is often understood as limiting the involvement with the observed, but is data gathering without any participation of the researcher really an alternative? Strictly speaking, being present along with other people in a room is a form of participation. As a research method, observation covers a wide range and is applied in multiple forms, which lie on a spectrum from passive to active. Being passive could mean no direct involvement or not being in the same space or location, such as when observing internet game play. At the other end of the spectrum, active observation involves participation in the form of actively directing and guiding participants by asking questions and making gestures. McMurtrie's (2022) systematic review of wayfinding studies in the museum context revealed that labels (i.e., descriptions of objects) direct movement for some but not for all visitors, and because of this the curator should consider multiple movement choices in exhibition design. Collecting data about movement patterns should focus on seeing, as opposed to purposefully guiding the visitors where they should go. Alongside the researcher's involvement, other forms of observation are considered, which relate to the research environment and highlight different aspects of observation. In structured or systematic observation, formal rules of what should be observed are established in advance and the results recorded. In unstructured qualitative observation, no formal rules are established (e.g., studying automation processes or recording sustainable supply chains in the fashion industry). Experiments carry an element of observation, often in form of interventions, such as changes to behaviours. Experimental observations are often strictly defined with parameters and criteria to enable the experiment to be repeated when required. Archival observation focuses on existing records, while the laboratory setting focusses on observation under controlled conditions, and structured observation references a manipulated environment as opposed to a natural setting. The choice of type, form, timing, and location of the observation should be part of the research design and be flexible enough to remain adaptable to any changes in the situation.

Being a good observer is not just an important research skill, it also serves us well in everyday situations. In research studies, observation works when studying dynamic situations, such as the behaviour of large groups of festivalgoers; how visitors move around a gallery; or in an immersive theatre performance wherein participants are encouraged to get involved, instead of simply watching. Being less intrusive can be useful when studying the interrelationship of people or situations, by preserving integrity within the study groups and giving the participants time to explore the environment in their own time. In the CCI, we see an increase in the use of everyday technology as a participatory activity. People film their participation to document and promote a desirable lifestyle. Experiences are documented in the moment, instead of experiencing the moment. Documenting events is an integral experience and therefore interactions between technology and people plays an important role in observation.

In many research studies, observation is used to preclude the adoption of other research strategies or when we know very little about the topic. Most research ideas are born out of observation or carry an observational element in the early stages, often not understood as relevant for later research. This highlights the preconceived notion of observation that could act as an inherent drawback: we see what we want to see, and our interpretation follows what we expect to know. There is no instant solution. Instead, we must acknowledge that we are human when participating in research. As a result, we should include self-reflective analysis prior to, during, and after the observational stage, as an integral part of the study.

Observation technologies might make it easier for researchers to gather data. I am referring to drones or other surveillance tools, but the right to privacy is just one aspect that would need to be respected in consented research. Observation also carries other methodological risks. It is resource intensive, and the implication of working with limited consent touches on difficult ethical implications. Forms of consent for large gatherings, such as pop concerts, can be included in ticket sales, but ethical issues remain (e.g., at politically motivated demonstrations and art activist actions). Be aware that evidencing situations through documentary media, such as videos, photographs, or screen shots, requires prior consent.

Regarding dissertations, observation might be one method that can be complimented by others, such as interviews or focus groups, which can help to build a larger pool of differing information. As a result, the research findings of one method could be crosschecked by comparing them against the findings from the other. In practical terms, while observation can be applied as a stand-alone method, it works equally well when used in combination with other methods.

Focus Groups

As a research method, focus groups place the emphasis on listening and communicating with and among people. Like interviews, focus groups are organised as conversations, but in small and diverse groups, instead of the one-to-one interview scenario.

Krueger (2014) argued that the group situation requires observational and moderation skills to understand the performative elements and group dynamics that are played out when several people come together to discuss a common theme or topic. Focus groups may sound attractive, since they are cost effective and efficient when compared with individual interviews, but the purpose of a focus group is not the same as an interview. The type of information or data that is collected needs to be considered and should cover thoughts, beliefs, and feelings. The focus is less on the variety of opinions, but on getting aggregated opinions and then using this data to observe how people respond to different resources. In focus groups, interaction and discussion among participants are encouraged, and lines of communication are created that help to understand how people adapt and deal with this artificially created situation as part of social positioning. Focus groups help generate new ideas, insights, and act as testbeds. They are popular in the field of consumer research to assess products, but they are also used frequently in CCI research to gather opinions and to test ideas.

The selection and recruitment of participants for focus groups can be time-consuming and costly. It has also become common practice in research to pay participants for their time commitment. Focus group participants are a selection of the target audience and capturing a truly representative sample requires planning. It can include demographic data such as age, gender, and location in response to the specifics laid out in the research design. In the CCI, this might relate to creative professions or groups (e.g., audiences, actors, cultural workers, or makers). There are several sampling methods that respond to practical concerns. Choosing people that are readily accessible to you (convenient sampling) or asking for volunteers on social media (voluntary response sampling) are both popular methods. Running focus groups for research purposes requires specialist training. This will help you to gain awareness of the role of the moderator as an inadvertent influencer who directs the content of the discussion and is able to manage the situation when other participants are acting in a similar capacity. Co-moderation with shared roles offers a chance to divide up the responsibilities (e.g., one to ask questions and the other moderator to handle the technology or take visible notes on a board). Alternatively, you could switch roles to cover different ideas and topics in the same session. A clearly written discussion guide that is distributed in advance can ensure that all participants are aware of the content and that all topics have a chance to be covered during the session. The order of the guide should stay flexible and follow the natural flow of the conversation. Questions that work well in a focus group setting are open ended, flexible, and have a short introduction that is understandable to everyone. Provocative questions or controversial topics often result in participants taking sides and reduce topics into binary thinking. Engaging participants with questions that put them at ease and make them comfortable are good starting points that set the scene for participants to explore the topic in detail afterwards. Finishing the focus group by offering to discuss points that have not already been raised gives participants a chance to control the ending. Choosing a convenient time and easy-to-access location will help motivate people to participate.

Focus groups that are held online have the challenge of accounting for technical barriers, while the flow of the conversation requires additional pointers and interventions. Falter (2022) argued that since the pandemic, online focus groups have seen a renaissance and have shown to provide easier access for some participants and to result in more engaged participants. For example, managing silence can be fruitful in allowing people to take a minute to think through their potential answers, but it can create a situation where people lose interest and turn their attention to their phones instead. Keemink et al. (2022) concluded that when familiarity with the medium, the sensitivity of the subject, and internet accessibility are accounted for, online synchronous focus groups yield no significant difference in data quality and offer an effective alternative to face-to-face groups. Most focus groups are either set up in real-time (synchronous) or they happen as online conversations over several days, such as in chat rooms or social media platforms (asynchronous). In these groups, the focus is on the text that is partly moderated and occurs as a form of conversation. Given the number of chat rooms and the experience students bring from being active social media users, asynchronous focus groups offer an alternative to real time face-to-face or online groups if equal care is taken when preparing and collecting the data.

To sum up, focus groups work well, but require careful planning, and experience moderating group discussions will be greatly helpful. Professional moderators are available at a cost, but dissertation projects do not usually have the budget to cover this. So, please bear this in mind when considering this method for your next research project.

Case Studies

The use of the case study as a research method is rooted in several disciplines and in CCI research we can learn from multiple forms. Establishing legal precedence in the field of law is one of the oldest forms. Legal practices aim to examine the facts of a case and the legal principles that apply in order to draw conclusions about the law and its future application. The best practice case studies follow a similar approach, extracting the general principle that works for other cases, without ignoring the special circumstances in which the case developed. In sociology and anthropology, case study research became well-known through the study of communities in which aspects of the community were examined and all the data collected and put into one large pool of information. In arts management, case studies are used to illustrate the complexities of specific groups, individuals, or phenomena. A case could be an art event, such as a performance, exhibition, festival, or an artwork. It could be an institution such as a gallery, company, network, venue, policy programme, or public body/funding council. The case can focus on a person/role, such a key individual or a durational/biographical study. I am thinking of Bernardine Evaristo, who jointly won the Booker Prize with Margaret Atwood in 2019. You could investigate a particular funding stream such as the Wellbeing Fund, which is a technology-focused support fund, or investigate the relationship between curators and artists, as seen through a cultural policy lens.

For example, instead of focusing on finances, as one aspect of the running of an organisation, you could apply a dynamic and holistic view to deliver an in-depth examination of the organisation, to consider its multiple tasks, locations, and functions, including content production and management. As a result. you can produce a case study that examines the complex environment in which the organisation operates, which goes far beyond purely financial data.

In general, case studies are a good choice when you want to explore key themes/questions in relation to a detailed example, when you have access or you can find plenty of relevant material, and when your research questions ask for an understanding of the context and development of a case or several cases. Yin (2018) defined a case study as an empirical inquiry that investigates a contemporary phenomenon in which the boundaries between context and phenomenon are not clear. Gaining insights into larger trends can be achieved through a detailed analysis of a single case. This counteracts the idea that generalisations are not possible in case study research because of the specific character of each case. As a method, case studies may not work in population studies, but they offer a focus on detail that is combined with a holistic view and, working together, they can demonstrate tendencies and new insights.

As an example, a researcher investigated the work pattern of freelance playwrights in rural communities and collected data using a questionnaire to establish initial information and contact with the playwrights. This was followed up with narrative interviews and an observation study of the participants in their homes. Further sources were collected in the form of the work they produced and was publicly available through social media channels and websites. The combined analysis revealed that most of the playwrights established a daily routine that corresponded, was adapted, and changed frequently in relation to community needs. Also, being embedded into community life acted as inspiration for their creative output. One playwright organised a reading club during the darker winter months, by hosting local participants, but in the spring and summer months, discussions with farmers and local traders began with walks in the fields. As a result, a small seasonal community fund was established to support the community work of playwrights. This funding scheme was later replicated in several communities to support community engagement of playwrights in rural areas. This case study started by collecting specific information about the playwrights' work patterns and demonstrated replicable community engagement as a result. It demonstrates the validity of a case study in one region, while capturing what became a trend soon after.

The focus in case study research is on finding out what information is available. This is achieved by using a variety of data collection methods, including the reviewing of records, documents, and reports (i.e., literature review), observation, interviews, and questionnaires. In this respect, the case study as a method combines other methods of data collection into one to achieve the most comprehensive understanding of the case.

As with the question of how many interviews are needed, the same question is often asked in relation to case study methods. There are some indicators, but it is always the individual approach that would need to be considered. The three-case model (e.g., traditional, innovative, and radical; or small, medium, and large) are widely applied, but so are multiple case studies. If the logic of classifying research into types of comparisons is followed there is no limit other than workload and time. Rueschemeyer (2003) argued that comparisons are key for multiple cases, but "a single case can force the rejection of a hypothesis or its modification, provided that the proposition in question was not formulated in probabilistic terms" (305). Discussing in advance what realistically can be achieved with case study research, either single or multiple cases, will help develop a robust design that demonstrates validity and best research practice.

The cut-off point for data collection relates to the number of case studies you have chosen, bearing in mind that multiple methods will generate a large amount of data. Yin (2011 & 2018) suggested using the four principles of data collection as a guide:

1. **Use multiple forms of evidence:** Each method delivers different sets of information. Documents augment evidence from the other sources, such as information mentioned in interviews. The internet can provide initial information about a topic and retrieval searches, such as those from archival/library materials, may help to clarify the context and what has been discussed in various disciplines and fields. Interviews are understood as verbal reports in case study research and Yin (2018) recommends focussing on actions when interviewing. Observations are often part of the data collections because of the live or real-world setting that determines relevant social and environmental conditions. Data triangulations help to develop converging lines between the different sources of evidence.
2. **Create an overview guide (e.g., database, table):** Finding ways to sort through and collate information requires some form of categorisation. Databases or simple tables help but will need to be established, ideally, as part of the research design.
3. **Maintain a chain of evidence:** Documenting the process and the sources helps to validate the findings and will encourage cross-referencing your results. Case studies are not set up to be replicable, but future research projects will benefit from understanding what data has been left out or will be accessible in the future. Being able to evaluate and critique the research practice is made possible for others. Having said this, the main benefit of reliable documentation becomes obvious during the analysis of the data and helps to confirm the researcher's confidence, simply by keeping an accurate record.
4. **Exercise critical care in collecting from reliable sources (e.g., reports, internet, social media):** Knowing how to select the right data is an important skill to learn for any type of research. Exercising critical care goes beyond the idea of being accurate, complete, and relevant. Case study research demands a deliberate and vigilant approach that includes being attentive and flexible, able to recognise and respond to unforeseen circumstances, and able to adjust the research design whenever necessary. Being reflective involves caring for oneself as much as for others. It enables us to recognise and think through our own assumptions, then identify their impact on the research.

The difference between approaching case studies as methodology or using them as a method, depends on the research question and the overall research design. Methodology includes broader ideas and frameworks that are applied to the research approach. They act as underlying objectives and aims that impact and inform the methods. The assumption that reality is complex and multifaceted informs the understanding of using multiple methods, and applying holistic thinking and incorporating context helps to uncover the connections between actors, structures, and practices. Other theoretical principle such as subjectivity and triangulation (see Chapter 3) define how to approach the research. Case studies, as methods, are tools that reference the techniques and procedures used in collecting and analysing data, thereby ensuring rigour and validity in the results. In Chapter 3, I explained the different types of case studies that all carry specific properties (e.g., exploratory, archetypical, composite, pragmatic, instrumental, descriptive). When selecting a method, we make a choice based on what kind of data is to be prioritised.

Collecting data for an explorative case study often extends into new, unfamiliar, and unchartered territory. In the beginning, it will be challenging to see where the research will lead, but key ideas will emerge out of the chain of evidence that is collected. Archetypical cases tend to focus on the known highlights and unique principles that best (or dominant) practice can demonstrate. For this case, it is important to first identity the familiar categories, while working out how best to capture the leading principles or trends that are of interest to the wider research community. The composite case study relies on the variety of examples that are mapped out, while focusing on demonstrating complexity and flexibility. Most data collected in these cases is often layered, and the challenge is to identify and understand what comes across as messy and unstructured. In pragmatic cases, it is common that the initial data collection has been carried out and leads to the development of a project idea in which a clear distinction between collecting data and further development of the project cannot be drawn. In this case, it is important to understand the opportunity of the moment and collect data ethically. Instrumental case studies carry a distinctive message defining the data that should be collected and therefore preselecting data that needs to be evidenced. The descriptive case study gathers information from a detailed explanation of processes and practices. Therefore, exact documentation is the key component for successful data collection.

To conclude, case studies bring contemporary phenomena to life and the hear-and-now approach allows us to collect data in real-life situations that are often messy, complex, and full of surprises. The challenges of collecting valid data remain regarding which data to select, how to cope with the sheer quantity of data, and how to structure the selection in order to support a meaningful analysis in the next steps.

Surveys and Questionnaires

Most of the methods discussed here relate to qualitative research, but questionnaires and surveys work for both quantitative and qualitative methodologies, though they have been often associated with a positivistic paradigm. The primary aim is to collect information to gain insights into the opinions and behaviours from a sample group through predetermined questions.

This written schedule of questions describes the process of designing and conducting the study, as well as collecting the information. The difference between the survey and questionnaire lies in the size and comprehensiveness of the information gathered. A survey is a comprehensive study designed to measure opinions and data, while the questionnaire gathers single sets of information and can be included in a survey. The choice to carry out a survey is influenced by the complexity of the information presented. Key features of survey design include standardised questions, meaning that all participants are asked to answer the same set of questions and are in most cases self-administered. This can help to limit social desirability bias, in which participants' answers are guided by expectations instead of what they actually think. A large sample size is required to facilitate statistical analysis. In surveys, it is common to use closed questions that allow participants to choose from a set of pre-defined response options. For example, *the Likert scales* (Joshi et al., 2015) asked participants to rate their level of agreement and disagreement over a spectrum of given choices. Importantly, questions should be broken down into simple pieces of information and allow representation (e.g., when measuring numeric change over time). Collecting financial information about art organisations or audience figures are common examples in CCI. Reliable data can be collected with questions that are dependable and consistent and that are able to be validated. It is also best practice to ensure that surveys measure exactly what they are intended to measure.

Braun et al. (2020) argued that primary qualitative surveys are less widely used, but they can produce rich data, covering subjective experience, positioning, and narrative. As a survey, they are self-administered and contain open-ended questions that are arranged in a fixed order. The wide-angle lens (Braun et al., 2020 643) together with the rich, but focused, data allows for the capture of a different and wide range of voices that would not be possible with a pre-defined response option. Compared to face-to-face interactions, the survey offers an unobtrusive and less burdensome way of gathering data. When the anonymous mode is applied, it might offer participants an opportunity to answer back without directly confronting the researcher. Additionally, this sense of being in charge of the answers might empower the participant to direct their answers more freely.

There are several practical elements to consider as part of the survey design. For example: Who is asking the questions (e.g., researcher, intermediaries)? Where is it taking place (e.g., in person, phone, or online)? and What impact does it have on the overall research design? In the past, some students were quick to adopt online surveys as a suitable method because they thought that they could be prepared and carried out quickly. On the contrary, survey design requires training, as does the analysis of the surveys. Unless you are already conversant with the field of database management, please seek advice beforehand. Having said this, online surveys do allow for more automated data collection, not to mention that they save a great deal of paper.

In the meantime, the following steps will help you to think through some of the parameters:

- Determine that the survey questions help you to meet your research objectives. A table identifying which question meets which objectives can help relate them to each other.
- Identify the target participants and make sure the questions are tailored to their demographic needs. The questions should reflect the language practices of the participants. For example, using formal language for young people who have developed their own phrases and slang might have a negative influence on the response rate.
- Choose an appropriate format. For example, response rates vary for online and paper-based formats. Find out what are most used among the targeted participants. Not everyone has a computer, so think of ways the survey could be read and answered on all electronic devices (e.g., tablets, smartphones, etc.).
- Write clear, concise, and objective questions, then test your survey on a small sample.
- Include a timeframe for how long it will take to complete the survey, explain to whom the survey is being distributed, and how long the survey will remain open, if online.
- Build in and facilitate any ethical requirements. This includes obtaining consent before starting the survey or, if the survey takes place online, before access to the first questions is given (see Chapter 9).

Conclusion

Collecting data forms a key component and sits at the very heart of any research project. It requires careful planning, starting with the selection of the most suitable methods that will deliver accurate, reliable, and varied data that fully supports the research questions. For example, interviews and focus groups work well for capturing experience, while the literature review summarises discourses (secondary data) and describes theoretical frames that correspond and respond to data collected through other methods that focus on primary data. Linking paradigm, methodology, and method in the research design ensures that all three components support each other and make sure the aim of the research is met. Together they act like glue, holding information together and providing a reliable study, while generating creative and innovate research results that will help to inform future decision making in the CCI.

Collecting data is the first step that delivers actionable insights in how to deal with the primary data. But without analysis, the value of data cannot be defined. In the next chapter, I will present some analytical tools that will help to draw out the results and make sense of the data collected. In the beginning of the chapter, I mentioned the analogy of the house, in which the methods are the tools that enables us to live comfortably in the house. In the discussion about data collection, we have placed the furniture and the amenities in the house, but we now need to try it out to see if it makes sense. This will involve moving and rearranging ideas, until we feel completely at home. Next, let me show you how data analysis can help you to put down roots in the new home.

References

Bechhofer, F. & Paterson, L. 2012. *Principles of Research Design in the Social Sciences*. Routledge.

Berner-Rodoreda, A., Bärnighausen, T., Kennedy, C., Brinkmann, S., Sarker, M., Wikler, D., Eyal, N., & McMahon, S. A. 2020. From doxastic to epistemic: a typology and critique of qualitative interview styles. *Qualitative Inquiry*, 26(3–4): 291–305.

Braun, V., Clarke, V., Boulton, E., Davey, L. and McEvoy, C. 2021. The online survey as a qualitative research tool. *International Journal of Social Research Methodology*, 24(6): 641–654.

Brinkmann, S. 2007. Could interviews be epistemic? An alternative to qualitative opinion polling. *Qualitative Inquiry*, 13(8): 1116–1138.

Brinkmann, S. & Kvale, S. 2018. *Doing Interviews*. Sage.

Department of Culture, Media and Sport2023. *Taking Part Survey*. https://www.gov.uk/guidance/taking-part-survey.

Falter, M. M., Arenas, A. A., Maples, G.W., Smith, C. T., Lamb, L.J., Anderson, M. G., Uzzell, E. M., Jacobs, L. E., Cason, X. L., Griffis, T. A., & Polzin, M. 2022. Making room for Zoom in focus group methods: opportunities and challenges for novice researchers (during and beyond COVID-19). *Forum Qualitative Sozialforschung/Forum: Qualitative Social Research*, 23(1): 1–27.

Joshi, A., Kale, S., Chandel, S., & Pal, D. K. 2015. Likert scale: Explored and explained. *British Journal of Applied Science & Technology*, 7(4): 396–403.

Keemink, J. R., Sharp, R. J., Dargan, A. K., & Forder, J. E. 2022. Reflections on the Use of Synchronous Online Focus Groups in Social Care Research. *International Journal of Qualitative Methods*, 21: 16094069221095314.

Krueger, R. A. 2014. *Focus Groups: A Practical Guide for Applied Research*. Sage.

McMurtrie, R. J. 2022. Observing, recording, visualising and interpreting visitors' movement patterns in art museums: A mixed method approach. *Multimodality & Society*, 2(2): 93–113.

Onwuegbuzie, A. J. and Frels, R. 2016. *Seven Steps to a Comprehensive Literature Review: A Multimodal and Cultural Approach*. Sage.

Rueschemeyer, D. 2003. Can one or a few cases yield theoretical gains? In James Mahoney & Dietrich Rueschemeyer (Ed.), *Comparative Historical Analysis in the Social Sciences* (pp. 305–336). Cambridge University Press.

Yin, R. K. 2011. *Applications of Case Study Research*. Sage.

Yin, R. K. 2018. *Case Study Research: Design and Methods*, 6th edn. Sage.

5

DATA ANALYSIS METHODS

Introduction

In most research projects, data collection and analysis go hand in hand. Furthermore, with some methodologies, such as the case study approach and grounded theory, collecting and analysing data run in tandem. This does not mean that the techniques are mixed. Instead, a clear division between the two different parts of the research design is set out from the very start. An important aspect to consider is that the methods for collecting data and the methods for analysis of it are suited to each other, thereby providing a complementary match.

This chapter focuses on what can be done with the collected data, and how they can be analysed in a systematic way to evidence, support, and answer the research questions. It adds another piece to the research puzzle that is being constructed in this book. Referring to the analogy of building and living in the house: at this stage, you have just moved in. You are living in the house, checking that everything works, and discovering how to organise your life to get comfortable. This involves rearranging things, cleaning, ordering, and coming up with new ideas to help you completely enjoy your new home.

Analysing data is organised and works in similar fashion. Making sense of data involves findings ways to order ideas, to extract and summarise information, as well as to arrange the findings in a meaningful way. Statistics are commonly used in research that deals with numbers (e.g., summarising data in the form of means, median, mode, variance, and standard). Larger population data is analysed with specific methods, such as regression analysis, confidence intervals, and most commonly hypothesis testing. In qualitative research, the focus is on capturing the complexities, not with numbers but with words – as texts, narratives, and discussions. Students have used content or thematic analysis, as well as discourse analysis, in the past, and these are discussed below.

DOI: 10.4324/9781003161912-5

Due to the increased use of social media and the fast-growing amount of data available on the internet, data mining has become a common method for identifying patterns and relationships in large, computerised datasets. Network analysis is another method that foregrounds relationships in social settings, often comparing financial data with other entities. CCI research applies network analysis, for example, to identify the flow patterns of visitors at cultural events, or how posts and messages on social media travel though different platforms.

In this chapter, I follow the same pattern as in the previous chapters. I introduce the commonly used data analysis methods in the form of an overview, with the aim of selecting the right analytical tool for different research projects. I focus on qualitative data analysis and will discuss one method at a time. First, I introduce thematic analysis, followed by content analysis, including coding and pattern building. I describe the basics to understanding data mining and network analysis, before moving on to discourse analysis. In the latter part of the chapter, I introduce explanation building, template analysis, and narrative analysis.

Depending on the research design, several methods can be utilised to complement and compare the analysis. This mixed method approach enables researchers to combine qualitative and quantitative data, aiding the ability to understand complex issues, and I will return to this again towards the end of this chapter.

Thematic Analysis (TA)

A simple and straightforward method, thematic analysis (TA) has been widely used to analyse data, such as from interviews. Whether you are a novice or experienced researcher, it makes a good starting point to go through collected data. The task in TA is to identify and analyse patterns through searching and examining, mainly in the form of text. This can be a transcript or audio from a podcast, videos, or any other literature, such as reports, webpages, blogs, and social media postings.

TA suits a variety of methodologies, ranging from discourse analysis to critical theory to feminist approaches (see Chapter 3). As an analytical tool, TA is flexible enough to adapt to all these various theoretical frameworks. It helps with answering the research questions that aim to capture people's experience and it supports the investigation of constructing or representing a specific phenomenon. TA can handle large or small data sets and the analysis can be data driven, theory driven, or a mix of the two. Being closely related to everyday pattern searching (e.g., in choosing matching or contrasting colours to wear), we rely on a basic understanding of ordering things into categories, such as colours, shapes, and forms. As a result, many of us are familiar with the concept, and as researchers, we can build on and learn from for our research projects.

Braun and Clarke (2006 and 2019a) identified six phases of TA practices that act as guidance. These are not set in stone, but help in formulating individual TA approaches:

1. **Data familiarisation:** This is achieved through reading/listening and rereading the data transcript. While being immersed in the data, a familiarity develops that enables us to make initial analytical observations.

2. **Coding:** This should not be confused with coding as applied in computer science, although the processes may be similar. It does not require knowledge of a specific (computer) language. Coding data means labelling important information and broad ideas that are relevant for answering the research questions. It goes beyond reduction or summarising because it aims to capture the semantic and conceptual readings of the data. At the end of the coding process, a list of all the codes is generated, which can be done manually or in electronic format.

3. **Searching for and conceptualising themes:** Finding coherent and meaningful patterns consists of organising the codes into broader themes, based on the codes that have been generated in the previous step. As a final step, all codes are arranged into meaningful conceptual themes. Themes cover a central idea with multiple facets and are not a topic summary. All codes related to one theme are collated together under this theme and this is carried out until all the codes are grouped into meaningful themes. For example, codes such as *grants, sponsorship, budget,* and *cash flow,* are categorised under the theme of *finances.*

4. **Reviewing themes:** This involves checking if the themes are relevant to the research question and to the codes that are collated under the theme. Defining the nature of the themes and how the themes are related to each other often results in rearranging or splitting the themes, assigning codes to different themes, or discarding those that do not support the story you want to tell with your data.

5. **Defining and naming themes:** Writing a detailed analysis of each theme helps to identify what it covers, and the story it is intended to tell. It is also related to the overall story you are setting out to communicate. Assigning a concise and informative name will finalise this phase.

6. **Writing up:** The analytical narrative and data extracts are woven together into a coherent and persuasive story about the data, which contextualises it in relation to existing literature. This might become a writing and rewriting exercise, until the narrative convinces the reader.

TA best practice comes with some warnings about what should be avoided. Do not use the data collection questions as themes. Instead let your themes be informed by the research questions and go beyond the questions you asked participants. Data familiarisation and coding are important steps to capture a systematic and deep engagement. As a result, they should not be skipped while going straight for identifying themes. In deciding if codes are relevant features of the phenomenon or the experience, removing the data sets from the codes in an exercise enables you to check if the codes help to answer the research question. Overall, applying and developing TA includes understanding that it is not a rigid method; retaining contextual fluidity remains important. Therefore, the phases mentioned above are not a step-by-step guide, but an invitation to think about how you approach analysis.

As with most qualitative methods, TA relies on researchers' reflexivity. Braun and Clarke (2019b, 2022) added the adjective *reflexive* to the name, emphasising that both technique and philosophy are united in being an interpretivist paradigm. It allows us to understand our role in the process and how we situate ourselves in the research. This includes addressing the assumptions that we bring to the research, so that we bring meaning to the data in the form of interpretation, while forging an argument and telling a story. Getting the balance right between the different stories that emerge (e.g., between your story and the story of the data) demands reflecting on what we do in theoretical and practical terms. This extends fluidity with regards to time. Analysis does not stop; it is a continuous process that is only interrupted when finalising a project. We capture snapshots, moments of conversations in time, that are not absolute but continue to shape our research journey.

Content Analysis (CA)

As a research method, many people are familiar with content analysis as they have tried it before and practice this method in their daily lives. While analysing and interpreting the content that we consume in the form of text, images, and recordings, we search for patterns, themes, and meaning that we can connect with other information (Krippendorff, 2018). Often, this technique has become so ingrained in our daily routines, such as when we select music or swipe through social media platforms several times a day, that we hardly recognise or reflect on what we are doing. Analysing content as a research method serves the same purpose, which is to extract information in a meaningful way, but with the difference that we tend to plan in advance and this involves a preselection of techniques, such as coding.

When described as a process, content analysis can be organised and broken down into several steps, and every step can be aided by tables, grids, and spreadsheets:

1.   With the selection of the data collection method (e.g., interviews), the type of data that are going to be analysed has been defined, but checking data suitability is another important step. For example, you must determine whether you are going to include all interviews, or select specific ones for transcription?

2. In coding data, we rely on either predetermined categories or we develop them though an iterative process, as part of the analysis. The categories form the skeleton of the analysis, and the content is allocated, and often summarised, under one or several codes (see pattern analysis section below).
3. The coded content is then collected, often in the form of a table or spreadsheet, to gain an overview and identify patterns or other insights.

Before starting to code, it is important to consider and think through how we approach data in the first instance. The two most common forms are the deductive and the inductive approach. Both are logical reasoning tools and come in many shapes, sizes, and colours. They serve the overall purpose of analysing data as a form of extracting information that we deem useful when answering the research questions. The deductive and inductive approaches define the process we use to work with the data, and researchers think this through before coding can start. Using the **deductive reasoning** means that a theory or a theoretical framework has been predefined, and this approach requires testing. With **inductive reasoning**, we aim to develop a theory from and through the data. Inductive reasoning moves from specific observations to broad generalisations, while deductive reasoning works in reverse. The deductive approach links research to an existing body of knowledge and the variables, components, and issues are defined up front, as are the predicted or presumed relationships between them. For example, precarity and inequality among the workforce in the creative industries has been documented and discussed regularly in recent years. In a new research project, you set out to prove that issues of inequality extend into many corners of the industry (e.g., into the small dance group you have been working with). Using a deductive approach means you utilise theoretical frames that are already part of the wider discourse, and this could include looking at the issue through a specific lens, such as feminist theories or meritocracy. You apply the information, knowledge, and passion gained from these insights (i.e., theoretical frames) to your data. You will code accordingly, looking for specific evidence that proves or disproves the theory. For example, meritocracy, as a concept, claims that everyone has the same chances to climb the ladder of opportunity to become a well-known actor, but your research might find evidence that the starting points (e.g., entry into drama school, access to training) depend on access to facilities that not all people can afford. Therefore, chances are taken up by people who have the means (i.e., privilege). As a result, the data provides the evidence, and you have deduced specific information that has enriched the discussion about inequality.

This approach often works with a hypothesis that is the result of an interpretation of the theory. Many research projects work with hypotheses in one form or the other and not all are clearly formulated. They exist in our minds but not on paper.

Josef Beuys (1921–1986) a German artist and professor, set out to challenge the academic establishment in a way that was, in retrospect, recognised to have been organised like an experiment. It was not a research project as such, but it illustrates the deductive method through radical action. Beuys summarised the longstanding debate about artistic talent and creativity, both in his art and in his theoretical writing. In short, he argued that "everyone is an artist" (Beuys & Bodenmann-Ritter, 1975 189), and questioned the discourse that creativity requires possession of special talent, a kind of inner gift, and rejected the artificial divide created by the myth of the artist as a genius. His counterargument questioned the existing theory. Following from this idea, he used his position as an admissions tutor in the art academy to provide proof or evidence against the myth of the artist as genius. He pushed for abolishing the entrance exam for art students, on the following hypothesis: since anyone can be an artist, there is no need to run entrance exams for art schools. So, he offered places to any applicant who wanted to become an artist and he ended up with far more students than he could teach. As a result, the university administration intervened on the grounds that not everyone can be accepted, as it was highly unlikely that all students would be able to practice art after completing art school. Together with his students, Beuys occupied the university headquarters, and he was arrested for trespassing.

In this case, the theory of the artist as a genius prevailed as a logic. Beuys was never able to prove that everyone is an artist. This extreme case of experimenting with one aspect or one form of deduction (that no proof of talent is required to enter art academy) shows the power of the method that reaches beyond the remit of research into art activism. In CCI research, deduction has been a common feature because researchers are interested in political conflict, recognising marginalised and underrepresented voices, and covering resistance and alternatives to the main policy agendas. The differences between research and an activist agenda are less clear, but the research process asks for documentation using a systematic approach that can be replicated. In research, we emphasise that the process is just as important to the results and actioned outcomes.

By contrast to Beuys's activist deductive reasoning, we can imagine what it would have looked like for him to apply inductive reasoning. He might have sat in pre-academy art schools listening, observing, conversing, and conducting interviews to find out what potential applicants had to say about their ideas of becoming an artist. As the inductive approach works with no defined theoretical frame, the researcher identifies the relationships between data and then uses the data to develop a question, proposition, or hypothesis. Both the ideas that the artist is a genius and everyone is an artist might have arisen among other issues that relate to creativity and talent in the conversations. But perhaps a richer picture could have emerged that linked career practicalities with other theories, such as financial assistance, equality, and artistic freedom. Inductive approaches work best when little is known about a topic, yielding results that are grounded in the data. The methodology *grounded theory* relates to inductive reasoning.

Pattern Analysis (PA)

Both inductive and deductive reasoning apply coding and pattern analysis. Patterns are used to identify regular sequences of events, objects, or characteristics that are embedded in the data.

For the deductive approach, predicted theoretical patterns are compared against an observed empirical pattern. Hammond (cited in Sinkovics, 2018) has based this idea on the underlying assumption that people make sense of the world by comparing what they observe externally to their internal mental models. This can be achieved either through the interplay of dependent variables that you have identified in the academic literature as possible outcomes (deductive) or the independent variables, arising from another unknown variant that you discovered in your research (inductive). Another way to predict a pattern is to build on the idea that variables are all independent of each other and, as a result, there must be several explanations for the findings, although only one may be valid.

In research, a variety of pattern analysis techniques are applied, including clustering, association rule mining, sequence analysis, and social network analysis. In clustering, the emphasis is on finding data that carry the same characteristics. In audience studies, for example, attendance frequency patterns (e.g., nonattendees, once per week, once per month) are collated in clusters. Association rule mining is based on identifying relationships or associations between different variables. Following the example in audience studies, we could investigate what kind of events people who attend the venue frequently choose and reference this in future programming decisions. Depending on the research question, sequence analysis is another common analysis tool used to understand trajectories, processes, and events that involve time, or temporal data. As an example, in researching artists' career trajectories, I am investigating factors that contribute to changes in their artistic practice to understand how changes impact other factors, such as social mobility, the artist's reputation, and age. Episode analysis tracks recuring sequences of events and processes, such as when milestones are reached or how often a policy is evaluated in comparison to other sequences, like election cycles.

Data Mining (DM)

This method is related to pattern analysis, but researchers have been using data mining as a research method in its own right. But because it usually applies mathematical, statistical, and computational techniques, data mining sits in the quantitative realm of methods, which are a lesser focus for this book. However, CCI research is no stranger to data mining and research has been carried out, mostly in conjunction with other methods. In CCI, data mining is applied to identify trends and preferences in attendance, consumption behaviour and the marketing of cultural organisations. In academic research, AI supported data mining is used as a tool to deliver data for critical analysis. The data requires interpretation because data lacks critical capacity. Data on its own makes little sense, and instead needs to be scrutinised through critical thinking. Currently, what AI promises for the future is referencing the discourse of usefulness and positivity that surrounds technological development. This includes *thinking algorithms* that are used for solving specific problems. Algorithmic capacity moves from purely categorising to dynamic adaptation, while breaking down problems into more manageable steps. This can involve observation, collecting a variety of data, or forming and then testing a hypothesis. This sounds like a fantastic tool for analysing data. However, it is worth considering critical voices in your research design that can counteract an overtly one-sided view. Strictly speaking, we would need to define what thinking means. Is thinking the same as breaking down issues in smaller units or executing step-by-step processes? Instead, should we approach thinking in an holistic way, which includes creative, critical, and reflective thinking that is based, not just on logic, but on perception and memory? Ideally, these research components should be discussed at the start of the project, thereby addressing potential flaws in the initial design. At the data analysis stage, it is impossible to iron out these issues retrospectively. Instead, when they become noticeable at this stage, they can jeopardise the validity of the entire project. The unwavering belief in solving problems using technological developments can overshadow other questions that impact data mining analysis in relation to ethical considerations (see Chapter 9). Issues of data privacy and protection need to be addressed from the beginning. They cannot be addressed retrospectively, so if data security is not correctly followed it can render the data useless and put people's privacy at risk. Having said this, data mining remains an efficient, flexible, and scalable method (Zong et al., 2021). It collects and analyses data quickly, thereby saving time and human resources. It is a key method for identifying patterns and relationships in large data sets and can act as a risk-detection tool for cultural organisations (e.g., in crowd and in finance management). As with personalised medicine, cultural organisations started to personalise their offers, developing loyalty schemes with the help of data mining. CCI research using data mining continues to highlight and fight inequalities related to class, gender, and ethnicity. Studies related to content generation (e.g., music, text, and image), content enhancement (e.g., image, VR) and information analysis employ pattern and relational analysis as their main tools.

Network Analysis (NA)

This method operates with similar ideas to searching for patterns, but in this method they are called links, nodes, or simple connections. Easley and Kleinberg (2010) defined basic networks as a collection of objects, in which some pairs of objects are linked, and the connection is placed centre stage. Relationships between objects or humans are described in patterns. For example, ties or links are measured as strong when frequent and intense interactions occur, and weak when there is less frequent connection or when fewer commonalities are identified. Granovetter (1973) argues that the weak connections offer access to diverse perspectives and new information. The strong ties tend to provide social support through shared value systems and frequent connections. For example, belonging to the same friendship groups could be interpreted as being embedded in a social network. Both strong and weak ties shape network dynamics and contribute to the overall health of the network through their different contributions. In network analysis (social network analysis), clusters of influencers are identified by studying the relationship between different members of a network or group, as well as what kind of dynamics are at work within networks. In social media research, opinion clusters that document various precarious working conditions, for example, could emerge as a result of the analysis. Studies of how information spread remain popular like density and hierarchical clustering (i.e., grouping information into a hierarch). Both are used to understand how networks form and operate. AI uses neural networks as the underlying technology for machine learning, which operate in the same way as the physical brain functions. Weizenbaum (1983) pioneered the first chatbot, called Eliza, over half a century ago. Today, chatbots that generate text and images are a timely adaptation of advanced network analysis.

In research practice, network analysis is often used in combination with other data analysis tools, such as machine learning, as explained above. Identifying topics in text analysis works with network analysis and can be employed for thematic analysis (see data mining section) as well as in combination with coding (see coding section). Game theory and network analysis are sometimes used intermittently to understand social interactions. Network analysis investigates the structure of the network, how information flows through the network, in much the same way that game theory predicts, through mathematical models, how people will behave and interact in specific situations. In short, it is concerned with what kind of strategies people employ to play the game. Easley and Kleinberg (2010) used auctions as an example to illustrate how network analysis and game theory analysis work together. In an art auction, bidders compete for the same piece of art and the highest bidder wins, paying the amount that they bid. Bidders have different information about the value of the piece and researchers can model bidding behaviour as a game. Network analysis can deliver pattern behaviour, such as who is the most active buyer and what kind of connections exist between the different bidders. As a result, auction fraud can be detected by uncovering pre-agreed auction strategies from a group of buyers.

In summary, all these different forms of pattern analysis work well for gaining insights into larger and complex datasets, where the relationships between the different variables is less obvious. In qualitative research, we tend to search for underlying patterns, their meanings and interpretations, and the theories are then either based on or developed from the pattern identified.

Coding (C)

As a student favourite, coding is another pattern analysis tool that generates the most common themes and patterns following a systematic approach. But being popular among students does not mean it works for everyone, so I recommend that you test it for yourself before you choose to code all your primary data. Paying attention to details and being disciplined are two useful personal traits that will help you make the most of coding.

Coding initially involves breaking down data into units, but it is not about labelling data. Instead the emphasis is on discovery, linking data to ideas and leading from the data to the idea. Coding runs through several cycles, and with every cycle data is refined and rearranged. Before coding can start, the data will need to be prepared and put into a format that allows for close reading. For example, interviews or focus groups are transcribed and the text generated laid out in a manageable form. This includes adding line numbers that will help with the identification of text passages later. AI-guided transcription services often provide transcripts without line numbers. Additionally, the quality of the transcript can vary from provider to provider, so it is advisable to go through the transcript to check for accuracy. Words can be misunderstood and distort the meaning. For example, in one of my research projects AI read *research* as *missiles* and confused *interviewee* and *interviewer*. If you intend to include interpretation of emotions and feelings into your analysis, an extended verbatim transcription is required. This captures not just the words, but also how the words were said and the circumstances that they were spoken in. This means pauses are noted and it could include gestures as well as intonation. Keeping a code book will help to manage the sheer quantity of codes you will generate and can double up as a notebook to record your initial thoughts and any reflections that cross your mind while coding (see analytic memos section).

When the preparation of the transcript is complete, read though it and highlight any *codable moments* that strike you as significant and worthy of attention. Layder (1998) named this pre-coding. In the first round, or cycle of coding (open coding) you read through the data word by word, in phrases or sentences that cover specific interpretations in the form of meanings, feelings, and reactions. These initial codes can be jotted down (e.g., by using the comments section of a word document), but you will notice that this space will quickly get rather crowded. A solution to preventing the overcrowding of codes is to copy the codes into a separate document, together with the line numbers, to enable you to trace back the code to the original text later. In larger studies covering multiple interviews, codes are repeated. Saldana reasoned that this is due "to both natural and deliberate causes, because most actions contain naturally repetitive patterns and actions, so it is the researcher's task to find and interpret them" (2021 5). Sometimes you will have two codes for the same word or phrase (simultaneous coding) and there can be patterned variations in the data. For example, capturing educational experience in a code will vary depending on the different belief and value system of artists. So, you code a commonality that consists of differences. Hatch (2002) summarises pattern characteristics that relate to frequency (i.e., often or seldom) and to sequences, actions that occur in a certain order. The characteristics of correspondence addresses actions that happen in relation to other activities or events, while causation captures one activity that is caused by another.

Following Charmaz's metaphor (quoted in Saldana, 2021 8) coding generates the bones, while integration (categorising, sampling) assembles them into a skeleton.

Saldana (2021 66) summarised the various coding methods into seven sub-categories (i.e., grammatical, elemental, literary, language, exploratory, proce-dural, and theming) that can be mixed and matched according to the research design. A selection of the most used methods recommended by Saldana are shown in Table 5.1. Please note that the table only provides an overview, so further literature needs to be consulted to explain the coding method in detail before it can be put to good use. Johnny Saldana's (2021) reference guide to coding provides further details and an explanation of how to successfully code data, illustrating the process through a wealth of examples. Depending on your research design, the choice of the coding methods will vary. For example, stu-dents that used grounded theory as a methodology to capture experiences applied affective coding in combination with attribute, in-vivo, process, and causation coding. Most data are analysed using coding techniques and all the previously discussed methods involve coding data. The mix-and-match approach conforms to a logic that either favours triangulation in testing one coding method against the other, or the accumulation of meaning through the use of different methods that complement each other, instead of being tested against one another. Remember, both ways of code method selection (i.e., tri-angulation and accumulation) work when unified and assessed as being suitable for supporting the research design.

The last coding technique in Table 5.1 points toward the next step, which is to categorise. This entails organising and grouping similarly coded data into relations by applying classification reasoning as well, as your tacit and intuitive sense, to determine what data can work together. Getting coding right rarely happens at the first attempt, often it requires several attempts to unlock the keys to the data, but trust your experience, knowledge, and motivation, and you will get there. As you progress through the coding cycles you will rearrange and reclassify, going constantly back and forth (see Figure 5.1). Imagine you are standing in front of a painting. In the closeup view you are dealing with the data. But take a few steps back and reposition yourself, gaining a broader view of the painting and allowing yourself to see the context, read the attached label, and unpack the way it relates to the surrounding pieces of art. Coding and recoding works in a similar fashion. Some subcategories might emerge under scores of categories, such as codes that harbour subcodes. But in general, cate-gories come out of several clusters of codes and not from other categories (see Figure 5.2). By thinking about the concepts, we can get to more abstract

TABLE 5.1 Selection of coding techniques (adapted after Saldana, 2021)

Name of technique	Shortcut description	Example	Use
Grammatical methods			
Attribute coding	Logging of essential information and demographic characteristics for managing data	Interview: 12 Participant Pseudonym: Anaconda Age: 35 Ethnicity: Black Social class: Upper Date of interview: 23 March 2023 Time: 2pm Duration: 2h	
Magnitude coding	Adding of a supplemental alphanumerical or symbolic code indicating intensity, frequency	Often (O), Seldom (SE), Not at all (N), Strongly (STR), Positive (POS)	
Sub-coding	Second order tag assigned to a primary code to enrich and detail primary code	Studio Artwork • Artists' friends work • Ancient artefacts • Artists' own works • Inspirational work • Works found on travels	
Simultaneous coding	Two or more different codes are assigned to one word or phrase		
In Vivo coding	Code is the exact phrase or word that is used by the participant themselves	BEING AT HOME IN THE FLOW	
Process coding	Actions are noted in gerunds (words end in -ing)	Adapting, emerging, drawing, remembering	
Affective methods			
Emotion coding	Labelling recalled emotions by participant or inferred by researcher about the participant	Tension, fear, relief, surprise	

Name of technique	Shortcut description	Example	Use
Value Coding	Participants attitudes, beliefs, and values that represent their worldview	Theatre is exclusive, future is scary, success is happiness	
Versus coding	Using binary terms that stand in conflict with each other to describe systems, organisations, processes, and concepts	Intrinsic vs instrumental; participants vs organisation	
Evaluation coding	Assigning judgment of merit, worth or significance of programme or policies (activities, characteristics, and outcomes) by participants	Boring services, powerful opportunities, new ideas	
Literary and language methods			
Dramaturgical coding	Apply conventions of play and performance (i.e., script, production analysis), use of character analysis	Objective: CONFRONT Conflict: DISTRUSTING Tactics: DIRECT, UP FRONT Attitudes: IRONIC Emotions: ANGER Subtext: LOSING MOTIVATION	Capturing social drama; intrapersonal and interpersonal experiences
Motif coding	Using previously defined index codes from folk tales, myths, and legends (i.e., smallest element in a tale that has something unique about it)	Story-based data; transformation to become an artist	See Uther (2011)
Narrative coding	Holistic approach to examine phenomena, issues, and people's lives, combines literary, sociological, psychological, and anthropological perspectives		To understand human conditions through stories (i.e., oral histories)
Verbal exchange coding	Uses identifiable units: ritual interactions, ordinary and skilled conversations, and personal narratives and dialogue		Used to interpret culture, such as theatre culture, requires detailed notation system for transcript

Name of technique	Shortcut description	Example	Use
Exploratory methods			
Holistic coding	Grasping basic themes, sorting self-standing units, such as stories, dividing text into broad topic areas		Using tentative labels for preliminary reading of data
Provisional coding	Developing a predetermined start list of codes to revise, modify, delete, and expand during the coding		Applied content analysis
Hypothesis coding	Uses researcher's preselected code to prove or refine hypothesis	Artist's Voice Childhood initiation to art Responses are preformulated and divided into possibilities such as: right, same, more, don't know. These are the codes used to analyse the data	
Procedural methods			
Protocol coding	Codes are predefined by other researchers, guidelines for conducting experiments		Educational research instruments for coding learners' behaviour
Outline of Cultural Materials (OCM)	Provides coding for categories of social life in ethnographic description	Indexing system for cultural artefacts such as clothing and garments	
Causation coding	Captures the everyday causal explanation people give, by plotting an attribution sequence on a chronological matrix	Housework skills transferred to Business skills, Performance skills led to leadership performance, and this helped create leadership skills	Discerning motives, beliefs systems, exploring why questions
Theming the data	Stands for an extended phrase that captures what a unit of data is about or what it means. In short, it is an implicit topic that organises a group of repeating ideas	Theme covers different aspects of being (i.e., what being an artist means and being an artist is)	Most forms of coding will have theming as a follow up step

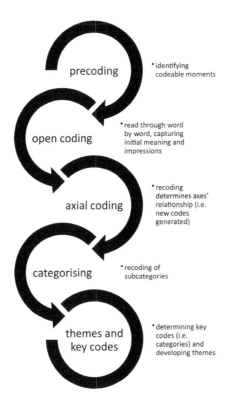

precoding
• identifying codeable moments

open coding
• read through word by word, capturing initial meaning and impressions

axial coding
• recoding determines axes' relationship (i.e. new codes generated)

categorising
• recoding of subcategories

themes and key codes
• determining key codes (i.e. categories) and developing themes

FIGURE 5.1 Coding cycle and stages (by the author)

constructs, called themes, and from there we could assert a theory, if following an inductive approach. When using a deductive approach, we call on the pre-informed theoretical frames, such as those outlined in a literature review, discussing coded data according to those theories and, therefore, no new theories are generated. Instead, evidence is provided for known knowledge.

In coding, the use and the meaning of terminology requires further thought because they can be confused with other common interpretations such as themes, topics, and categories. *Themes* are outcomes in coding, and do not exist by themselves, while in other uses themes are recurring ideas. A *category* has an explicit meaning in coding and the themes cover the subtle and tacit processes that are informed by several categories. For example, *happiness* can be a code or a category, while *love is expressed through happiness* could be a theme. In grounded theory, axial coding is performed as a step toward identifying the relationships between different categories. As an iterative process, going back and forth between initial (or open) and axial coding, will refine the analysis. In practical terms, codes and categories are laid out together and connections are drawn that are related to a central axis point in terms of meaning. This is often a pivotal moment, when new categories are discovered or drawn out of the data and themes emerge or are highlighted. It is when the properties and dimensions of the categories and themes are defined. Afterwards, the conceptual framework can be outlined, linking themes together into a coherent and narrated written format.

The methodology of grounded theory (see Chapter 3) uses a set of procedures with three cycles of coding (i.e., open, axial, and collective). It approaches the text line by line for analysis, coding the text with a choice of multiple codes that such as exploratory, grammatical, elemental, and effective codes. It then reassembles the fractured data to find the dominant or key codes that form part of the theoretical framework that is emerging from the data. This process is repeated until theoretical saturation is achieved.

Coding manually is a good starting point for novice coders and small research projects. More comprehensive projects, such as research studies covering multiple interviews or focus groups, will benefit from the help of software to enable the coding to be done electronically. There are several software programmes that can be employed and many help by providing a systematic view of the data, allowing researchers to code, while keeping records and an overview of the entire process.

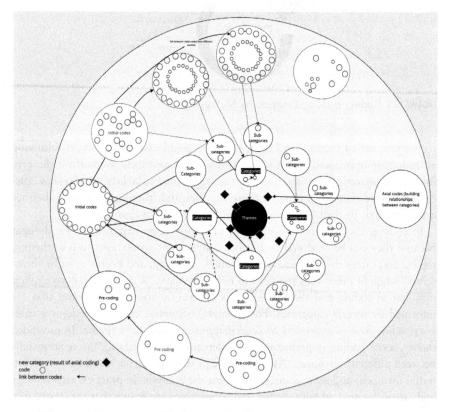

FIGURE 5.2 Coding structure illustrated with connections between the coding stages (by the author)

Some code video recordings, while others provide transcripts. Depending on what kind of data you have collected, it is worth shopping around for the programme that is best suited to the requirements of the project. Universities provide computer-assisted qualitative data analysis software (CAQDAS), but it is important to understand the pros and cons of the different programmes, including what they provide and how they generate their analysis. Some, such as InVivo, count repeated phrases or words as do many of the AI-assisted transcription programmes. This might be helpful, but it does not generate codes. Trying out coding manually enables researchers to connect to the data by touching sticky notes or paper, and sometimes these haptic encounters indirectly add to the researchers' understanding of what is important, as the codes are generated electronically.

Visualisation of data has been a fast-developing field that can help organise and examine codes through word processing programmes. By using *tags*, the software gathers words according to their frequency, and categorises them according to size. The most used term appears as the largest, and as the frequency of the words decreases, so does the size. Researchers tend to use code landscaping tools in the beginning to get an initial feel for the data, but I have used it intermittently throughout the research process. This is partly to gain reassurance as to where the coding is heading, and partly for motivational purposes to break with the routine of coding for days and weeks on end. I noticed that the frequency or size mattered for an initial view, in an aesthetic sense, but the familiarity with the data compensated for the size and a form of axial coding happened automatically with the visualised data landscape, helping with the basic outlining of the codes. AI-driven data visualisation will provide further analysis, enabling dynamic coding, which could be particularly important for the revision of predetermined coding techniques, but for the moment the electronic software helps mainly with the sorting and ordering of codes.

Analytic Memos (AM)

Taking notes to capture, and subsequently recall information, is another common tool and skill that facilitates research. In coding, it fulfils several functions. Firstly, memos not only record thoughts and memories, but also act as conversations that researchers have with themselves about the data while researching. It provides a chance to note down any thoughts about participants, processes, and phenomenon that trigger or prompt reflections, much like writing a letter to a friend or relative. Secondly, memos perform a role as critical friends or alter egos that allow researchers to question the extent to which preconceived ideas are read into the data. This helps guide the coding, including the weight that researchers give to assumptions, emotional investment, and motivation as data. In these nonverbal conversations, researchers will formulate ideas, disregard them, then further refine them. Thirdly, memos form a concurrent relationship with the coding. the activities of writing, coding, and memos help to develop the coding system and allow the phenomenon to evolve. In qualitative methodologies, memos are understood as data, can be coded, and need to be labelled with a descriptive title and date. When coding electronically, finding out in advance how codes and memos are labelled and how to access them later in relation to the original text is paramount.

Memos can be written throughout the process, starting with the initial ideas, formulating the research questions, collecting data, analysing it, and finally writing it up. In this sense, memos resemble research diaries and, judging from my experience, writing down thoughts following a "brain dump" allows me to deal with ideas that would not pass my initial judgment, but might turn out to be useful and important at a later stage. For example, when coding I remember the interview and not only feel close to the interviewee, but also to the context of the interview – the location, circumstances, and even weather conditions. Because memory is implicated in the present but referenced in the past, I compare memos written on the day of the interview with my reflections written during coding, both of which add yet another layer of data. When it comes to memo writing, it should not be delayed but carried out the moment the thought occurs. It reminds me of the epiphanies that happen when they are expected least. The abundance of electronic devices that we carry or use daily, offer the ability to memorise our thoughts instantly, so there is no excuse not to record what occurs in the moment.

Discourse Analysis (DA)

Continuing with text-based analysis, the focus shifts from coding to the framework of discourses and context. The emphasis is on the plural of discourses that are amalgamated and woven together into a new coherent discussion, critically reflecting on the multiplicity of exchanges and social interactions. The text remains an important underlying feature in the analysis, but greater emphasis should be paid to the interconnectedness of the text, its context, and the practices that are associated with both text and context. Fairclough (1992) developed a three-dimensional analysis framework (see Figure 5.3) that aims to help make sense of the text, the context, and their broader implications. The idea is to analyse the three dimensions together to fully understand the complexities of language used in social interactions.

1.   The text dimension is concerned with how the language in the text is organised and structured, what meaning the words convey, and what messages they carry. The bottom square contains the text description that is set out to analyse language using grammar, vocabulary, and syntax, and includes how those linguistic features form and support meaning making.
2.   The discourse dimension refers to the social practice of the language in use. As a practice, it is concerned with the cultural and social context. As illustrated through the square at the back of Figure 5.3, this dimension

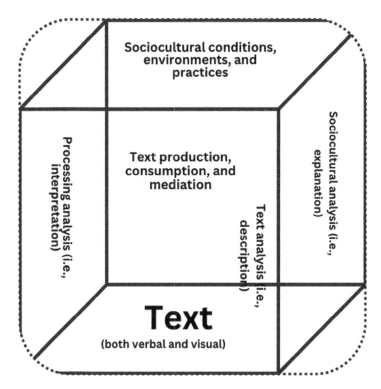

Sociocultural conditions, environments, and practices

Processing analysis (i.e., interpretation)

Text production, consumption, and mediation

Sociocultural analysis (i.e., explanation)

Text analysis (i.e., description)

Text

(both verbal and visual)

FIGURE 5.3 Fairclough's three-dimensional framework for discourse analysis (adapted by author)

looks for guidance toward other discourses and practices that deal with similar ideas, covering text production and consumption, which is also known as processing analysis. For example, it focuses on how power relationships shape and are shaped by other practices.

3. The third dimension covers sociocultural practices, including cultural, political, economic, and historical factors that influence the text. Made visible in the square on the right, it covers social analysis, the experience of the environment, and the negotiation of social relations and processes, including precarity and inequality in the CCI, for example.

It does not matter which side or square you start with, all sides of the cube are valued equally when developing the argument. Typically, the text is considered as a whole, but identifying typical discourse fragments (Wodak & Meyer, 2015) that cover repeating points, which are also raised in other text passages, remains a good option. The detailed analysis depends on the criteria set beforehand and usually references the context (i.e., author, occasion, structure, and selection of the text), text surface (i.e., layout, headings, topics), rhetoric (i.e., form of argumentation, underlying logic, idioms, symbols, vocabulary, style, and references made), and content statements (i.e., ideology, societal viewpoints, and outlook). Not all text lends itself to typical fragmentation and it is worth bearing in mind that discourse analysis favours the connections between multiple discussions and discourses. This can be achieved through combining the detailed analysis with the bird's-eye perspective. By zooming in and out, it constructs and conveys (new) meaning.

Discourse analysis puts the emphasis on unpacking the text to discover the underlying issues. For example, the philanthropic rhetoric of the Arts Council England (ACE) as expressed in numerous reports and policy documents (i.e., text), relates to the neoliberal understanding that as little state support as possible should be given to the arts. This is because the market will regulate demand and therefore the arts do not need government intervention. This is not explicitly spelled out in published documents, because it is a grant awarding agency, but it is implied as an underlying assumption and the language used in the documents gives us a lot of references that cite free market dominance. The Arts Council England's four published investment principles (i.e., being ambitious and quality, dynamism, environmental resilience, and inclusivity and relevance) sound rather innocent. But the detailed explanation of those terms – for example, the appeal to arts organisations to "reduce cost, maximise income, and become entrepreneurial" (ACE, 2022) – demonstrates how business language is used to communicate, illustrate, and assess grant proposals. It could be interpreted that the ACE is interested in making an investment, only in the sense that returns are expected in the future. The term investment is not value free and attracts thinking in terms of assets, stocks, and money. Consequently, generating a profit seems a desired outcome that is written into this word choice. Other forms of investment, such as professional development, might be possible but, because the word is used mainly in a business context, it is worth questioning its choice in the first place.

Critical Discourse Analysis (CDA)

The example of the interpretation of ACE philanthropic rhetoric points towards critical discourse analysis (CDA), which is a specific method of discourse analysis focuses on power relations and dominant ideologies (see Chapter 3). CDA follows principles that are similar to discourse analysis in that it analyses word choices, sentence structures, and rhetorical devices for the textual analysis. Any discursive analysis focuses on the way in which language expresses, shapes, and constructs identities, beliefs, and values. In cultural policy analysis, attention is paid to political structure and social norms, which are engrained in multiple discourses. The term CDA hints at the importance of being critical about the content of your data and yourself by, for example, looking at your positionality and setting those reflections in relation to the broader social and political implications that dominant ideologies include and perpetuate. CDA draws on insights from other fields and disciplines, like cultural studies, sociology, and linguistics, which research power relations (e.g., hierarchy building, subordination, and privilege), ideological structures (e.g., liberalism, democracy, and socialism), and it is therefore not surprising that CDA applies an interdisciplinary approach.

Discursive Psychology (DP)

This method also belongs to the discourse analysis family and follows similar interdisciplinary guidelines for studying how people use language to construct meaning in social interactions. Taylor (cited in Wesner & Woddis, 2022 12) extended the phrase "the personal is political" to "the personal is also social". She emphasised that the shared understanding of what is considered common sense is based on a selection of ideas that follow established ways of doing things, and which is also expressed, among others, in language practices. For example, the use of pronouns and metaphors, which carry commonly understood meanings are foregrounded in exploring social behaviour including values, emotions, and feelings. Wetherell's affective practice (2012) provides further advice about what being affected means, as a core social topic, in shaping and understanding discourse. In her book *Emotions and Affect*, she responded to a general affective turn in cultural studies and social psychology at the time, but her work resonates today in relationship to the collection of online data for discourse analysis. The shift towards practice includes a reformulation of the discursive practices that are linked to research practices. For example, multiple texts are generated in the public domain of the internet. While this provides easy access to data in the form of posts, tags, blogs, and comments, the conveyed text is limited in length, size, and appearance by the platforms, which impacts affective practices. Often affective behaviour analysis, as expressed in the language that is generated through a series of threads and stories, is in high demand for research. Scrolling through Twitter (or X) accounts offers contextual information, using hashtags that are directed from the source, and which generates an information loop on the platform. Strictly speaking, this structural selection should be considered in the analysis, as it directs the discourse.

Overall, it goes beyond the scope of this book to provide a comprehensive overview of the multiple forms of discourse analysis. Using a kaleidoscopic approach helps to pinpoint not just a single method but puts emphasis on the constantly changing ideas and patterns that make up the discourse analysis family. As with many methods discussed in this chapter, there is no universal canon of data collection. Researchers will define their personal approach through experience and CCI researchers are able to employ research skills gained through extensive essay writing in their respective programmes. Remember, most essays that are written in degree studies follow the same logic of analysing and discussing discourses. Making good use of these skills, including self-reflection, will be helpful for dissertations or final project write ups. Being mindful and understanding that research is intellectually challenging, rigorous, and critical in the application of methods and arguments, will also support the discursive nature of this method.

Explanation Building (EB)

In this section, I aim to introduce analysis techniques and tools that are applicable to a variety of methods and that suit several methodologies. Explanation building is commonly applied in qualitative and quantitative research, and it is fair to say that the majority of research is perceived to be using causation, the hallmark of explanation building. Constructing a causal explanation in abstract terms involves manipulating one variable and then measuring its effect on another dependent variable. Using the cause-and-effect relationship has been applied in experiments to test out hypothesises in order first to revise them and then test them again. For example, exhibition design (one variable) can be manipulated to evaluate how visitors (another variable) react in terms of time spent in the exhibition, engagement, and the satisfaction of their experience. As an experiment, two different versions of exhibition designs could be offered to the same visitors and their feedback analysed to capture their experience. The process is revised by exchanging and rearranging objects until a satisfactory result is achieved.

Cultural organisations are subject to ongoing change and managing this change can be challenging. With the help of explanation building, a theory of change can be developed and implemented to ensure that change can be achieved. For example, many cultural organisations have sustainability as an objective or a value in their mission statement, but there is no or little evidence of this in the activities they offer. A solution would be to either change the mission statement, by removing sustainability, or by designing activities throughout the organisation to justify the statement. In other words, provide a clear understanding of the causal relationship between objectives, activities, and outcomes.

The quality of the evidence and ruling out of alternative explanations accounts for the strength that explanation building can bring to research. Creative industries make good use of this method in understanding several phenomena. For example, to discover why a particular song has become a hit, researchers investigate the different roles of lyrics, chord structure, and instrumentation, as well as marketing strategies, each of which might have an impact on the popularity of the piece of music. Similar studies have been conducted to explain the popularity of films, video games, and exhibitions. Explanation building has been used for exploratory case studies, in which you collect information in several rounds of research and repeatedly return to test and revise your approach. The policy cycle of developing, implementing, maintaining, and evaluating policies is a good example of this form of analysis. All cases aim to bring a deeper understanding of the underlying mechanisms that drive human creative behaviour and innovation in CCI.

Template Analysis (TEA)

As a predefined layout, templates are commonly used. They include stencil templates for creating repeated patterns on fabrics, walls, or traffic signs, as well as manuscript layout templates for writing, such as for essays or dissertations. Blueprint templates in architecture enable ready-made houses, while, in marketing, consistent branding templates deliver better product recognition. Website templates allow us to design and arrange information by adapting and playing with a given format. In research, templates represent pre-existing sets of categories and themes that help in organising and analysing the data (King, 2012). In this sense, templates provide a consistent framework, ensuring that other new patterns can be extracted from the data that would otherwise have gone unnoticed. Choosing codes for the coding process (see coding section) is one example. The frame is provided through the different codes (see Table 5.1), but it is for the researcher to decide which codes help to analyse the data best. In short, template analysis uses codes, but these are predefined and come in lists and categories. Relationships between the themes and codes are often explored by applying a hierarchical order of codes. Planning, executing, and monitoring are common divisions in project management research that uses this method extensively.

Sometimes the familiarity of the template and the systematic approach makes us assume that they provide a one-size-fits-all approach, but this is far from reality. Instead, researchers refine, modify, and adapt templates as the data is analysed to capture emerging themes and topics. Remember, templates are useful tools to organise your data. The section on pattern and coding discusses this further.

Narrative Analysis (NA)

The final method of analysing data focusses on everything related to narration in terms of its meaning, structure, and functions (Riessmann, 2008). Stories, trajectories, and other forms of literature and film are examined through close reading, and the application of storytelling elements, like plots, characters, settings (including cultural background and environmental perspectives), points of view (i.e., who is telling the story), conflict (i.e., problems and challenges that drive the plot), and dialogue (i.e., conversations between characters). Narrative analysis is the opposite of fractured data. Instead, it analyses the story as a whole, only applying limited fragmentation of data. Narrative analysis uses the same questions that many of us are familiar with from our early schooling: What is the story about? (i.e., the main argument being presented); *What happens to whom, where and why?* (i.e., characters, events, and locations); *What are the consequences of this?* (i.e., results); and *What is the significance of these events?* (i.e., interpretation within the wider context and how this can be applied or used in different situations).

In social research, the emphasis of this interpretative approach is to unpack and discover the underlying themes, patterns, and messages that are told in oral histories, news articles, and personal narratives. CCI is packed with examples and narrative analysis has been used to address questions of identity related to professional, political, and cultural practices. Art activism, habits, and agency are analysed in relation to concepts of time, memory, and power.

Narrative analysis relies on storytelling characteristics, but not exclusively. It employs other methods, including discourse and thematic analysis, to capture experiences (e.g., how cultural workers make sense of the cultural worlds they inhabit). Narrative can be understood as forms of social life in which the personal life merges with public conduct and a shared understanding between people, perceptions, and conditions in society develops. For example, my own research (Wesner, 2018 and Wesner & Woddis, 2022) shows that artists' careers are sometimes built on the expectation of a breakthrough, in which recognition, reward, and success come together all at once, thereby compensating for the long and difficult struggles of the past. In many cases it never happens, but the expectation that it will happen one day motivates the artist to pursue their career. Instead of experiencing the breakthrough, a gradual development occurs that becomes visible through the analysis of narrated expectations that are perpetuated in society.

Conclusion

Data analysis methods demand rigour, subject expertise, advance planning, and good time management. Students tend to overlook the fact that the bulk of the work will involve the analysis of the data. Novice researchers take longer overall, but it is also not uncommon for experienced researchers to neglect time management when absorbed in the analysis. Having said this, analysing data is ultimately a rewarding exercise, especially as the fruits of the labour materialise when data are transformed into meaningful insights. Data literacy skills are long-lasting, sustainable, and are transferable into many tasks that require critical thinking, combined with paying attention to detail. Bear in mind that this process is hardly ever linear or a one-time and straightforward exercise. Instead, it makes sense to expect a continuous learning process that requires ongoing monitoring, reflection, and evaluation to ensure the reliability of the data. Looking at the research process overall, it is one of the later steps that comes before the final written piece can be produced.

There are plenty of methods for analysing data. Choosing suitable methods requires that they are paired with methods for collecting data. Both the type of methods for collecting and for analysing must speak to each other. Matching methods for collection with methods for analysis is part of the research design and is ideally dealt with early in the research process. But it is worthwhile checking that both types of methods work well together as the research progresses. For example, structured interviews with predefined questions that correspond to already selected themes will fit with template analysis and thematic analysis.

Remember, as a researcher, flexibility is important, and processes will need to be adapted when carrying out original research. The idea of staying flexible means being responsible to the ongoing technological developments that might make data analysis more accessible, but also reinforces the idea that critical questioning should be applied to all research data and processes, including those that are generated with the help of AI.

One final point raised in this chapter relates to the reason why data is analysed. I am referring here to an understanding data as evidence. This is a notion that raises the familiar debate about evidence-based policymaking, which is commonly used in the CCI. Belfiore (quoted in Majone 1989) in 2022, arguing that evidence and data are not synonymous. Instead, evidence is a form of the interpretation of data, which is purposely developed to persuade a particular audience. Belfiore (2022) reasoned that in academia we tend to read or translate, thereby providing evidence as research, but this should include questioning evidence. For example, if policymakers and researchers consider multiple sources (including data, grey literature, expert advice, and anecdotal evidence) as useable and valuable proof, but without also questioning those sources, then this can lead to incorrect findings. Consequently, with data analysis in CCI, we should bear in mind that researchers must verify not just the meaning of data, but the data itself. In practical terms, this accounts for transparency, verifiability, and reproducibility of the data of which the evidence is the result. For example, with a dissertation the implications are that transcripts of interviews are added to the appendix, or when stored on the university servers, it is mentioned where they can be accessed. In the dissertation, interview quotes are cited and referenced to count as proof of evidence, but to ensure transparency these need to be traceable to the original transcripts.

References

ACE (Arts Council England) 2022. *Investment principles*. https://www.artscouncil.org.uk/lets-create/strategy-2020-2030/investment-principles (27 August 2023).

Belfiore, E. 2022. Is it really about the evidence? Argument, persuasion, and the power of ideas in cultural policy. *Cultural Trends*, 31(4): 293–310. doi:10.1080/09548963.2021.1991230.

Beuys, J. & Bodenmann-Ritter, C. 1975. *Documenta: Jeder Mensch ein Künstler: Gespräche auf der Documenta 5/1972*. Ullstein.

Braun, V., V. Clarke, G. Terry, and N. Hayfield. 2019a. Thematic analysis. In P. Liamputtong (Ed.), *Handbook of Research Methods in Health and Social Sciences* (pp. 843–860). Springer.

Braun, V., and V. Clarke. 2019b. Reflecting on reflexive thematic analysis. *Qualitative Research in Sport, Exercise & Health*, 11(4): 589–597. doi:10.1080/2159676X.2019.1628806.

Braun, V., Clarke, V., & Hayfield, N. 2022. 'A starting point for your journey, not a map': Nikki Hayfield in conversation with Virginia Braun and Victoria Clarke about thematic analysis. *Qualitative Research in Psychology*, 19(2): 424–445.

Easley, D. & Kleinberg, J. 2010. *Networks, Crowds, and Markets: Reasoning about a Highly Connected World*. Cambridge University Press.

Fairclough, N. 1992. Discourse and text: Linguistic and intertextual analysis within discourse analysis. *Discourse & Society*, 3(2): 193–217.

Granovetter, M. S. 1973. The strength of weak ties. *American Journal of Sociology*, 78 (6): 1360–1380.

Hatch, J. A. 2002. *Doing Qualitative Research in Education Settings*. Suny Press.

King, N. 2012. Doing template analysis. *Qualitative organizational research: Core methods and current challenges* (pp. 426–450). Sage.

Köhler, T., Smith, A., & Bhakoo, V. 2022. Templates in qualitative research methods: Origins, limitations, and new directions. *Organizational Research Methods*, 25(2): 183–210.

Krippendorff, K. 2018. *Content Analysis: An Introduction to Its Methodology*. Sage Publications.

Layder, D. 1998. Sociological practice: Linking theory and social research. *Sociological Practice* (pp. 1–208). Sage.

Lê, J. K. & Schmid, T. 2022. The practice of innovating research methods. *Organizational Research Methods*, 25(2): 308–336.

Majone, G. 1989. *Evidence, Argument and Persuasion in the Policy Process*. Yale University Press.

Riessman, C. K. 2008. *Narrative Methods for the Human Sciences*. Sage.

Saldaña, J. 2021. *The Coding Manual for Qualitative Researchers* (pp.1–440). Sage.

Sinkovics, N. 2018. Pattern matching in qualitative analysis. In C. Cassell, A. L. Cunliffe & G. Grandy, *The Sage Handbook of Qualitative Business and Management Research Methods* (pp. 468–485). Sage.

Uther, H.-J. 2011. *The Types of International Folktales: A Classification and Bibliography*, vol. 284. Suomalainen Tiedeakatemia.

Weizenbaum, J. 1983. ELIZA—a computer program for the study of natural language communication between man and machine. *Communications of the ACM*, 26(1): 23–28.

Wesner, S. 2018. *Artists' Voices in Cultural Policy*. Palgrave.

Wesner, S. & Woddis, J. 2022. Artists and cultural workers in cultural policy and creative practice: From the big break narrative to mutual aid and collective care. Simone Wesner and Jane Woddis in conversation with Stephanie Taylor and Greig de Peuter. *Journal of Cultural Management and Cultural Policy/Zeitschrift für Kulturmanagement und Kulturpolitik*, 8(2): 9–30.

Wetherell, M. 2012. *Affect and Emotion* (pp.1–192). Sage.

Wodak, R. & Meyer, M. (Ed.) 2015. *Methods of Critical Discourse Studies*. Sage.

Zong, C., Xia, R., & Zhang, J. 2021. *Text Data Mining*. Springer.

6

FORMULATING RESEARCH QUESTIONS

Introduction

As with any other discipline or field, in CCI research is driven by questions that demand answers. Those answers then help with the development of CCI as a field, and the result is that the whole of society benefits. Applying the analogy of the house, we must take a step back focusing on the build. The research questions are the main pillars holding up the structure of the house with the rooms divided up around it. The research questions guide the research process, providing focus and specificity, and holding the essence of what researchers want to learn, explore, and investigate. The characteristics of the pillars shape the surrounding rooms, including the roof. Regarded as the starting point of research, it comes with multiple issues and problems that arise during the framing of the research process. However, most research arrives at questions only after being on a journey of discovering interests, topics, and concepts that require further thought – a kind of scoping exercise, as it is called in research method textbooks. In short, do not expect to come up with a research question straight away. Instead, allow yourself to be taken on a journey.

Following the same idea, this chapter invites you to join the travel party, discussing what should be considered when developing a research question. It contains practical pointers with examples and will guide you through some of the tools that aid the discovery process. The chapter introduces Layder's approach (2012) which develops a research question through formulating initial ideas linked to the themes and topics of interest, before moving on to problem questioning. Different types of research questions are introduced to aid conceptual approaches, before the final step, which uses examples to connect research questions to the trio of research design. Please note that there is no formula for developing a research question. Instead, many different approaches

DOI: 10.4324/9781003161912-6

will lead you to a good research question. It is a matter of discovering what works best for you. This chapter is designed to help you on your journey.

To start with, many ideas might not make sense at first, as they are often contradictory or might simply be puzzling. When I find an issue interesting, I usually cannot let go of the thought. I might have a hunch that with further reading and some initial research it will start to contextualise. I begin to imagine what the house will look like when fully constructed. At this stage, I have an inkling of what the pillars will look like. There may be several questions or pillars that I keep in mind before I eventually work out what the main pillar might look like and from what it can be made. In terms of research design, I argue that the research questions direct the emergence of the design, which is made up of pillar pieces, including:

1. Defining the discussion about the scope of the research. In CCI, the scope is broad and multifaceted, including social, economic, cultural, and technological research. CCI covers different aspects of creative activities, including cultural values, funding, policymaking, and labour practices, to name only a few.
2. Aiming to point towards key variables and concepts (paradigms) that could be employed (e.g., those relating to creativity, cultural production, intellectual property, cultural habits, participation, collaboration, intersectionality, and decolonialisation).
3. Allowing speculation about the methodology and the data collection and analysis methods. What methodology (see Chapter 3) and methods (see Chapters 4 and 5) would be best suited to enable the research question to be answered?

Another common assumption about research questions is that, when satisfactorily framed and formulated, it remains the same throughout the research process. Bear in mind that research questions are open ended, allowing for several answers, and because the very nature of the research is empirical, change is inevitable and should be accounted for in the research process. Keeping a flexible approach to the research questions throughout the research process helps to adapt to inevitable changes.

Having said this, I recommend students post their research questions in a prominent position, such as a wall, fridge, or smartphone, as a reminder of where the research is heading overall. Sometimes being too deeply involved in the details lets the birds-eye view dwindle, so a visual reminder of the research questions helps to bring the focus back to the overall research agenda.

Thinking About a Topic

When formulating a research question is understood as a process, how and where to start is a key question to ask? As expected, there are many ways and no clear formula, but here are a few pointers worth considering. For example, I could write down all the known parameters that I have been thinking about, such as the timeframe or expected outcomes, and put this to one side. I also know topics, people, and fields of interest, so I could try to bring them together in a brainstorming session. A more structured way would be to ask a set of questions that clarify the parameters of the project. In any case, I need to tread carefully by interrogating what it is I want to research. Firstly, what is it that I aim to understand? Is it a concept such as memory, or the artistic myth, or provenance? Secondly, are my interests focused around investigating specific research agents (e.g., institutions, structures/frameworks, people, interrelationships)? Thirdly, does it make sense to investigate different ways of enquiry, such as how do I ask questions? Is it an exploratory study or do I aim to prove a hypothesis? Would designing an experiment be the most suitable way to investigate my interests? Fourthly, shall I start casting a wide remit and read extensively and loosely around the topics I jotted down earlier, or would a discussion with a fellow student or colleague help to kickstart the process? This fourth question depends on the previous answer and is related to the process or the trajectory I will follow. Answering these questions depends on researcher's habits and ways of translating an interest into a research journey. In short, searching around a topic of interest and discovering what the key issues are can take many forms, but finding out what has already been written about the subject makes for a good start.

Thinking about the different fields or the discourses that tackle arts management and cultural policy ideas will help you to understand where your personal interests lie. Are you driven by the generation of new knowledge, or do you want to investigate the meaning of concepts? For example, do you want to know how the concept of "common practice" is understood among your co-workers? You could explore what common practice means conceptually in the first place and expand upon that common understanding of a shared set of norms and expectations to identify explicit (e.g., written policies and procedures) and implicit (e.g., unspoken understandings of how things work and are done) aspects. You could investigate the benefits and the challenges that arrive from a common practice for workers, organisations, and society as a whole to expand and go beyond the meaning of common practice as a rationale for efficiency and effectiveness. In a slightly different approach, the relationship between ontology (i.e., knowledge and meaning) and technology could be questioned by focusing on specific organisations, such as, for example, how art collectives engage their audiences with digital technologies. In the first instance, attention might shift to a more marketing-based topic that focusses on the relationship between ticket sales and programming. However, there are numerous ways to explore the relationship by taking a critical point of view. For example, how is technology used to control creative content or how can this be compared to traditional forms of art censorship?

In the past, students liked to know what makes a good research topic. There is no definite answer, as it very much depends on your own understanding and the personal interests that drive your curiosity. These interests are not always obvious when seen through the lens of learning or study, but they are there. Ask yourself what you would like to engage in; imagine situations, events or look back at an art-related or cultural moment in which you felt at home but perhaps also bewildered or puzzled. Ideas that can be generated from these little common moments have the potential to develop into a motivational topic that will maintain your interest and encourage your search for more information. Another way to focus your interest is by reviewing previous reading materials to see what you remember and then take this interest further.

In the case of dissertations, reading materials from modules or courses you participated in, or podcasts and talks you have listened to will help generate areas of interest to start.

After noting down some areas of interest, your focus could turn towards a topic that is more specific. In my research, I have a longstanding interest in visual artists' career trajectories. This stems from my initial MA dissertation, in which I investigated art galleries in Dresden/Saxony and noticed that I knew little about the artists' careers, even though some artists were friends. Given that German unification remained a constant topic of discussion at the time, I was curious to find out how artists had weathered life amid the changing political turmoil since unification. Many artists that established a career in the former GDR lost all their contract work overnight, but due to the political interest in GDR art that occurred at that time were able to sell their work after German unification. Accompanied by these factually driven changes, the behaviour of artists was by no means straightforward, and this caught my interest. Working my way through related ideas and problems, I formulated questions that would capture the topic and the problem separately. As a next step, I tried to pin down from what angle the topic could be approached. This could be expressed through their artistic practice, through their cultural, political, economic, social, or media environment. I could have studied their lifestyles and interviewed their partners, or I could have focused on celebrity artists and studied their behaviour. My interests were driven by several ideas, but political and artistic curiosity merged into the more specific topic of visual artists' careers in Saxony after German unification. As an exercise, the topic was translated into a question trying to pin down specifics without losing the broader view: What have artists' career ambitions been since German unification? Have their career perceptions changed prior, during, and after German unification? At the time these questions were noted but left aside.

From Topic to Problem

Formulating a research problem allows for a broader remit. Approaching research through problems and issues that are known stimulates and motivates us more toward solving the issue, which may be the preferred option in our daily lives. The aim is not to fix the problem but to explain and analyse in-depth what causes the issues.

In a next step, issues were translated into the following questions: How do social settings influence artists' careers? How does this impact on the pro-fessionalisation of artists in society? What is the role of artists in the art world? Do they have power? How do they interact with other players in the art world? Adapting the topic into a question and formulating the issues into questions helped to shape ideas further. In the example, the topics of interest and the problems were linked with the idea of advancing the topic into a problem – and similarly for the questions. The topic questions (i.e., Why are artists reluctant to market themselves or to engage more actively in their career development in the first place?) developed into the problem questions (i.e., How do social set-tings influence artists' careers?). How does this impact the professionalisation of artists in society? What determines an artist's career? The challenge is that it is impossible to investigate artists' careers as such, without further clarification. I am also not interested in all artists in the world; my motivation is linked to German unification. In the next step, the problem question is adapted to specific conditions and environments, while maintaining a broad and analytical approach. This enabled the researcher to carry out a specific investigation in a defined geographical location (i.e., the administrative region/land of Saxony), and it does not refer to artists covering all fields, only visual artists specifically. Furthermore, in this case a timeframe that is linked to the historical event of German unification was set, arriving at a research question: How have visual artists' careers in Saxony developed over time since German unification?

Defining the parameters that specifies research makes it unique and ensures that a certain degree of originality is built into the design. However, being specific does not mean that the broad aspect is lost, as previously mentioned. I keep the broad frame of careers, which as a concept contains practice and theory at the same time, but the underlying concept that runs through the question is change. The research question captured change as the key research topic without referencing the word *change*. So, why did I not use *change* as a term when asking what changed in artists' lives since German unification? Using *what* in the question assumes that change happened. This might be a fair assumption since the regime change is accepted as a proven fact, but it drives the investigation in a different direction to what I wanted to achieve. Asking the *what* question locates the characteristics of change relative to artists' lives. Following this approach, the results of the study would be describing the impact of the political change from the artist's perspective. In a sense, I would try to find evidence for change and examples of change. I would not be ques-tioning the concept of change. Instead, change is taken for granted. It frames artists' life experience, as fixed to the changes triggered by German unification, a specific historical event. In other words, the research question reduces the investigations' remit and implies that it seeks to find evidence that captures change. However, capturing artists' career trajectories might reference or include other aspects, such as childhood exposure to creative practices, that would perhaps be disregarded as evidence. This selection, as set out in the question with the wording of *what*, would appear to contradict my exploratory approach. As I mentioned above, I want to stay as openminded as possible. I began questioning change at the same time as I was investigating the change expressed in the research question. Following a process-driven approach, as implied through asking *how* instead of *what*, strengthens the exploratory character of the study. The focus on process still establishes a focus but shifts this toward methods – or, as in my case, toward the description of how artists go about their daily lives without the prior judgment of evidencing change. In this sense, the question seems to be best addressed using an exploratory methodology, and the question acts as a pointer or hint toward the exploratory approach. Asking *how* indicates the exploratory character of the research, enabling us to study experience, including the emotional involvement of the participating artists.

Types of Research Questions

Overall, the types of questions (*what*, *how*, and *why*) frame the study, while connecting methodology and methods as the supporting elements from the very beginning. White (2017) argued that different types of questions fulfil different purposes and address different aspects of research. The most common are: (1) explanatory, (2) exploratory, (3) evaluative, and (4) predictive questions.

1. **Explanatory** questions handle causal relationships with the aim of explaining how one variable affects another. They work in the same way as causal analysis (see Chapter 5). Hypothesis-based questions often cover expected explanations in the form of binary choices, as expressed in yes and no. For example: Does exposure to immersive theatre lead to increased participation in performance related activities? Goal-oriented questions often guided the natural sciences. For example, in 1988 the Human Genome project set out to determine a completed DNA sequence. It achieved the identification of 90% at the end of the project in 2003, while the first fully complete human genome sequence was achieved in 2022 (NHGRI, 2023).

2. **Exploratory** questions seek to discover new areas that have been under-researched, with the aim of finding new insights. Exploratory studies often ask open questions, not knowing where the investigation will take the research, while trying to gain insights into ideas. My research is informed by such an approach, which was based on questions related to, for example, how ideas travel or how policies develop. The focus is not on the possible success of the policy, but instead explores areas that we know little about. This will produce results that are not fixed at the start of the research. Artists are often seen as being on the receiving end of policy

decision-making, in the form of support. But my research shows that artists create policies throughout their career, by developing, informing, and acting out practices that guide governmental policy in indirect forms. Most of the initial thinking is based on assumptions, but exploratory research tries to approach a study by being reflective from the outset and keeping an open mind throughout, as much as possible.

3. **Evaluative** research questions, in policy analysis, focus on impact and the effectiveness of policies, programmes, and interventions. For example: How effective were performance indicators in evaluating organisational performance of cultural organisations in the UK?

4. **Predictive** questions relate to trends and attempt to seek predictions and future outcomes through the analysis, based on facts or current data. AI-generated data and large data sets are used to answer questions, such as: What is the likelihood of AI-generated exhibitions superseding traditionally curated exhibitions in the next ten years? This type of question also relates to speculative research that is sometimes described as thinking outside the box. They ask questions that, in the first instance, seem to rely on possibilities and futures, aiming to find alternatives, or develop sensibilities for specific issues that we might have to face in the future. For example, some of the important speculative questions relating to art funding ask: Who will support the arts and culture when neither public nor private support is forthcoming? How could we develop alternative funding models that do not rely on currently available resources?

These four types of questions demonstrate one way of thinking about how to conceptualise research questions, but there is more to consider when linking the question to a specific methodology. For example, critical theory is interdisciplinary as a field of study, aiming to challenge given assumptions related to power, power structure, and oppression. Research is carried out to point toward an issue or a problem that comes across as unjust, unfair, or is understood to be false. Criticality needs to be reflected in the research question and should be designed to encourage criticality, reflexivity, and enable critical analysis. This research can be either exploratory, evaluative, or explanatory, using questions that ask how and what. Developing a research question using a critical theory framework can build the critique into the question. For example, asking the question of what cultural factors contribute to inequality in the CCI assumes that inequalities are embedded in its practices. Critical theory can take a stand and address the social and cultural wrongs in societies, but that is not a given. Critical theory studies can maintain a neutral approach in the questions, but still aims to uncover societal wrongdoing while uncovering underlying issues. For example, asking the question of how neoliberalism shapes cultural values avoids initial judgment and gives no immediate indication, but the term *neoliberalism* itself entails a judgment against the subsidy of art by the state, favouring free markets as linked to general market dominance. Consequently, the term carries the underlying critique as part of the research question. When discussing terms and concepts such as this, the research questions for this type of work can be politically motivated, carry emancipatory interests, and are often practice-based. An example of this could be an investigation into the unjust treatment of women in society. Unequal pay for women in the arts sector is well documented and critical theory-based research would ask further questions of how, where, and when these conditions were established and for what kinds of reasons, thus criticising the status quo of male-dominated pay and remuneration policies.

When formulating a research question, thinking through methodologies can provide helpful pointers, and continuing this journey of conceptualisation leads to the next layer of knowledge provision, which are referred to as paradigms (see Chapter 2). These summarise the positions, convictions, and values that we apply to the underlying ideas of what knowledge is, what we perceive as new knowledge in the first place, and what limitation we apply when trying to understand and define knowledge. For example, Karl Popper (1902–1994) and Hans Alberts (1921), two philosophers of the critical rational tradition, pointed out that there is no absolute knowledge and that the best we can do is to refute or falsify. Referencing the two philosophers' positivistic approaches, scientific development is based on rectifying mistakes. So how could this be applied to the process of formulating a research question? Popper (2005) and Alberts (2014 [1985]) argued that research questions are required to comply with the principle of falsifiability and need to reflect the idea that knowledge must be proven wrong or false to be able to advance. In other words, all knowledge claims are fallible and subject to revision in the light of new knowledge. Apart from providing evidence of deep thought that is linked to formulating hypotheses and thinking about the research question, this statement argues for learning though trial and error. When applied to the process of refining research questions, it helps us to realise that researchers should not be afraid to change the question and to adapt questions as many times as necessary. Understanding the development of research questions as experiments allows for sorting out what works and what does not.

Referencing the trio of paradigm, methodology, and methods as the underlying link or the clue that informs and holds the research question together, highlights the various and diverse information that comes together in one or several questions, thereby defining the character of the research design. In the initial phase of discussing ideas, topics, and problems, the trio of paradigm, methodology, and methods might be less obvious, but should be foregrounded when refining the question. Linking the research question with the trio ensures that the enquiry is laid out in such a way that an answer to the question can be achieved. Importantly, it relates to the personal values and ways of thinking that suit and support the researcher's motivation and working practices, which are defined as part of the research design.

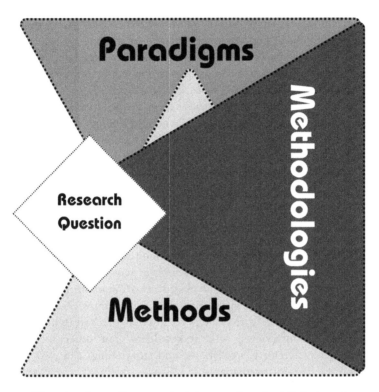

FIGURE 6.1 The trio of paradigm, methodology and method linked to the research question (drawn by author)

From Question to Design

To demonstrate the benefits of linking the research questions with paradigm, methodology, and methods, I consider four examples:

1. The research question aims to contribute to the wider debate of diversity as a concept, while focussing on the cultural and political influences of diversity policies. This is to be investigated by focussing on how this plays out in a contemporary art collective, resulting in the following research question: What are the cultural and political influences on diversity policies in contemporary art collectives? This research is approached through the interpretative lens, using critical theory as a qualitative methodology thereby enabling the researcher to address, for example, the underlying power relations and promote just social relations. The question has no references to power relations and appears neutral, or at least it does not promote one specific influence over another, but potential conflicts between cultural and political factors and diversity policies could be read into the question. In terms of data collection methods, semistructured interviews with selected members of several art collectives could be carried out and analysed. However, the question lends itself equally well when using other methodologies.

For example, discourse analysis enables a research focus that discusses the variety of standpoints, opinions, and ideas, analysing the critical text (e.g., memorandums, policy pamphlets, manifestos) of the art collectives. Applying a case study approach that investigates the unique diversity policy from one collective could be studied in-depth as another option or as an alternative.

2. What are the ethical implications of using artificial intelligence in creative and cultural industries management? This question points toward practice and seems to rely on meaning making among CCI managers. It asks about ethics as a notion of care in relation to AI as a technological development. It relies on constructs, opinions, and attitudes that address ethical issues (e.g., copyright, human rights, or censorship). As a paradigm and as a methodology, constructivism emphasises the importance of social experience and meaning making, and these are the concerns this question raises. Constructivism asks how people or individuals negotiate meaning in their interactions in the world and what influences those interactions. Common methods for constructionistic research reflect the active role the researcher plays (e.g., the cocreation of knowledge between participants and researchers). Working together as collaborators plays a central role in creative practice and in research into meaning making. Suitable methods that help to answer the research question are focus groups or interviews with stakeholders, but other methods (e.g., developing games, creative workshops, and storytelling) can also work well when coproduced with participants.

TABLE 6.1 Example 1

Research Question(s)	Paradigm	Methodology	Methods: Data Collection	Methods: Data Analysis
What are the cultural and political influences on diversity policies in contemporary art collectives?	Interpretative lens	Critical Theory (i.e., addressing underlying power relations)	Semistructured interviews with Art collective members	Thematic analysis (TA)

TABLE 6.2 Example 2

Research Question(s)	Paradigm	Methodology	Methods: Data Collection	Methods: Data Analysis
What are the ethical implications of using artificial intelligence in creative industries management?	Interpretative/ Constructivism	Constructivism	Focus groups and semi-structured interviews; developing games, storytelling, and other creative workshops	Thematic analysis (TA), Explanation Building, Content Analysis

3. How do craft producers distribute their products in the craft cottage industry? This research question focuses on a practical explanation that would work with a case study approach by using pragmatism as problem-solving and action-oriented research. The methods could range from structured interviews and document analysis to an examination of strategies and practices that are applied during distribution. Evidence could be collected from a range of craft organisations or from various individual craft producers. The results of the study are likely to explain the process and provide evidence for the variety of distribution methods that are applied. As a practical outcome, the study could recommend the fastest or the most efficient route for distribution, but the focus of the question relates to the exploratory investigation of distribution. Focussing solely on efficiency might side line multiple distribution channels, as well as disregard potential experiences that carry other values.

4. What are lived experiences of emerging art dealers in the digital art sector? The fourth question focusses on the participant perspective as individuals or as a professional group. Phenomenology as an interpretivist paradigm and as a methodology explores subjective experience, aiming to uncover the underlying meanings that emerge from the participants' perspectives. Grounded theory is another methodology that explores perceptions and experiences, so could be applied to study this question. For both methodologies, phenomenology and grounded theory interviews with art dealers would be a good choice. A small sample size of three to five narrative interviews can provide sufficient data to explore and unpack the underlying themes and patterns that emerge through the data analysis (see Chapter 5). Using coding as a data analysis method for the interviews (see Chapter 5) works well with the choice of grounded theory as a methodology, while for a phenomenological study thematic, interview analysis has been commonly practiced. This research question is adaptable to any other professions and art forms that are covered in CCI. The exploratory character of the question relates to the experience that as a topic is broad and unspecific and through the research, themes such as memory, identity, and digital conditioning will emerge to allow for further study. In the case of a dissertation, these themes will guide the literature review retrospectively.

TABLE 6.3 Example 3

Research Question(s)	Paradigm	Methodology	Methods: Data Collection	Methods: Data Analysis
How do craft producers distribute their products in the craft cottage industry?	Interpretative/ Pragmatism	Action research	Structured interviews, document collection, analytical memos	Pattern analysis (i.e., coding), content analysis of distribution practices

TABLE 6.4 Example 4

Research Question(s)	Paradigm	Methodology	Methods: Data Collection	Methods: Data Analysis
What are the lived experiences of emerging art dealers in the digital art sector?	Interpretative/ Phenomenology	Phenomenology, Grounded Theory	Narrative interviews with art dealers, document collection, analytical memos	Coding, narrative analysis, discourse analysis

Conclusion

Research questions contain a great deal of information about the character of the research, the concepts that are implied, and the specific parameters relating to time, location, and the field and group of people at the centre of the investigation. Learning to read research questions in reverse provides some training (see the exercise below) to handle the complexities of the research design. Formulating a research question takes time but getting it right will be rewarding in all the later stages of the research. Moving from topic, to theme, to problem, while utilising the experience or asking questions, offers a way to become proficient in developing research questions.

Choosing a suitable type of question enables the move from abstract thinking to practical application. The final approach to thinking through the research question's implications are applied by matching the trio of paradigm, methodology and methods with the question. The examples discussed here highlight the connecting force that is built into the design, enabling the ability to move back and forth from research questions to research design, testing it out and refining it along the way. This process shows that the research question demands attention beyond the remit of the initial inception. Returning to the house analogy with the research questions as central pillars, I suggest making a feature of them by giving the research question as much exposure as possible. This will demonstrate the raw beauty of the design, allowing the question to be accessible and adaptable throughout the research process.

EXERCISE: REVERSE READING OF RESEARCH QUESTIONS

Instructions: Take the research questions outlined in the table from the section, then move from question to design and fill in the gaps using the answers given as examples, including:

1. Identify the topic to which this question relates/alludes
2. Note any potential issues and problems in relation to the topic and research question
3. Decide the type of research question to use according to the assigned numbers

TABLE 6.5 Reverse reading of research questions

Research Question(s)	Type of RQ (1) Explanatory (2) Exploratory (3) Evaluative (4) Predictive	Topics	Issue/Problems Implied
What are the cultural and political influences on diversity policies in contemporary art collectives?	2		
What are the ethical implications of using artificial intelligence in creative industries management?		Duty of care, copyright	
How do craft producers distribute their products in the craft cottage industry?			Distribution channels remain undocumented, are limited, and not accessible
What are the lived experiences of emerging art dealers in the digital art sector?			Consider focusing on a regional or local art sector

References

Albert, H. 2014. *Treatise on critical reason.* Princeton University Press.

Layder, D. 2012. *Doing Excellent Small-Scale Research.* Sage.

NHGRI(National Human Genome Research Institute) (2023). Fact sheet Human Genome. https://www.genome.gov/about-genomics/educational-resources/fact-sheets/human-genome-project (accessed 30 August 2023).

Popper, K. 2005. *The Logic of Scientific Discovery.* Routledge.

White, P. 2017. *Developing Research Questions.* Bloomsbury Publishing.

7

IMPLEMENTING RESEARCH

Introduction

Research requires planning and having discussed research design in previous chapters, this section continue to advance our discussion of the research process by turning attention to many practical aspects researchers will face. In short, research practice involves a variety of actions and processes, as well as strategic thinking, and includes considerations like fieldwork, timings, and connecting and organising research.

In this chapter, I explain and analyse how the overall research design is put into action. I discuss objectives as a helping hand to check and organise research. I explain the basics of how to organise fieldwork, how to approach research participants, and what can be done to mitigate common mistakes researchers making regarding time planning, using familiar networks, and professional practices. In the final section, I discuss *the practice turn*, including the nuances of practice-led (i.e., operational significance) and practice-based (i.e., by means of practice) research vis-à-vis other approaches. I touched on this in Chapters 5 and 6 in theoretical terms, but in this section the discussion focuses on the practicalities of answering the question of what it means to maintain a research practice that must be specifically engrained in practice and why it makes sense to highlight practice in this way.

In research planning, practical steps and parameters are often foregrounded because of their proximity to our everyday life. Using transferable skills to set up meetings and approach people as research participants might be considered easy tasks, but the details require careful planning. Some research parameters, such as timeframes and how outcomes will be presented, are set. For example, dissertations or major projects come with submission deadlines and a minimum word count, as well as set style conventions regarding citations and referencing.

DOI: 10.4324/9781003161912-7

Set parameters frame the research because they tend to be non-negotiable and any planning that is carried out must relate to them. While this can be restrictive, researchers are free to negotiate the *in-between space* and planning involves filling the space with meaningful action.

Research Objectives

As stepping stones from the research design to the practicalities of organising the research, objectives break down the research question into manageable parts. And because many everyday work activities are objectivised, or incentive oriented, we are familiar with what an objective should look like: clear, measurable, concise, and achievable. The SMART mnemonic acronym, which stands for specific, measurable, achievable, relevant, and time-bound, has been adapted for research purposes. By exchanging measurability with evidence-focused, adding a *T* for *targeted*, and an *R* for *rigour*, it creates a new mnemonic acronym – STARTER. Like the first course of a meal, it offers a lighter, but definable introduction that prepares the taste buds for something more substantial to come. This plays with the adaptable meaning of objectives, which are not set in stone, but remain adaptable during the process of research, while at the same time setting the scene.

S stands for **specific,** to be detailed and clearly defined. References are made to specific locations, spaces, or organisations. The research questions contain sufficient detail to reformulate this into an action. For example, take the question: How do millennial digital makers perceive their careers in contemporary CCI in Accra/Ghana? It can be rewritten into an objective: To explore millennial digital makers' careers perceptions in contemporary CCI in Accra/Ghana.

The first **T** stands for **targeted,** which refers to the actions that are aimed at someone or for something. This could be a CCI organisation or people. In the example used in the prior paragraph, it refers to millennial digital makers.

The **A** stands for **achievable.** The actions that are expressed in the objective need to be attainable. In other words, objectives, as planning tools, need to ensure that the research is realistic. This asserts that the research is completed in a limited timeframe, that deadlines can be met, and sufficient resources have been allocated or need to be redirected to achieve the objectives. Referring to the research question above, it would be impossible to explore all makers in Accra at one given time. Let us assume that the research resources allow for ten days of fieldwork, then the objective must reflect the given resources. For example, the objective would be defined as investigating the relationship between engagement and career satisfaction of millennial digital makers in one or two meeting places.

R stands for **rigour,** ensuring that the objectives follow set frames of references including ethical compliance. Research is documented so that it can be repeated in different and changing circumstances. Again, referring to the above example, an objective that is rigourous could read: To identify and ensure ethical compliance in advance of fieldwork actions for the project, including the obtaining of consent from the makers.

The second **T** relates to the **timing** of the research. For example, when is a good time to carry out fieldwork? How much time can participants spare for interviews? What are suitable times for makers to be observed? Being time-bound is essential to meeting deadlines and, combined with the resources, it should be reflected in the objectives. Adding a timeframe to the already discussed objectives above will provide an answer: To explore millennial digital makers' career perceptions in contemporary CCI in Accra/Ghana during July 2024. This timeframe provides a clearer idea and leaves sufficient flexibility to carry out ten days of fieldwork in July 2024.

The **E** stands for **evidence** that is provided as proof and this should not be confused with measurability. In qualitative research, numbers might provide some evidence in the form of statistical analysis, but they are never proof on their own. Evidence takes many forms, ranging from expert opinion as expressed in published research, to empirical data that has been collected and analysed. Importantly, evidence is used to support claims and helps develop arguments on the basis of analysis. In combination with rigour, evidence provides reliability and validity. As an objective, it is not directly expressed, but when added to the methods of data collection, it helps to give readers the opportunity to understand the source of the evidence. In the example, this could be added either as a separate objective (e.g., to collect data through semistructured interviews and participatory observation). Alternatively, it could be added to the end of an already existing objective (e.g., to explore millennial digital makers' career perceptions in contemporary CCI in Accra/Ghana in July 2024, through semistructured interviews and participant observations).

The last **R** refers to the **relevance** of the research and how it is placed in relation to the broader context of originality and knowledge generation. This could be best achieved by bringing existing knowledge to the table and using existing references to make the case why this research needs to be undertaken, in the first place, and what it can contribute to the people involved, including the participants, stakeholders, funders, and readers.

Using the STARTER acronym ensures that researchers will meet the essential parameters of research as part of the research process.

FieldWork, or Developing a Practice

Fieldwork as an activity means collecting the data where it is produced. Anthropologists in the 1920s would have referred to this as natural setting. This would have involved travelling to places and living with the community while studying the communities, phenomena, and interactions with nature. After this exposure, researchers would travel home and write up their findings by relying on their research diaries. Over the years, this separation of desk and field research has become less practical, but the term *fieldwork* has remained, albeit taking on a different meaning. Just as research comes in many shapes and forms, fieldwork can be interrupted or suspended for a while and continued later. It can consist of extended periods of collecting data, or it can be continuous for a set amount of time. Fieldwork might not involve travelling; instead, data may be collected in different settings, such as social media or through computer-generated interactions (e.g., how audience avatars interact within an immersive digital performance). Research practice is a continuous process, and it depends on the individual just how useful the distinction between fieldwork and other forms of research are, including desk research. In the practical sense, fieldwork can help to structure the research process because it changes the focus from predominantly reading and writing to listening and analysing. If desk research runs alongside the fieldwork, the balance might shift toward listening in the case of conducting focus groups or interviews. Occasionally, knowledge gaps become apparent and there is nothing to worry about at this stage, but making a mental note of it will help when analysing the data later.

Historically, the nature of fieldwork changed over time, exposing the attitudes of 'the *us and other*' of the colonial era that remained ingrained in our understanding for far too long (Anderson, 2006). Today, research should be directed though collaborative, intersectional, and interdisciplinary approaches, with the aim of engaging and empowering communities. Importantly, researchers' responsibilities need to reflect this in the choice of their methodologies, which are geared towards interaction and participation, instead of simply studying reactions. For example, action research and community-led research are now accommodating methodologies. Using geospatial technologies, mapping, and data visualisation are other common examples that were embedded in colonial practices and therefore require careful consideration. Who is drawing maps, for example? Is it the experts, or could AI help to visualise networks? What are the pitfalls, biases, and limitations that are built into choosing these methods? Digital humanities offers plenty of critical materials to explore associated issues (see Chapter 8), but it is a matter for the researcher to reflect on their position in the field.

Self-reflection, including thinking about the positions we take and arrive with, seems an obvious necessity throughout the research process. As a white, female, middleclass researcher, I radiate privilege. But having been brought up in the underprivileged German Democratic Republic and being a foreigner in the United Kingdom (UK), nuances these stereotypical attributes. This should not be understood as an excuse, but it demonstrates that positioning includes thinking through multiple roles and functions. Thinking through these impressions of myself influences my position and how I present myself to, for example, the research participants. Few textbooks consistently promote self-reflection as a requirement. Instead, researchers must read between the lines and learn from experience. There is nothing wrong with learning from mistakes, but careful consideration can avoid hurting people's feelings. Often these are the little gestures and behaviours we demonstrate. Unconscious bias refers to attitudes and behaviours, including the stereotypes we use to perceive, evaluate, and treat others, of which we are often unaware. Selecting participants for the research study is one example. We tend to approach people that we think are most likely to answer, or we choose people that are likely to give us the answer we are keen to hear, resulting in answers that support our hypothesis or that we perceive as favourable for the research outcomes. Mitigation of some of these behaviours can be achieved, but they can never be completely eliminated. What we can do is to define, as objectively as possible, participant selection criteria. Documenting research enables a third party to replicate the data collection and peer reviews can help to raise researchers' awareness of bias.

In research aimed at a dissertation or a project, the practicalities of gaining access to participants requires careful consideration. For example, choosing family and friends as interview participants provides easy access and, in most cases, they will support the research, but do they meet the selection criteria? The answer depends entirely on the study's content. While I can see friends' participation in audience studies or research relating to the use of artistic products as being part of a larger group, people we know tend to be homogeneous and is only appropriate if this is a selection criterion, otherwise it will not be possible to fulfil the aim of capturing experiences from a diverse group of people. In short, choosing family and friends as research participants depends on the remit of the research. They may provide easy access but should not be used as a shortcut to gather participants or to fill gaps when time is running out.

During data gathering, researchers are on a quest for information. They want to collect primary data from people, and this is never just an exchange of information. As embedded responsibilities are in the research design, it is the research practice that relies on the human qualities of the researcher. As a result, fieldwork demands multitasking. As researchers interact with people, research content needs to be scrutinised and reflected on. To gain a temporal overview of partial results requires time and effort to be organised while the fieldwork is ongoing. By design, collaborative research often builds in reflection time, using evaluation techniques that help to take stock or the project. Reminders could be established in the planning (e.g., memo writing, see Chapter 4). Ensuring that all the people involved participate equally is another challenge that requires the researcher's attention. Researchers take on different roles simultaneously: organiser, interviewer, observer, analyst, carer, and many more. All these roles and functions come with their own set of expectations, which require attention. For example, is the time and location suitable for an interview? Will I be able to get there on time? Is my phone charged to record the interview? Is the video camera booked for the focus group? Who will operate the equipment? Are participants comfortable in the chosen setting? Has this been mentioned before? How are we doing timewise?

Simple details such as these should by no means be underestimated. They will all have an impact on the quality of information. Above all else, they affect how participants will feel afterwards and determine if they will take part in future research projects. As researchers, we are part of the research community that learns from other researchers' conduct, so being mindful of this general research responsibility helps to ensure that we can all keep exploring.

Power relations between participants play an important role and as a result can influence research outcomes. For example, interviewing a familiar group of people demands an understanding of what power relations are at play before and during the research. It also requires an understanding of how these might impact the research outcome. The sense of solidarity among friends or like-minded people can be fruitful to get a discussion going in an interview, but it can also hinder an understanding of what this sense of solidarity might mean for the individual. There is no set recipe for how best to communicate and a great deal will depend on the specific situation, the participants involved, and how the researcher reads the situation. For example, recordings can free up notetaking for information purposes but checking what has been covered against a list of topics and themes in semistructured interviews requires multi-tasking, and the pressure of maintaining the natural feel of a conversation can shift power relations. In focus groups, several people may try to work out power relations at the same time, often without noticing it. For this reason, it might be advisable to run focus groups as a research pair (see Chapter 4) with one researcher observing and taking notes that include reflection on the power dynamics that are at play.

Some of these human qualities might come naturally, but to ensure you get the most from every session these skills should be practiced in advance. This can be part of the training, practiced when using observation as a method for collecting data, and extended to general awareness exercises that are used for research purposes. Running a pilot or testing out your approach in advance will help build confidence and is highly recommended for the novice researcher.

Approaching research participants starts with the selection criteria. This aids in developing an idea of what kind of participants are needed, and does so before participants are invited with a personal email or call (depending on how familiar you are with the participants). I would suggest researching the background of potential participants, which could involve studying their artistic outputs and following them on social media to see what story the internet tells you about their public lives. The amount of information that can be studied in advance varies, but participants will expect you to have done your homework so that you do not waste time clarifying and repeating information that is in the public domain. Instead, aim to build your fieldwork by expanding on the initial information research. Approaching participants in the form of a personal email should provide hints that you are familiar with their work, explain why you are approaching them in the first place, and should set out the parameters of the fieldwork. For example, in the case of interviews it is advisable to mention how long the interview will take, that with their permission you intend to record the event, and therefore a quiet location would be needed. Good research practice involves clear and kind communication (see Chapter 4).

Like in any work environment, mistakes are part of the research parcel, but that does not mean that we should not try to avoid making them (see Chapter 8). Mistakes such as arriving late for the interview or having a room double-booked and having to cancel a focus group can be mitigated by admitting to the participants that these things happen and explaining what you have learnt from it so you can avoid it happening again. These occurrences do not require long explanations, but participants will appreciate an apology. In research practice, dealing with mistakes will translate into experience, but there may be consequences that require further mitigation. For example, participants might not be willing to reschedule in cases where you were unable to attend because you missed the appointment. People's time is precious and business practices should be applied in equal measures when carrying out research. Many of these good behaviours are common sense, but sometimes little reminders will help to make sure you comply when under pressure or in stressful situations. All research participants, including the researcher, come from a variety of cultural backgrounds, and stereotypical behaviours should be questioned to ensure they are correctly interpreted. Arriving late, for example, might be appropriate for some participants, while others demand being on time. Situational behaviours require you to adapt quickly and react accordingly, raised awareness can be achieved by discussing and reflecting on assumptions, both in advance and during data collection.

Planning fieldwork is as essential as adapting the plan to allow for eventualities to be addressed. Setting a realistic timetable is easier said than done, but some advanced rule setting might work, depending on the individual arrangement. For example, I tend to plan for twice the amount of time that I think I will need. This gives me room to manoeuvre and alleviates the stress associated with lateness or upcoming deadlines. The need to take extra care when in an unfamiliar environment should therefore also include time for orientation and being able to develop a feel for the place. Everyone will have their own personal mechanism for taking in an unfamiliar environment. I like to take a walk around the neighbourhood beforehand to familiarise myself with the location. Many organisations that CCI researchers investigate are based in communities, and when taking a walk to help with general orientation you can also get an idea of what the cultural organisation's community location is like. The same applies to virtual organisations, the internet neighbourhood, for example following up links that are provided on the organisation website are good starting points. When carrying out field research, the amount of data paired with the latest information can become overwhelming. So, deciding which information to absorb and which to discard is an important exercise that can be part of the interim evaluations. Depending on the length of the fieldwork, this can include taking stock, checking for data saturation, and making sure that the information is as diverse as set out in the research design.

Dissemination of the research comes at a later stage, after the data has been analysed and written up, but preparation for the dissemination begins during the fieldwork itself. Participants need to know when and if they can access the outcome of the research, so giving an approximate timeline helps to ensure that they trust that the data will be handled with care. Collaborative research often involves dissemination events that are developed together as part of the research.

The distinction between data collection, analysis, and dissemination is best understood in relational terms by highlighting the dependency of the various parts to each other. Analysing data in part during fieldwork will happen naturally, as the urge to understand what has been said, observed, or experienced triggers comparisons and initiates other forms of analysis. Memo writing, as part of the self-reflection process, during the fieldwork helps to clarify the process (see Chapter 5). I tend to write a lot of memos during my fieldwork and have even sat at a bus stop to write up a reflection of a just-completed interview. Others might record voice notes. Iin either case, it is crucial to document these self-reflections while still fresh in the mind. Because I use grounded theory as a methodology, the notes are understood as data that will be woven into the overall analysis. These snippets and pieces of initial analysis reveal emotional attachments that are obvious during the fieldwork but are likely to be seen and interpreted differently in the later stages of the analysis. Besides the main aspect of collecting data, I value fieldwork as an essential part of my continuous learning journey. None of the fieldwork I carried out were the same, but all were full of excitement, involved steep learning curves, and many motivating moments. The unexpected moments have played out through memory, and I call them the fieldwork myth. This idea of the myth covers misperceptions that fieldwork might be always productive and easy to carry out while navigating complex social and cultural dynamics. Research reality is different: a great deal of time is spent dealing with the practical aspects of the fieldwork that are important but can leave you with a feeling of not having done enough. Productivity is often measured in terms of the generation of content work, such as researching, reading, and interviewing. The work that has gone into setting up this type of research remains underestimated and undervalued, but without it, content work could not take place. In short, redefining what productive work contains will both assist and motivate researchers during fieldwork.

A safe research environment is crucial and should be made a priority. Important practical arrangements include choosing a safe place to meet people, letting a friend know where you are going, and only arranging interviews or focus groups in semi-public places. The feeling of being in a safe place translates into what is called a controlled environment, such as those provided in laboratories when experiments are conducted. Fieldwork operates under different conditions and the researcher needs to take this into account. Objectivity as a requirement in research refers to standardised procedures and replicability that are not excluded from qualitative research. However, the researchers' experiences are subjective and embrace their personal viewpoint and therefore the emphasis is less on generalisation and more on finding common ground, depending on the research design. The relationship between being objective and subjective is negotiated between all participants. During fieldwork this becomes apparent as it is played out between participants' understandings and ways of thinking and is therefore made recognisable. Paying attention to these relational frames opens avenues for analysing and reflecting on the behaviours of participants, including the researchers'. Conflicting arguments, things that seem puzzling or strange, often provide rich data and can propel fieldwork. But at the same time, it may leave the researcher feeling uneasy because they can come across as challenging and difficult to navigate. These issues highlight some of the complexities of field research that researchers can expect and often seek out from the start. In short, thinking through the fieldwork myth in advance saves time, while good planning will pay off and should include expecting the unexpected.

Accidents or things that go wrong are unforeseen circumstances that in research can range from getting diary mistakes, last-minute cancellations, phone or computer malfunctions, and many more. For example, once I deleted two interview recordings by accident before I had a chance to upload them to my secure university cloud workspace. On another occasion, a traffic accident blocked the road on my way to a focus group, resulting in my turning up half an hour late. People understand that issues such as these are beyond our control and are the result of external circumstances. Accidents aside, there are oversights that are avoidable, so communications between researchers and participants is vital to work through these to prevent them happening in the future. For example, ethical violations can be complex and, in many cases, happen unintentionally, owing to a lack of planning and preparation. Following ethical guidelines is paramount (see Chapter 9). Actions such as interviewing participants without obtaining their consent in advance can jeopardise the research outcomes and put their validity into question.

Implementing a research checklist:

- The STARTER (i.e., objectives) has been prepared.
- Research participants are selected, invited, have received research information in advance, and confirmed their participation.
- Documentation methods are set up and their functionality has been checked (e.g., power supply for recording devices, ensuring the recordings are secured).
- In case of travelling to a meeting place, the directions are clear to both the researcher and all participants.
- Following the research data collection, thank you letters to participants are sent out, together with follow-up information about when the outcomes of the research will be available.
- Data is secured according to institutional guidelines (e.g., uploaded onto a university server).
- Data analysis and the writing up of research outcomes are given sufficient time for discussion and rewriting.

This list is far from complete, and it will have to be amended and updated appropriately, but it covers the essentials for novice researchers.

The Practice Turn

In social science, what is known as "the practice turn" focuses on the study of social practices, how social practices are constructed, and how life is shaped through practice instead of analysing abstract concepts. Schatszki argued that practice is constituted through the actions of individuals, objects, or materials and spaces. He argued that the field of practice addresses the social as "a field of embodied, materially interwoven practices, that are centrally organised around a shared practical understanding" (1996 12). Watson et al. (2012) is interested in change of practices and Wenger (2009) points at communities of practice. All three are relevant in research practice and have formed the backbone of methodological thinking for the last forty years. Participatory and collaborative approaches are the most notable examples that study social practices in their habitat or settings, with the researcher being part of this context, and participants involved in all aspects of research, including the design and shaping of the research environment. Therefore, the research process is viewed as a practice and becomes less compartmentalised or is seen as a linear process. Both the many nuances of practice-led research that focuses on the operational significance and practice-based research that stresses the means of practice are discussed in Chapters 5 and 6. CCI research benefited from the increasing popularity of practice-based research, helping to investigate themes and topics such as precarity, hidden exploitation of the workforce, and under-represented groups. Decolonising research methodologies are foregrounded, and new methodologies emerge that emphasise context-sensitive and activist approaches that prioritise reciprocity and the empowerment of marginalised communities. This could mean participatory approaches, giving research participants equal roles in conducting research, or by being led by participants, thereby creating natural conversations. For example, in the living lab methodology, the emphasis is on user-centred design, cocreation, and open innovation (Dekker, Contreras, & Meijer, 2020). While this methodology originated in innovation research, it has been adapted for other CCI environments and used to foreground marginalised communities in the craft sector.

In practical terms, the practice turn remains tautological, expressing the same idea of focussing on practice twice, but its meaning is set in the context of fostering practice as a holistic approach, including empowering participants. Therefore, implementing research must be approached in a similar fashion and conventual methods may be questionable and unsuitable for approaches of this kind. For example, as interviews make a clear distinction between interviewee and interviewer, this method reinforces existing power relations, if not carefully negotiated. Participatory approaches (e.g., when all participants work together as equal partners) cocreate a research practice that is informed through and by communal and collective practical actions. It requires advanced planning, but equally relies on ad hoc decision making and negotiating skills, as well as an evaluative reflection practice that is applied throughout the whole research process. Casual conversations, spontaneous workshops, by-chance meetings, and trying out novel approaches to the collection and analysing of data are as common as carefully planned and developed approaches (e.g., playing a board game together and developing a new research idea). This type of research is resource intensive, requires high-level awareness training, and has financial implications, because participants acting as researchers should be paid.

Individual practice-led research is common in art subjects, when creating a piece of art forms part of the research process (see Chapter 3). Practice-led dissertations contain the artworks (e.g., film, piece of art, design) that are specifically produced for this occasion, as well as the analytical part. Universities set appropriate proportions in their guidelines, depending on the weighting of one part over the other, in the degree.

Conclusion

This chapter explains the practicalities of research. It focuses on what needs to be considered when data are collected. Objectives are meant to link research design and fieldwork. Like stepping stones, objectives are used to focus and clarify what the research sets out to do. Using the STARTER acronym (like the first course of a meal), objectives are defined as being special, targeted, achievable, rigorous, (having) appropriate timing, (using) evidence, and relevant. Fieldwork, or developing a practice, refers to the fact that planning remains essential, paying attention to detail, and employing communication skills to help radiate confidence into the research practice. Questioning the kind of research practice (practice-led as an operational tool or practice-based as a means of research) helps to clarify the overall research approach. It provides sufficient space to discuss participatory approaches that can be informed by natural conversations, allowing reflection on existing power relations. The implementation checklist can be ticked off, amended, and reordered, according to the requirements of the research project.

References

Anderson, B. 2006. *Imagined Communities: Reflections on the Origin and Spread of Nationalism*. Verso Books.

Dekker, R., Franco Contreras, J., & Meijer, A. 2020. The living lab as a methodology for public administration research: A systematic literature review of its applications in the social sciences. *International Journal of Public Administration*, 43(14): 1207–1217.

Schatzki, T. R. 1996. *Social Practices: A Wittgensteinian Approach to Human Activity and the Social*. Cambridge University Press.

Schatzki, T. R. 2005. Introduction. In *The Practice Turn in Contemporary Theory*. Routledge.

Watson, M., Pantzar, M., & Shove, E. 2012. *The Dynamics of Social Practice: Everyday Life and How It Changes* (pp. 1–208). Sage.

Wenger, E. 2009. Communities of practice: The key to knowledge strategy. In E. Lesser, M. Fontaine, J. Slusher (Ed.), *Knowledge and Communities* (pp. 3–20). Routledge.

8

EVALUATING RESEARCH

Introduction

As explained in Chapter 7, a comprehensive guide to setting out and advancing research projects is essential, but the best planned and considered research does not always translate into a smooth ride in practice. Using critical internal evaluation tools will strengthen research practice and validate the results. But even after taking the greatest of care, unforeseen circumstances, accidents, and mistakes can occur. The fact is that they are all part of the research process, so it is advisable to acknowledge and consider those throughout.

This chapter starts with an introduction to the limits to research and briefly discusses common assumptions about generalisations. In the following section, I explore the concept of evaluation, how research is evaluated, and what evaluation means in the context of the accidental turn. In the section on bias, I introduce conscious and unconscious bias, while placing an emphasis on reflection regarding limitations and how to translate pitfalls, mistakes, and accidents into enriching the research process, instead of portraying them as obstacles that cannot be overcome. Even though I present accidents and opportunities as separate sections, they should be read together as a single entity leading up to the final part, which covers success and failure in research. Therefore, the discussion is concluded by examining success and failure as interdependent concepts. While success and failure are commonly perceived as opposites, I demonstrate the pair in their relational character. This is inspired directly from recent momentum in the CCI sector about changing business models, showing how to integrate thinking about failure as a way of enriching the research experience.

DOI: 10.4324/9781003161912-8

Limits

Finding the right balance between what can be and what ought to be achieved is defined by the limits that have been set for the research. In short, limits cover the constraints or boundaries that researchers encounter when designing, implementing, and evaluating research projects. The immediate attention often turns to resources, with financial resources being defined as the most important means to set the remit of the research. However, depending on the subject field, not all research requires substantial amounts of financial resources.

Dissertations or final extended pieces of work in degree courses operate mostly without budgets and individual researchers manage expenses within the provision of their degrees. Archival research may incur travel expenses and labour costs but does not rely as much on equipment as the research carried out in other fields. Research projects can cover costs through research grants, donations, and collaborations with industry partners. A detailed discussion of financial resources goes beyond the remit of this book and therefore only a few limited pointers are set out here. Other boundaries are set by the time that is available and is often expressed through deadlines. The amount of expertise required could be another element that limits the remit. Ideally, project ideas can be costed and expressed in budgetary means after the idea is conceived. In practice, ideas and the availability of grants need to be seen in relational terms, and they are often developed in tandem. This indicates how ingrained neo-liberal ideas have penetrated research thinking and how much pressure is passed down to researchers in university structures.

The scope of the research has limits and needs to be defined in relation to the research questions, objectives, and other resources, such as the availability of time and expertise. The same applies to methodological boundaries that have been discussed in previous chapters. For example, a questionnaire is chosen to reach a larger spectrum and number of responses, while narrative interviews extract a different type of information and can require a smaller number of interviews. Ethical limits apply to research involving humans and should be guided, for example using informed consent.

Williams (2000) discussed generalisability within an interpretivist paradigm as an issue that is often raised as being impossible to achieve because of the emphasis on socially, politically, culturally informed, and experience-based research. But he concluded that most research makes generalising claims when discussing findings and outcomes. It may be expressed in different words, referencing, for example, external validity or transferability, or in outputs related to theory, but the content and the research process will have to handle general viewpoints. Williams argued that aiming to improve the representativeness of research enables researchers to adopt alternative strategies. This in turn might help to foster a willingness to admit the limitations of one's own research. Following the idea of generalisation, research papers of any type will have to address limitations in some form or another.

Evaluations

Covering and discussing the limitations of the research process and the resulting implications for the content of the research yields a variety of opportunities for reflections and for taking stock, both during and at the end of the research. As a formal process, evaluations are common practice across all fields and, in CCI, funded projects are assessed at several points throughout the duration of the project. For example, midterm or final evaluations are often written into the budget as part of the project activities. Measuring and assessing the critical processes and content of the research translates into several forms. This includes an assessment of effectiveness, impact, and intervention, or can be directed to analyse the research methodology that has been developed and used in the research project. CCI and higher education evaluations are similar, in the sense that both sectors operate with accountability and critical assessment. Depending on the nature of the research, evaluations involve a mix of methods, including the same forms of data analysis that are detailed in Chapter 5, such as using numbers in the form of a statistical test or simply summarising audience numbers at dissemination events. In qualitative terms this could include peer reviews, expert opinions, interviews, surveys, and observational studies to capture what has been evidenced and what has been achieved.

Overall, evaluation assesses whether the means are appropriate and to what degree the outcomes have been achieved. Evaluators will discuss their methods or mix of methods in advance at the beginning of the project, before applying an agreed approach. There are various recipe books for evaluations that elaborate on their different forms. For example, the choice between internal or external evaluators depends on how best the research project could benefit from critical analysis. Some funding bodies will spell out in the funding guidelines exactly what type of evaluations should take place. Peer review is a common approach in academia to assess the validity of the idea, the research design, and its implementation, assessing how much academic rigour has been applied, or what type of mechanism has been put in place to self-assess and reflect on the proposed work. The aim of the evaluation is to provide feedback, to make suggestions about how to improve the quality of the research, and compare the research project, including the results, against other projects to identify if academic standards have been met. Peer reviews can take place at several points during the research but are applied when a funding application is made and when the results or outcomes are ready for publication. This is mainly to check if the integrity and credibility of the research findings have been maintained. Much has been written about the fairness of peer reviews, which are usually anonymised. So, novice researchers should be aware that unfair practices exist, but these are not best practices. Most peer reviews provide helpful feedback and are written with a view to improving the research findings and the research process before the work is published. Research network contacts, fellow students, and colleagues can be helpful in providing alternative or informal peer reviews at every stage of the research. But the kindness of colleagues and fellow students in commenting on a research project should be reciprocal, a give-and-take process, especially considering that this is not part of everyday work activities.

Bias

Limitations take many forms and bias is a formal term used in research practice to explain potential pitfalls. The origins of bias date back to the French word *biasis*, which refers to the oblique line in weaving that deviates from the horizontal and vertical lines of thread, thereby indicating a departure from the perpendicular. Given the numerical nature of weaving, counting the number of threads and the mathematical order of pattern, it is no surprise that the term is commonly used in science to debate the limitations of research. In general, the term applies a metaphorical meaning, as figurative slant or a systematic inclination, prejudice, or judgment. In research, this translates into systematic error or deviations from the objectives that can influence the validity and reliability of the research outcomes.

The possibility of bias features in all parts of the research process, starting with selection bias, extending to measurement bias, confirmation bias, and publication bias. The selection of research participants or subjects can raise questions about how well the target population has been represented. When the sample is not representative, the results are deemed unreliable. For example, a study about audience preferences might include only white, middleclass women, but the results claim that the preferences apply to all audiences. Smaller studies and most qualitative research projects choose not to rely on representative samples and instead place their emphasis on capturing the richness of experience through other means. Measurement or information bias occurs when variables are wrongly assessed or measuring errors have been made such as, when socially desirable answers are provided by participants when this might be a result of an assumptive or leading question.

Confirmation bias is closely related and refers to a tendency to find the expected answers or select data that conform to the researcher's assumptions and expectations. Finding what one is expected to find, while neglecting other results that do not fit, is one of the most common biases. Objectivity is often regarded as an achievable research value but please note that this is not suitable for all research. Instead, societies focus on science interpretation includes the accompanying logic and rationales that we tend to apply directly to all forms of research, without acknowledging it as another common bias. Equally, seeing research results through a societal lens may mean favouring positive or significant results, while neglecting the less favourable interpretations. The gap between the dissemination of results to a wider or nonexpert community is often blamed for publication bias, but if the researcher explains results in an accessible way, this will mitigate senseless positivity. Having said this, I am not arguing against positive results or positivism, but when an overemphasis is placed on portraying pleasing results without critical discussion, this can raise concerns.

The funding bias, which is similar to the publication bias, relates to research that relies on third-party resources from organisations that have a vested interest in the outcome. For example, private companies might favour agenda-driven research or market- and trendsetting investigations that support their overall aim of increased profit margins, while paying less attention to niche or unconventional research projects. In the film industry, we see this played out outside of research, when mainstream blockbusters receive large amounts of investment, while smaller independent productions struggle to raise sufficient funding. A similar mechanism could be applied to CCI research. Agenda and advocacy-driven research has been at the forefront of evaluation research, delivering the expected positive results in CCI. It created a funding cycle that supported the same type of research and therefore the breadth and depth of knowledge that is generated for the CCI could have been curtailed. What CCI research needs are diverse research agendas and interdisciplinary collaborations, celebrating a more comprehensive understanding of CCI.

Being aware of potential bias will not protect researchers from employing biases, but thinking through the implications of potential biases raises awareness of pitfalls. If this is discussed in the published results, then the process of mitigating this kind of natural behaviour becomes an integral part of the reflective research process. This type of bias is known as conscious bias because of conscious thoughts, beliefs, or attitudes. It supports the opinions, behaviours, and explicit actions of people, based on characteristics such as race, religion, age, and gender. In short, it leads to the discrimination against certain sectors of the population. In the UK (United Kingdom), the Equality Act 2010 legally protects people from discrimination in the workplace and in wider society. It aims to regulate discriminatory behaviour as unlawful through the definition of protected categories. Having said this, having regulations or laws in place does not mean that discrimination does not occur. For example, hiring practices that consciously favour individuals of a certain age, race, or religion are signs of conscious bias and are against the law in the UK. In CCI, the discourse on institutional sexism and racism highlights these issues, while movements such as #MeToo and Black Lives Matter have propelled the problems into the wider consciousness of society, but this still needs to be translated into every arts organisation, including their hiring practices.

While explicit bias can be addressed because people are aware of it, implicit bias is much harder to capture. This is because of normed and unintentional behaviour, outside of conscious control, as suggested by the word *unconscious*. This form of bias is based on social and cultural influences, as well as personal experience, and can be acquired through learned associations that operate at an unconscious level. Hence it describes behaviours outside of our conscious awareness. This can mean that differential treatment or unintentional discrimination is happening, despite researchers holding egalitarian beliefs. Acting without being aware of our own behaviour seems difficult to comprehend. There is no obvious solution apart from raising awareness that may lead to a change in behaviour. For example, through unconscious bias training that is now offered in many organisations as standard training for new employees. As part of this training, I learned that in an interview situation it is not appropriate to congratulate a pregnant woman on her status, even when this would be my personal instinct as a fellow mother and woman.

Perceiving individuals as more or less competent can be based on societal stereotypes. For example, many years ago at a conference in London, I met a group of Germans from Western Germany living in the UK. My regional German accent outed me as an East German studying in the UK, which was met with bewilderment by the group. Shortly after German unification it was perceived as impossible for East Germans to have the means to study abroad. Working and being able to live abroad was a privilege that was reserved mainly for West German citizens. This left me with a feeling that I was perceived as being less worthy of living abroad. This type of bias could easily affect the choice of topic for research. For example, focussing on dominant narratives or mainstream topics will result in neglecting marginalised voices. The same could be seen in the choice of research participants or in the data collected. Favouring studies that have been conducted by well-known researchers is another example. Unconscious bias perpetuates systemic inequalities in CCI research and therefore it is essential for research training to include awareness training to learn about unbiased decision-making processes. If this is not available, it can be requested at an institutional level so that it is subsequently incorporated into all research practices.

Perpetuating inequalities has been a serious issue affecting all areas of society and hindering fairness and equality. It requires action to actively counter this behaviour. The first step is to recognise that everyone holds unconscious bias to some degree. From here, the aim is to find out what the unconscious bias is, how deeply ingrained it has become, and how it can be addressed. Advancement of knowledge only makes sense if it is achieved in a manner that is inclusive and represents everyone involved.

Accidents

Commonly, we associate accidents with the damage or harm caused by unexpected or unplanned events. The literal meaning of the accidental turn as a wrong turn when following directions applies equally to when everyday routines are interrupted through unexpected occurrences. Navigation tools are programmed to automatically suggest alternative routes as soon as the wrong turn is recognised. In research projects, we can encounter obstacles, face unexpected situations, and discover alternative approaches, all resulting in deviations from the set design or plan. Unexpected shifts of topic conversations initiated by a piece of new information, a change in interest, or a misunderstanding can direct the research into unforeseen directions. As much as accidental turns are part of everyday life, it is the way we react to the event that determines the outcome. In research, accidental turns help develop adaptability and provide an opportunity to adjust plans and steer research into new directions. When unforeseen events impact the research process, they may cause distress and be harmful, yet the same events could present new opportunities to rethink practices and change processes. The accidental turn is known for its potential to find new solutions that would have been unthinkable without the unforeseen intervention. The changes and adaptations that emerge from them have enhanced research practice, so accidental turns have become common and widely accepted. While they require careful navigation when analysing the new situations, considering the implications and the development of alternative solutions, CCI research practice has embraced interventions of this kind. Alternatively, the accidental turn offers an opportunity to explore assumptions and could act as a diagnostic test, as existing assumptions may be challenged by the unforeseen event.

For example, during the planning of a recent research project, I assumed that blockchain technology will provide the most appropriate method for developing a provenance-based database. But through an informal conversation with participants about energy costs and their experience of power cuts, it transpired that they regarded the high energy consumption of blockchain technology as unethical. This informal exchange allowed participants to voice their concerns, highlighting the need to conserve energy to minimise the impact on climate change. Participants discovered a common interest that impacted the direction of the research project. While I had incorporated sustainability into the project from the start, this discussion foregrounded sustainability as a core value and led us to evaluate the impact of the project's technology in terms of energy consumption. As a result, it influenced the direction of the project, placing sustainability as a core value when creating provenance for craft materials. It shifted our perspective and clarified an underlying assumption as a core value. This happened early in the project and resulted in blockchain technology being abandoned and replaced by a conventional database that does not rely on power hungry information technology. This example illustrates that research values adapt meeting societal needs, while embracing the relational nature of conversations. It shows that accidents have the potential of changing not only CCI research but the sector and the whole of society.

Opportunities

Understanding accidents as opportunities enriches the discussion about the research process, instead of regarding mistakes or accidents as hurdles that cannot be overcome. As well as applying a positive frame of mind, opportunities can act as enablers as they present favourable or advantageous circumstances that can carry the research forward and discover new insights. At a personal level, to learn something new, for example, a language, skills, or to meet new people, are often the result of a specific task or event without seeking it out as an opportunity in the first place. Learning a language may intentionally be driven by the desire get to know the culture of a country or a region, but while immersing yourself in the language, a new business idea could develop that could ultimately lead to you changing your profession. This change may instil a level of confidence that will result in further exploration of your capabilities. Sometimes opportunities are unforeseen events that come uninvited and must be taken when they present themselves. They cannot be planned or written into the research design, but they can manifest themselves at various stages of the research process. This could be a conversation with a colleague in the corridor, a new dataset that has just been published, or an object that you came across while on holiday. In addition, new methodologies or new pieces of equipment can suddenly alter the remit and the direction of the research or can be used to support the research in alternative ways.

Addressing current and emerging issues, also known as trendsetting, can provide opportunities for fellow researchers to follow, thereby enriching the field of research by offering different directions. In CCI research, new bodies of literature are created through trends that address the lack of knowledge and information about specific topics and relations. Currently, a growing body of research has developed that focuses on decolonisation and around ideas of creative labour, work, and the precarity of workers in the sector. The reasoning why it is important has to do with the growing general awareness of the need to decolonise society as a whole, as fostered and channelled by mega movements like Black Lives Matter. Movements of this kind ripple through all fields and areas of society. Research communities have previously argued for these changes but were not noticed by the wider population.

"Being in the right place at the right time" is one of those sayings that can be applied to trendsetters. Seeking opportunities, being open for change, and taking risks are all common attributes for trendsetters. The reward for this behaviour lies in the future and can only be known when sufficient time has passed. In research, references such as milestones or legacy publications that are evidenced through citations, fulfil a similar role to understanding the meaning of research opportunities that have occurred in the past.

However, there are two concerns that need to be considered alongside this discussion. Firstly, most research findings relate to prior research and references, then build on these findings and outcomes. In short, many other people and research projects have laid the foundations for new directions or new discoveries. Attributive claims to a single author must be seen within the context of a wider body of accumulated knowledge. Secondly, without an underlying demand for change, for example, related to equity and inequality, research alone cannot change society. Research often aims to be at the forefront of trendsetting, aiming to bring about societal change through discovering and highlighting new and original knowledge and experience. While this discussion links to the wider importance research plays in society, it goes beyond the remit of this book. In research projects, inclusive of dissertations and major projects, opportunities matter. But because of their unforeseen nature they can be disruptive, come at the wrong time, and are not always feasible for follow up. The meaning of opportunity here highlights the developmental aspect of research, favouring a positivistic approach, but research is equally built on reflection. Opportunities should be assessed using critical research tools. Questioning the opportunity may highlight other unintended consequences. As a result, not everything that can be seen as an opportunity turns out to be beneficial.

The following questions provide an initial guide, designed to inject criticality into thinking about opportunities as part of the research design, the research process, and the research outcomes:

- What does the opportunity present and for whom? Despite an agreed research approach, personal research interests differ, so what is beneficial for one person may be harmful or could disadvantage another researcher.
- Do the potential changes need a distinct set of expertise and research skills?
- Will potential changes impact the methodology and the methods?
- What is the overall impact on the content of the research? Does it require changing or altering the research questions and what kind of consequences will this have on the outcomes?
- How has the opportunity arisen and what are the circumstances in which it was recognised?
- Does following up on the opportunity cause ethical concerns for the research project and for all participants involved? This could include changing information that was provided to participants, including asking for additional consent.
- If the research process takes a new direction, has this been discussed with the supervisor in the case of a dissertation, or, in the case of research project, does it require further discussion with the research funding bodies, coinvestigator or line managers in the case of institutional concerns?
- Does the new idea or change to the timeframe, resources, and workload, have implications for participants?
- Do the changes have financial and budgetary implications?

Success and Failure

When research produces the desired outcomes, it is evaluated as a success. When the project does not go to plan, the concept of failure is often associated with any deviations from the original plan or practice. In CCI, both outcomes are viewed as opposite ends of a spectrum, rather than a positive and negative binary. However, the relationship between the two is defined through the interdependence of success and failure.

In CCI, research success can be achieved through failure, as it incorporates a learning process that improves what was regarded as a negative result. It is harder to understand this relationship since we tend not to mention the failures that helped create the success. For example, securing research funding from prestigious UK funding bodies has a success rate of under 20%, resulting in the rejection of many applications. The same applies when attempting to secure high response rates to questionnaires or finding appropriate participants for interviews. Students have regarded securing insufficient participants for their studies in their dissertations as failure, admitting that they underestimated the time required and made mistakes in the research process. An example of this could be choosing the wrong time for their interviews, such as approaching participants during their summer holidays. The fact that they reflected on their shortcomings underlines learning capabilities to be gained from mistakes, but in this instance, it is the reflection that will improve the research practice. Put simply, it results in students enriching their research experience, as the next time they will plan interviews at a more appropriate time. When confronted with this issue, students may have felt unease as they thought they had to admit failure, enforcing the negative perception that this would impact their marks, while in fact the opposite was the case. Students who did not reflect on the situation in their dissertation raised markers' concerns about their reflective awareness and capacities. But students who discussed their experience initiated a learning process and received encouraging comments.

Research activities involve rejections, repeat applications, and revision, none of which are easy to deal with. But understanding failure as part of the research and creative process helps to mitigate the associated negativity. In CCI, studies of failure have received increasing interest in recent years and are associated with discussions about changing conventional business models. For example, we know this from the film, media, and publishing industries in relation to the challenges of open access, free content, and streaming models. Similarly, the entrepreneurial turn has overplayed success in the form of processes and products, hiding failure perceived to be negative, but researchers have been critically redressing this imbalance (Kerrigan et al., 2020, Landoni et al., 2020, Banks & O'Connor, 2021, Dana et al., 2021).

Conclusion

Research is a fluid process, which is continually evolving and changing. While dealing with surprises, unforeseen circumstances, and developing strategies to overcome obstacles, researchers adapt to the changing conditions and learn how to handle difficult situations thereby gaining professional experience and resolving these challenging allows us as researchers to grow in confidence. Evaluations can take many forms, but all try to access the work that is undertaken in a specific environment. Evaluating research helps to ensure quality and rigour in the research process. It gives research the seal of approval and makes sure that the knowledge and insights gained have been achieved with due diligence. Evaluation involves judgment and demands analytical and reflective skills that help to navigate the complexities of human behaviour. It is essential to understand bias, in both conscious and unconscious forms, and to become aware of its dangers. To be effective, it will need to go beyond understanding and involve reflection and active behavioural changes, as well as discussions about the personal and professional values that are applied in research practices.

Both accidents and opportunities disrupt research practices and cannot be mitigated in advance, but instead require attention as they present themselves. Both encourage adaptation and changes that are part of everyday practice. Finally, evaluations tend to measure success against the research aims, neglecting failure as a leaning framework. However, CCI researchers can tap into a growing body of research about creative and management failures that value failure as a learning opportunity. It provides a platform to incorporate these findings into their own research practice, addressing bias, accidents, and opportunities as relational concepts that through their integrated understanding help to produce exceptional research.

References

Banks, M. & O'Connor, J. 2021. "A plague upon your howling": art and culture in the viral emergency. *Cultural Trends*, 30(1): 3–18.

Dana, L. P., Gurău, C., Hoy, F., Ramadani, V., & Alexander, T. 2021. Success factors and challenges of grassroots innovations: Learning from failure. *Technological Forecasting and Social Change*, 164: 119600.

Kerrigan, S., McIntyre, P., Fulton J., & Meany, M. 2020. The systemic relationship between creative failure and creative success in the creative industries, *Creative Industries Journal*, 13(1): 2–16. doi:10.1080/17510694.2019.1624134.

Landoni, P., Dell'era, C., Frattini, F., Petruzzelli, A. M., Verganti, R., & Manelli, L. 2020. Business model innovation in cultural and creative industries: Insights from three leading mobile gaming firms. *Technovation*, 92: 102084.

Williams, M. 2000. Interpretivism and generalisation. *Sociology*, 34(2): 209–224.

9

RESEARCH ETHICS

Introduction

All researchers, participants, and associated groups working in and with organisational settings must comply with the ethical and moral standards set against a rapidly changing environment. But what is sometimes regarded as an administrative burden, on closer inspection, reveals ethics as a thinking process, as a practical standard of behaviour, and as a cultural practice. What has been regarded as good ethical practice requires constant scrutiny, because without a sound understanding and application of ethics policies and procedures, the research results are in danger of being compromised. The safety and safeguarding of participants, including the researcher, is paramount. In CCI, ethics has always been an integral element and is woven into the fabric of every item that is produced and every performance given. Cultural rights contain and apply ethical thinking that connects normative and legal implications with cultural values. In CCI, research practice, ethical principles are enshrined in all aspects of research and cover legal, moral, and professional behaviours. With legality in mind, human rights, copyright, privacy rights and more, combine to set out in law what is good ethical practice. In moral terms, it is about fair representation and ensuring participants are credited and respected. In professional terms, integrity is expected to ensure that all research participants are treated with consideration. One way to ensure these qualities are applied is to provide clarity by using sources accurately and honestly.

In this chapter, I start by discussing ethics as a thinking process before explaining in practical scenario settings how ethics are applied. This covers choosing suitable locations, obtaining consent, ensuring access to the research results for participants, and compliance with data protection regulations. In a follow-up section, I explain the ethics procedures referring to the compliance

DOI: 10.4324/9781003161912-9

with the General Data Protection Regulation (GDPR) as expressed in data management plans, as well as discuss an example of ethics forms used in a higher education setting. The concluding section covers referencing as a form of ethical compliance, and I also consider how to use Artificial Intelligence (AI) text generating programmes as a writing tool while avoiding the dangers of plagiarism.

Understanding Ethics

When discussing ethics and ethical behaviour as a general idea, most people would agree that it involves judgement about what is right and wrong. But this right/wrong binary is seldomly expressed as simply the difference between the two choices. Instead, it may be better expressed as a spectrum of judgements. In formal terms, Fieser (2014) explained that ethics (also referred to as moral philosophy) involves systematizing, defending, and recommending concepts of right and wrong behaviour, while Rancière, (quoted in Lloyd, 2015 1) defends ethics as a mode of thinking in which an identity is established between an environment, a way of being, and a principle of action. When applied for the purposes of research, ethics should be considered as normative ethics, where practical considerations are included regarding the risks, threats, and rights of others during research and the subsequent mitigation of these.

Tracing back the meaning of ethics to ancient Greece, Aristotle (384–322 BCE) would have concurred with the idea that ethics should be seen as a matter of rational inquiry into what is right and wrong. But since then, this view has seen many alterations. I will briefly introduce the three main strands of ethics (1) consequentialism, (2) deontology, and (3) virtue ethics as discussed in philosophical terms. This will lay the foundations to locate and understand normative ethics when applied in researching creative and cultural industries, as they continue to influence contemporary ethical thinking and direct the way we approach ethical questions.

(1) For the consequentialists, as the name implies, the ultimate or the core of judgement whether something is right or wrong, relates to the consequences of one's conduct. Split into three versions of egotistic, altruistic, and balanced behaviour, favourable outcomes are weighted against unfavourable results. In ethics, egotistic actions are morally right if the positive consequences outweigh the negative consequences for the individual performing the action. For example, weighing up the consequences of pursuing a career move into strength and weaknesses without paying attention to the greater good, could indicate ethics egotism. As a counterpart, ethical altruism states that the consequences of actions must be more favourable for everyone, except for the individual performing the act. Fieser (2021) argues with the utilitarian John Stuart Mill (1806–1873), who understood ethics to be a combined effort of people's behaviour. He argued that an action is right, when the greatest happiness for the greatest number of people is achieved through the decision. In 1991 Beauchamp argued along the utilitarian view, deeming actions to be morally right if the value and disvalue derived from actions is, at the very least, balanced.

(2) In deontology, the discussion about what is right and wrong ethical behaviour combines right and duty, thereby foregrounding the relational characteristics, asserting that the rights of one individual lead to the duty of another individual. For example, the individual right to vote as a duty triggers the government to provide the means to vote. Immanuel Kant (1724–1804) centred the importance of individual autonomy in the pursuit of happiness as his ethical mantra. He reasoned that all duties can be summarised by what he called the "categorical imperative" (Kant quoted in Gregor & Timmermann, 2014), which is described as an end in itself, rather than a mere means to an end. He argued for an assessment of personal behaviour or actions through reasoning. Subsequently, if the reasoning or maxim (i.e., principle or rule) that was applied to an action can be applied to everyone as a universal law or guide, it is ethical. In short, it is an unconditional and necessary principle of reason that can be applied universally and consistently to guide ethical behaviour. To determine if an action is permissible or morally wrong, Kant suggested analysing it using a thought experiment. He suggested imagining a hypothetical scenario in which the principle that the action is based on would be followed by everyone in similar situations. To determine whether the personal principle can be applied universally it needs to be assessed for logical contradictions. If self-contradiction or logical inconsistencies arise or important values are undermined, the action is deemed impermissible and fails the experiment. If the opposite is true, it carries an ethical remit. Translated into everyday research practice, imagine the following: You promised a colleague help with writing a research grant funding bid, but close to the deadline you decide that due to other pressures to prioritise your own work instead. Your colleague is left unable to find alternative help at such short notice, and consequently the funding bid could not be submitted on time. Applying the thought experiment, the question arises what would happen if everyone behaved in this way, prioritising their own work and therefore being unable to help others. In a society that values care, helping other people as a form of taking care is essential. According to Kant's concept of the categorical imperative, the behaviour in the imagined scenario is unethical because it would have been your duty to help. While this principal refers consistency and coherence to ethical behaviour, it relies exclusively on explaining ethics through reasoning. The Scottish-English philosopher William David Ross (1877–1971) emphasised that in a time of conflicting obligations, such as prima facie duties (i.e., gratitude, fidelity, justice) they should be separated into duties where the more pressing obligations override other duties (1939). For example, imagine an interview situation in which the interviewee gets distressed, resulting in the interview being stopped and abandoned. Consequently, no data could be collected and your project results, which rely on this one-off interview, are compromised. In short, the duty to do no harm overrides the duty to contribute to research.

(3) The last strand, virtue ethics (i.e., ethics of character) followed a close reading of Aristotle's character traits, which indicated that there are ideal traits that a virtuous person would carry. The traits are built on natural internal tendencies

that when nourished throughout a lifetime will be stable enough to guide ethical behaviours. Being kind across many situations, repeatedly over a long time, is seen as part of a person's character and does not indicate that the person wants to maximise utility, gain favour from someone else, or fulfil a duty. Within the remit of this idea, the ancient concept of *eudaimonia* (translated from Greek as happiness, flourishing, or wellbeing) has been discussed. Bloomfield (2014) argues that living a good life includes happiness and virtue, insisting on a conceptual link between the two. Subsections of virtue ethics translate the character trait idea into an agent-based theory. Virtues are determined by common sense intuition that observers judge to be admirable traits in other people. The phrase "I wish I were like another person" translates some of this thinking into everyday life. Agency is given to the people we admire, or in other words, through our admiration the admirer gains agency, whereby the judgement of bad/good or wrong/right is linked to the motivational and dispositional states of exemplary agents (Zagzebski, 1996, 2017). Over time, our judgements become more refined, while encountering a wide variety of examples and by drawing systematic connections between them, our moral system also becomes more refined, thereby merging virtue with motivations. Aristotle (384–322 BCE) discussed this reliance on motivation or natural virtue as practical wisdom that relies on an understanding that people know how to live well (Aristotle, 2006).

In contemporary philosophy, feminist approaches to ethics in particular foreground the notion of care and the relation of natural caring as an important impetus for moral or ethical behaviours, arguing that care is a human condition that is morally good. Care is understood as a natural desire to be and to remain related (Nodding quoted in Tong, 1998). In this regard, care helps maintain humanity and supports society, while meeting the needs of ourselves and others. This includes understanding the relationships we form with each other and considers the interactive context in which we live. It allows us to reflect on specific circumstances in which ethical decisions are made and question the idea that ethics is based on universal principles. In CCI, an ethics of care is applied in pockets but not consistently. For example, in the case of managing people, the social responsibility agendas are being driven by aspects of wellbeing, care, and equality as well as equity. We see care addressed in the discourses about labour and work. Research on social class and on the living and working conditions of art practitioners have applied concepts of solidarity as an expression of care. But among policymakers, help in formulating the issues and problems that arise from a relational approach to care and wellbeing remains less appreciated. Despite the ethics of care being advocated since the early 1980s, progress has been slow. Better integration into everyday politics and management in CCI would help the concept to gain wider acceptance, therefore changing ethical practice into best practice could be a task for researchers to align ethics with decolonising and intersectional research agendas.

Tronto (1998) suggested four practical steps on how to translate moral qualities of care into a process of caring, which, following the work of Belfiore

(2022) and Alacovska, and Bissonnette (2021), has recently received increased attention in CCI.

1. This process is guided in the first phase by moral attentiveness, a kind of caring in which unmet caring needs are identified. Considering the increased politicisation of the role of the individual, this is not an easy ask. This is because it involves the suspension of one's self-interest and focusing on the perspective of the people in need, including being attentive to our own needs, as a collective undertaking.

2. Research comes with responsibilities that are captured by a sense of caring. Translated into action, or a process, the second step asks for stepping up, for doing the responsible thing. In short, when the needs are identified, they are required to be met. This means someone, some group, must be willing to take on the task. This relates back to Nodding's idea (quoted in Tong, 1998) of understanding care as a natural desire to be and remain related. Responsibility becomes a concept that fulfils needs.

3. The conceptual idea of responsibility translated into action involves the hands-on work of care or caregiving, which requires competence, another moral quality. The ethics of care stresses the emotional response that empathy is required in ethical decision-making and is one of the important components of competence. The feeling of empathy is translated into responsibility and actioned as competence. Belfiore (2022 67). Emphasising the moral implications, Tronto states that "to be competent to care, given one's caring responsibilities, is not simply a technical issue, but a moral one" (2013 34–35). Combining technical skills with emotional intelligence makes good practice, not just in care-related circumstances, it also applies to the general sense of how people relate to each other.

4. The fourth and final quality is responsiveness to receiving care, a kind of reflective evaluation from the people, groups, and environments who were cared for. Research methods of observation, analysis, and judgment are at hand to qualify the care received to be deemed as successful, sufficient, or complete.

In research, ethics of care provides a conceptual framework to think through and understand the ethical implications of the expected research outcomes and enables researchers to apply the concept in their practice as a process-focused activity. The challenge is to weave the conceptual understanding and thinking together with the practical behaviour into the research design, its implementation, and in its evaluation.

Thinking about care is a known quality in research through *duty of care*, a concept every researcher must apply and address at every stage of the research process. It stands for a combination of thoughts, actions, and behaviours regarding care, which summarise the responsibilities and obligations of the researcher in relation to research participants. Researchers understand that it is their duty to protect participants against potential harm relating to privacy and welfare. For example, researchers have demonstrated awareness of risk when promising blanket anonymity to research participants. They provide confidentiality agreements between participants and researcher and then applied a coding system during data analysis for deidentification of all data, leaving one identifiable key securely stored on a password-protected storage device to avoid reidentification.

However, this straightforward approach houses several difficulties and when put into practice, the lines of duty are less clear. Ensuring confidentiality and privacy requires thinking through all the eventualities that could lead to a breach of confidentiality, with the result that information could become accessible to the wider public, with unintended consequences. The handling of personal data is regulated through the European Union (EU) and the United Kingdom (UK) data protection acts known as General Data Protection Regulation (GDPR). Although this legislation delivers guidance, it is worth discussing some of the potential pitfalls that could emerge while researching and that fall within the remit of data protection. The first difficulty relates to the guarantee of anonymity that is often written into a research design, yet wrongly understood. It is judged to be sufficient to remove personal details from the raw data and to ensure that participant consent is provided to do so. GDPR guidelines require assurance that no traceability is possible using motivated intruder testing (Graham, 2012). This includes the requirement that an independent researcher is tasked with trying to find out if participants could be recognised in any way through combining data from the study with publicly available data from the internet, references, and other applications that aim to identity the participants. If participants can be identified successfully, then anonymity cannot be guaranteed. The same concept is applied in testing computer systems and networks through penetration testing or ethical hacking. Skilled, ethical hackers try to compromise the systems, simulating attack scenarios to determine how resilient the system is. Like the motivated intruder experiment, ethical hackers conduct reconnaissance missions to find as much information as possible about the system. They look for vulnerabilities in old versions of applied software, open ports, and weak passwords, then attempt to exploit this information to gain access and control over the system. For example, by elevating themselves to a position with administrative privileges, they can use this information to provide preventative recommendations to the system owners. As a direct result, any potential security flaws are identified in advance. Seeing anonymity testing through the eyes of a hacker adds to a researcher's understanding and why the importance of handling of personal data in a research setting should not be underestimated.

Pseudonymisation can be used as an alternative approach, especially when anonymity cannot be guaranteed. It does not provide the same level of security for participants, but it provides sufficient protection for participants with a low-profile internet or social media presence. Pseudonymisation, like anonymisation, requires that data can no longer be identified with a specific person. Instead of ensuring irreversibility of identification, it necessitates "replacing one attribute (typically a unique attribute) in a record by another" (Lee, 2014). It effectively introduces a key and is more appropriate in this instance when considering indirect identification. A simple application of pseudonymity could be to replace the name of the participants with a pseudonym, but other keys (e.g., age, profession, gender, location, social status, and stratification) will work equally well.

Further protection of research participants includes ensuring their welfare and, while researchers may have the best intentions, the practical execution is complex and requires unpacking the meaning of duty of care in relation to welfare. The obvious place to start addresses the challenges that convey the topics and themes that researchers investigate and what questions participants are being asked when being consulted for research purposes. Any topic can cause distress or trigger unpleasant memories amongst participants and not all can be anticipated, but topics and themes differ in their impact on participants, as does the vulnerability of participants. Themes and topics that are linked to personal experiences, such as discrimination, violence, mental and physical health issues, and any other harmful and hazardous events that result in personal discomfort are as common as in the creative industries as in other areas or industries. As researchers, we cannot rely on good will and hope nothing will happen. Instead, thinking about what could happen will prepare for eventual difficult situations, such as when participants are in distress, experience unpleasant feelings, or fall ill during the research. This should not be taken to imply that difficult social issues cannot be investigated, but the right precautions need to be in place in advance.

This could mean that when difficult issues are being discussed a process of care could be initiated like the ethics of care. When attentiveness is applied to the design of the questions, establishing the care needs of the participants is automatically included. It is worth noting that university ethics compliance forms ask about the content of the research, including a potential list of questions to support the consideration of participants' wellbeing. For example, formulating open-ended questions that are indirect, together with wraparound questions that prepare the participant in advance, both aim to mitigate potential hazards and distress. Other considerations include giving participants a choice of whether to answer questions of this kind, to indicate that the interviewer should move on to the next topic, or even halt the interview at their request. They all demonstrate that the participant's wellbeing is integral to the research and that this is communicated in the information provided before the data collection stage. A trigger warning in the participant information sheet helps with preparation of data collection. These actions deliver a message that researchers take their responsibilities seriously.

During data collection, the researcher's experience in dealing with tricky situations is often dealt with by using common sense and instinct, but there are also professional guidelines that will help mitigate any problems and should be at hand if a situation arises. People in distress require clear and supportive information, so researchers need to know in advance who can be contacted in such cases, an example of which may be a discussion of harassment in the music industry. A list of charities that provide support in emergency situations is a good starting point and should be included in the participant information sheet. Competent care demands actions, and being competent about care means acknowledging the fact that, in most instances, researchers are not healthcare professionals and therefore knowing how to access health and other support services is necessary for every researcher. The ethics of care invites us to reflect and evaluate.

After data collection, care involves not only a thank you email but an offer to provide further support to all research participants. This extends to researchers referencing self-protection and reflection as part of the research practice. In previous chapters, I outlined the importance of finding a research topic that relates to the researcher and that individual experiences are embedded in the form of motivation and interest, which could be manifested in a variety of feelings, like joy and freedom, but also vulnerability. Therefore, researchers should apply protective thinking to understand and mitigate any potential harm. This involves choosing safe locations for interviews, applying knowledge of how to handle difficult conversations, and knowing when professional healthcare or support are required. Thinking through worst-case scenarios including the potential for violence or abuse might not always be obvious, but as an exercise it will be helpful to develop a sense of awareness. In CCI, special safeguarding measures are applied to specific environments that can vary greatly (e.g., observational studies conducted in late night music and dance venues or in thinking through the potential impact of studying violent films). Safeguarding issues must be addressed by the researcher for the purposes of the research, but this often depends on whether people can be trusted in the way they behave, act, and communicate.

Trust is seen as an essential element that, when woven into the research design, will support ethical thinking and actions. Participants are trusted to act reliably, competently, and honestly, but in many research projects this is a challenge because trust rests on belief and is built over time. Meeting participants for the first time for an interview must be built on trust as a form of reciprocal behaviour. Therefore, declaring any conflict of interest is required to ensure its impact on the integrity of the research is fully understood and minimised. Interviewing family or friends demands a duty of care that must be maintained and should not compromise the relationship. Nepotism as a concept is one of the less obvious challenges that undermines trust. Asking friends and family to participate in research or to use their contacts is asking a favour. This might save time, but could be interpreted as preferential treatment, giving the researcher an advantage over fellow researchers, or providing privileged access to information. Granting advantages that are based on personal relationships rather than on merit could compromise research outcomes and can impact negatively on the research culture. Research might deliberately involve family and friends as a purposeful decision, but the potential for a conflict of interest should form part of the research rationale. Operating with honesty and integrity may sound banal, but Martyn Denscombe (2009) argues that ethical principles are guided by the assumption that researchers have no privileged position in society that justifies pursuing their interests at the expense of those they are studying, no matter how valuable they hope their findings might be. Denscombe sums up researchers' overall responsibilities, which connect all the distinct aspects of the duty of care into a monitoring process, as an integral part of the research process. Institutional review boards or ethics committees, in university settings, provide support and maintain oversight of any research carried out in their organisation. The ethics committee addresses any concerns relating to ethical principles. Most organisations have designed a set of forms and guidelines that helps staff and students to think ethically, including ensuring duty of care and indirectly referencing the ethics of care.

The role and function of ethics committees and procedures are not always well understood, and forms can sometimes be misinterpreted as an administrative burden and as unnecessary. In this case, ethics forms and the ethics process are understood as expressions of institutional oppression or as a kind of standardisation that leaves no room for interpretation. Resistance thinking is applied, and the forms that stand for the whole ethics process are misrepresented as an unnecessary mechanism, as a tool that the institution uses to enforce their authority. When the forms are regarded simply as a burden that must be completed, the process of thinking through the ethics is hindered. In my capacity as an ethics representative, I have seen students and staff struggling to make sense of the forms. This is not because they are difficult to complete, but because a negative attitude influences the reading of the forms and blocks ethical thinking as a notion of self-care for the researcher. Max and Michael van Manen (2021) argued that this fixed attitude underestimates the flexibility and dynamics in which ethical principles and the ethics of care operate. Occasionally, the same notion of being fixed, inflexible, and undynamic are projected onto the forms. Repetition of information between forms is seen as a sign of bureaucracy, despite this being required, as some of the forms are meant to be handed to the participants, while others stay with the organisation. Therefore, distilling the ethical approval process, and reflecting about the process, is equally as important as is filling out the forms. The process assures that the rights of participants and researchers alike are protected and underlines a commitment to excellence in research across a wide range of subjects.

Within a university, ethics committees tend to streamline the approval process across the organisation to ensure equal treatment with subject specific guidelines or best practice examples covering the ethics of care. Therefore, it is highly unlikely that a one-size-fits-all approach can work. Discipline or subject area specificities must be worked out as a collective undertaking, thereby fostering a shared ethical understanding. Discussion in CCI about working conditions, of reinforcing a work-life balance, and of adequate pay, are all connected to the ethics of care.

Creative workers are trying to find novel ways of thinking through the ethical process and apply methods that suit their investigations. As a result, they will challenge existing processes to adapt them to their own needs. For example, forms of collective writing can question concepts of authorship, so when research responsibility is defined around the individual this can cause tensions. Consequently, further discussion can be accommodated through the ethical approval process until a satisfactory solution is achieved. Research is a collaborative process, so ethical practice evolves, changes, and negotiates between participants, while generating new knowledge.

Students require ethical training that explains ethical thinking and the concept of the ethics of care, and regards research as an integral part of their degree education. Only when the link between the duty of care and the ethics of care as a principle and process is made, will the idea that following the ethics process is an administrative burden be lifted. As an educator, seeing students apply ethical principles and following the ethics process in their professional work environment shows the wider reach of the ethics of care as a lifelong learning approach, one that truly works when everyone is on board the ship.

The Ethics Process

The following section discusses the practical applications of the ethics process.

As an initial step, it is important to identify if the research to be carried out involves working with people at any point in the project, including dealing with confidential human data. In my workplace in the UK, ethical guidelines are integrated into the approval process and apply to research that involves any of the following participants and situations:

- Human participants (whether participating actively or through observation) – from the perspective of their welfare and interests and duties of care for their personal data
- Where there are legitimate concerns for the welfare and interests of those carrying out the activity, including where a researcher needs to travel to a location where the Foreign Office has issued advice to travellers, which raises concerns about the individual's welfare whilst in the country
- Animals – from the perspective of their welfare, interest, and duty of care
- The potential to damage or change our cultural heritage
- Changes to the natural environment
- The potential for damage to the reputation of the individual, the department, the college, the discipline, and academia as a whole. The welfare and interests of the wider community should also be considered
- When requiring an individual to step outside accepted regulatory or legal norms

- Collection or review of individual or case-level administrative data, or archival material, which is not in the public domain
- Collection or review of sensitive data derived from social media platforms (e.g. data from closed discussion groups or forums or posted by potentially vulnerable social media users) and in some instances for collaboration with international (academic or non-academic) bodies.

(Birkbeck, 2023)

In most cases, this will have been discussed in the research design and the methodology and methods that have been determined in what form and format participation will take place. In short, any research involving humans or their participation requires ethical approval from the organisation in which the research is based, to ensure compliance with the ethical principles set by the organisation. Ethics policies or ethical guidelines are designed to advise how to navigate this process. Approaches will vary between organisation, but the following forms or documents will be required in some form: ethics application form, information sheet and consent forms for participants, as well as a data management plan. Depending on the ethics process defined by the individual organisation, an initial questionnaire connected to a flow chart (see Figure 9.1) can be helpful to identify the information needed to accompany the application.

Any research can only be undertaken once ethical approval has been granted by the organisation. For students this could become a stressful situation if time implications have not been considered in advance. How long it takes to gain ethical approval depends on the nature of the study and how quickly applications can be turned around within the organisation. However speedily the administration works, applications must go through several stages and must be read by a number of reviewers, which takes time. The nature of the research gives an indication of how many stages the application must pass through. In a university setting, ethical committees at multiple structural layers discuss applications and classify them into routine, sensitive, and highly sensitive cases. Routine cases reference research that is commonly carried out in specific subject fields. For example, if a similar piece of research has been carried out before, a precedent is established that can be used as a guide for any subsequent cases. In CCI, this relates to the use of methods such as interviewing or social media investigations, which are widespread practices and therefore regarded as routine cases. Subject field guidelines will correspond with the ethical standards of professional bodies that offer guidelines, such as the British Sociological Association, Association for Computing Machinery (ACM), Code of Ethics and Professional Conduct, and the Academy of Management's Professional Code of Ethics. This applies when they are linked to accreditations of research, and they differ from subject to subject. Guidelines are explained and discussed in the ethics training that the researcher will receive before embarking on an ethics application.

Research funding organisations are also a reliable source for helping to understand ethics. Principles that are commonly used in research are referenced,

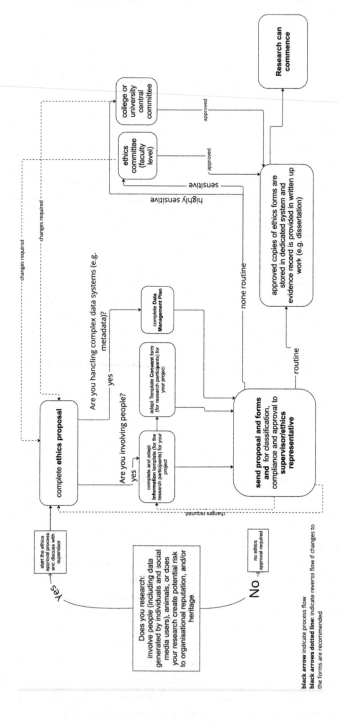

FIGURE 9.1 Flow chart ethics application process (by the author)

as is the case for the UK research councils, the primary government-backed research funding bodies. The Economic Social Research Council (ESRC) stipulates six principles on their website and defines the following general preconditions: (1) respecting the individual by maximising the benefits to individuals and society; (2) including the rights and dignity of individuals while minimising risk and harm; (3) participation should be voluntary; (4) guaranteeing integrity and transparency of the research process; (5) clearly defined lines of responsibilities and accountability; and (6) maintaining independence of research with a special reference that conflict of interest must be declared (ESRC, 2023).

While these general principles apply to all subject fields, interdisciplinary research might have to be considered by several subject fields. Despite efforts being made to address the nuances of interdisciplinary research, subject field thinking still dominates. Therefore, when the decision making at the subject level is inconclusive, the ethics application is referred to the next administrative level, which is usually one step removed from subject expertise. Additionally, any cases that are not routine (i.e., sensitive and highly sensitive) are discussed by ethics committees, which usually consist of academics trained in ethics and which are involved in helping to translate ethical principles into the ethics application process. Ethical principles in my own university states: "Do not put participants at risk, and respect vulnerable populations. Researchers need to have their research plans reviewed by the Institutional Review Board (IRB)" (Birkbeck, 2023). Note here the direct link to the ESRC principles. The quote references vulnerable populations including children, people with disabilities or impaired health, who cannot consent to the research being carried out. In those cases, additional steps are necessary to ensure the protection of their rights. In CCI research, working with children is common practice, but in ethical terms this work would not be routine but sensitive because of the vulnerability of the participants. In practical terms, the ethics committees might combine several subject fields, and there is usually an option to discuss applications at faculty or college level when dealing with the most complex cases that are classified as highly sensitive. Ethical approval for these cases may take longer and can require further safeguarding procedures to be put in place as part of the research process. If ethical thinking is treated as an add duty and is left to the last minute, timings become an issue, because research cannot commence before ethical approval has been obtained. Universities offer timelines (see Figure 9.1) explaining the procedural implications for research practices in their ethics training.

The research location, including the countries from which research participants come, may require further ethical clearance. For example, the introduction of the General Data Protection Regulation in the EU, extended its territorial scope compared with previous regulations. This applies beyond the borders of the EU when the research involves EU citizens and when EU researchers work outside the EU, for example in the UK. Data protection references legal obligations that must be put in place, ranging from obtaining consent in the form of a contract or individual consent to data processing. It might be taken for granted, but research must be legitimate, follow vital interests, and perform a public task. Some countries, such as Germany, follow stricter country-specific laws that have integrated GDPR guidelines, but due the historically based ethics culture, researchers in Germany tend to be highly sensitive to data protection. Most universities in the UK have specific documents that address the implementation of GDPR guidelines and other legal obligations as part of the ethics application process (see Figure 9.5). Location-based ethics must address further concerns when, for example, research is taking place abroad or if the topic of the research clashes with a country's cultural or ideological norms and practices, such as an investigation of corruption or the rights of underrepresented groups, such as the LGBTQ+ community. The questions asked in ethics applications relate to risk mitigation and ensuring the safety of all participants. For example, during the COVID-19 pandemic, specific measures had to be taken to minimise the risk of infection. Therefore, a risk assessment had to be carried out as part of the ethics application. Arts organisations translated these measures into their professional practices. For example, many dance companies would not allow any visitors backstage, long after lockdown measures were lifted. This was because high infection rates would jeopardise the safety of theatre workers and of performers, particularly those who express their work through body movements and must meet high physical demands. Research methods that include haptical elements, such as the touching and feeling of materials also faced increased risk of infection during the pandemic and therefore had to be discussed specifically, which under nonpandemic circumstances would have fallen under routine behaviour (e.g., when visiting a weaver's studio).

When thinking about risk, the nonvisible dangers that can cause harm to participants are often underestimated. Ensuring mental or psychological wellbeing during the research remains underestimated and demands careful attention. Methods such as focus groups, observations, and interviews can act as triggers for underlying traumas. As a result, it is important to discuss these eventualities in the ethics application and to prepare for potential interventions in case they are needed during data collection. For example, as mentioned in the section "Understanding ethics", a list of potential charities that participants could contact during or after the research encounter should be considered in advance of the ethics application. In some circumstances, a combination of potential wellbeing triggers could come together in both location and topic-based risks. These applications are complex and are usually discussed and assessed as highly sensitive. In CCI, this would include studies of children's art play in a refugee camp or a series of interviews with musicians about their underground practice in a country that forbids music as a cultural expression.

In practice, several enclosed documents make up the application appendix. If consent is required, this includes a written consent form and an information sheet that applicants will receive before data collection. Anything related to data handling is covered in the data management plan. This is designed to address the whole data journey, from the creation of data-to-data storage, what kind of data is produced, at what point and from whom data is processed, and for how long. A risk assessment might be necessary when handling specific materials and substances. The forms also cover written exchanges in the form of emails and other correspondence through social media channels, as well as communication such as videos or podcasts.

Ethics Application Form

Most organisations have developed a form that corresponds to their organisational policies, covering the following points:

1. **Personal information:** Name, position, department, programme, research project title, funding source, mentor/supervisor name or line manager, date of application, and proposed research starting dates
2. **Research project rationale:** Summarises the key aims and the research question, the benefits of the research to the public, as required in the research principles, associated risks and their mitigation in the project
3. **Participants:** Explain identification, selection and recruitment, number of participants, inclusion/exclusion criteria
4. **Methods of data collection and data analysis:** Explain the collection, processing, and use of data; describe the activities of participants, in the case of question-based methods; include an indicative list of questions; and explain how the data will be collected and how it is going to be analysed
5. **Protection of participants:** Identify methods of protection, such as anonymisation or pseudonymisation, and explain how to achieve this
6. **Data storage:** Comply with your organisational data storage arrangements. For example, storage may only be allowed on the organisation's cloud provider, but not on personal computers. This is relevant if the research requires anonymisation (see point 5) of personal data to break the link between the data and the personal details of the participant
7. **Consent:** Explain how to ensure that consent is given freely without coercion
8. **Certify:** Ensure that the information (including appendices) are complete and correct, that compliance is guaranteed, responsibility has been accepted, risks are identified, and that research can only commence when ethics has been approved
9. **Classification of research:** Select a classification suggestion (i.e., routine, sensitive, highly sensitive) according to your organisational guidelines and ethical principles.
10. **Signature and date:** Several signatures might be required prior to sending the application to the ethics representative. In the case of dissertations, this includes the supervisor who can also act as first port of call after the ethics training.

Name(s) of applicant	
Email address of applicant	
Date of application	
Proposed research start date	
Status (e.g., student, member of staff)	
Course of study (if student) – subject and title	
Department or School	
Supervisor name and email (if applicable)	
Thesis, dissertation, academic staff research	
Project Title	
Funding source for study (if applicable)	

Attachements: Please indicate the attachments enclosed with this form (delete as appropriate): Information Sheet, Consent Form, Data Management Plan, Materials (survey questions, advertising), Other (please list):

Please provide a rationale and description of proposed project: This should be a summary of key aims and research questions derived from your reasearch proposal. What question(s) do you aim to answer and why? What are the benefits of doing this research, what are the potential risks, how can they be mitigated?

Participant selection: How will participants be identified, selected, and recruited? How many participants will there be? What are the inclusion/exclusion criteria?

Methods: How will the data be collected, processed, and used? What will the participants be asked to do? Where will the data be collected? How will the data be analysed?

How will participants identities be protected?

What arrangements are in place to hold the data securely? (both eletronically and hard copies): Please consider questions such as at what point can you break the link between the participant's identification and the data.

How will you ensure consent is informed and freely given without any coerction?

Please confirm each of the statements below by highlighting yes or no.

I certify that to the best of my knowledge the information given above, together with accompanying information, is complete and correct. (**yes/no**)

FIGURE 9.2 Template for Research Ethics Application

I certify that to the best of my knowledge the information given above, together with accompanying information, is complete and correct. (yes/no) I accept responsibility for the conduct of the procedures set out in the attached application. **(yes/no)** I have attempted to idenify all risks relating to the research that may arise in conduting the project. **(yes/no)** I understand that no research work nvolving human participants or data can commence until ethical approval has been given. **(yes/no)**
Suggested classification of project by the applicant (please highlight): SENSITIVE / EXTREMELY SENSITIVE / ROUTINE
Signatures (if emailed hard copy signatures are not needed): Applicant: Date: Supervisor (if applicable):   Date: NB As the supervisor you are confirming that you have approved this proposal, its aims, and methods as relevant and worthwhile, and are satisfied that ethical issues have been addressed adequately.
For use of Research Ethics Representative (please highlight): Decision Refer Back, Acceptance, Refer to Faculty Ethics Committee, Rejection **Classification of project:** ROUTINE / NON-ROUTINE Signature: Date: (Research Ethics Representative)

FIGURE 9.2 (Cont.)

Consent and Information Forms

Within this framework of legal obligations, consent is one of the prime concerns and the consent form is where this is established as written consent (see Figure 9.3). The form is usually predesigned, and a copy or template is provided during the ethics training, which would need to be adjusted to the research study as appropriate. The consent form is only valid when linked to the research project information and is sometimes provided separately or attached to it. Both forms, the consent form and the information sheet (see Figure 9.4), are to be given to the participants before any data collection can commence. Importantly, in the consent form researchers need to make clear to all participants that they are taking part voluntarily and that they have the right to refuse information and withdraw at any time, to ensure that they are not being coerced into participating. The researcher needs to make sure that participants understand the study's purpose, so that they are clear about the nature of the research and what the impact will be for them personally. Researchers would need to explain the study's procedures so that participants can anticipate what to expect in the research. Participants always have the right to ask questions, obtain a copy of the results, and to have their privacy respected. Both the participant and the researcher agree to these provisions by providing their signature on the consent form (Creswell & Creswell, 2017).

Asking for consent for internet-based questionnaires is usually covered on the initial window of a webpage before the questions are introduced and after explaining what the study is about. In short, an information sheet and consent form are provided, for example, as an opening page, and through tick boxes or signatures written consent is obtained. After consent has been given, the questionnaire page opens, but if it is not, access is denied. Instead, the reader is redirected to the general page where contact details are provided to obtain further information.

Information sheets should spell out to the participants what the study is about and why participants have been invited to take part. It provides details on how the study will use the data collected and what is involved in the data collection and the subsequent data analysis. It explicitly spells out how the anonymity or pseudonymity is guaranteed and what actions are undertaken to keep the data secure and for how long. It also needs to answer the question of what will happen to the data if participants change their mind and wish to withdraw from the study. It explains how this process is organised and states the date up to which withdrawal is possible, which is usually at a point at which the data become amalgamated into a larger and often coded set of data. Participants may request a copy of the results or the write-up, and it is good practice to make this optional, while explaining how participants can access the findings. The information sheet should encourage participants to ask other questions and provide the contact details of the lead researcher. In the case of dissertations, supervisory details should be added as well. At the end of the information sheet, links to the organisational policies, for example, privacy protection information should be listed and the complaint procedure explained, together with address details and a contact person. In most cases, this will be the ethics representative of the organisation.

Data Management Plan

Data has become part and is seen in many aspects of modern life, but the need to be accountable and use data responsibly is easier said than done. Without further thought, we tend to sign away data privacy requests from companies far too lightly. However, the same attitude could jeopardise the research process and the results. The idea that nonhuman data requires less protection has been proven wrong on many occasions and data breaches continue to occur. Such breaches can be harmful and even put participants at risk. The data management plan helps to prevent data breaches by offering a step-by-step guide to think through the process the research data will take. Like the consent form and the information form, a template is often provided from the organisation that

Consent Form

Research Project	
Name of Researcher	
Institution	
Project Purpose	

	(Tick as appropriate)
I confirm that I have read and understand the information sheet dated [add date] for the above study. The study has been explained to me and I have had the opportunity to consider the information, ask questions and have had these answered satisfactorily. I understand that I may ask additional questions at any time.	
I understand that I have the right to refuse to answer any question without giving a reason.	
I understand that my participation is voluntary and that I am free to withdraw at any time, without giving any reason, until the data has been amalgamated into a larger dataset and it is no longer feasible to unpick it from the oher data. (Provide an estimation of how long this will be.)	
I understand that any information given by me will be collected and processed as follows: e.g., collected on a voice recorder and then transcribed and anonymised by the researcher. NB. if the data is being passed to a third party. such as a transcription service, then this must be made explicit. Identify: who will have access to the data. For example: all data will be identified by a code, with personal details kept in a locked file or secure computer with access only given to the immediate researchers. If personal data is being collected, explain how personal data will be kept separate from research data. State that there will be no way to link personal data (e.g., date of birth, name) with the anonymised research data. Please state that all consent forms containing personal information will be destroyed at the end of the project.	
(If appropriate.) I agree/do not agree to the interview being taped/filmed. (If this is the case, please cover the following: who will see/hear these recordings, how recordings are identified by a code and will not be used or made available for any purposes other than the research project, when the recordings will be destroyed, how the use of film or video affect your promise of anonymity.)	
I understand that I have the right to ask for the audio tape/video recording to be turned off at any time during the interview.	
I agree to participate in this study under the conditions set out in the Information Sheet.	
(Group interviews only.) I agree to keep the information shared in this interview confidential.	
Name of Participant: Signature: Date:	
Name of Researcher: Signature: Date:	
One copy will be given to the participant and the original will be kept in the file of the researcher or as an eletronic copy at [file location].	

FIGURE 9.3 Template for a Consent Form

Information Sheet
(Please make sure this is informative and user-friendly)

Project title:
Institution:
Name of researcher:
Contact details of researcher:
Name of supervisor (if appropriate):
Contact details of supervisor (if appropriate):
Invitation paragraph: You have been invited to take part in this study because [list reason(s)]. Before you decide whether to take part, it is important that you fully understand what you are being asked to do and why. Please read this information sheet and feel free to asl the research team if you have any questions. Take the time to decide if you want to participant or not.
Project summary: What is the aim of the study? How does the data intend to collect from participants fit in? When will this study be completed?
What is involved? How will the data be collected by the researcher? How will the data be processed and analysed by the researcher? How will the data be used (e.g., publications, etc.) resulting from this research project? What will be done before the data is made available for other researchers to use and why is it important that we make the data available for other researchers to test at the end of this research project
How will my anonymity be protected? What will you do to ensure that participant data is protected? Will the data be given a reference code rather that a name? Will the list that links the codes and names be held in separate locations? Who on the research team and associated bodies will have access to the data? How will anonymity be protected in publication? What will you do if you discover you are unable to protect anonymity?
What happens if I change my mind and want to withdraw my data? Explain how and up to what point data can be withdrawn. This is usually until it is anonymised and incorporated into a larger dataset, where it becomes impractical to withdraw. Give a practical timescale for this.
Will I be sent a copy of the findings at the end of the research?
The Researcher can be contacted as follows: The Reseacher's academic supervisor (who can also answer any questions you might have about the researcher) can be contacted at: [e.g., email address, phone number, etc.]
Privact protection information For information about data protection policy please visit: [website address]
If you have concerns or complaints about this study, please contact the Ethics Representative at [email address] or by post at [address].
You also have the right to submit a complaint to the Information Commissioner's Office.

FIGURE 9.4 Template for the Information Form

houses the research project. The following information lays out some of the similarities that most data management plans have in common, providing a starting point for thinking through the data creation.

1. A skeleton of the project data (name, project, contact details) provides an initial overview
2. A detailed description of the data that is created and used follows, to include secondary and primary data, the format and the scale of the data, and what kind of data has been collected (e.g., personal data or professional opinions). Personal data requires specific measures, as mentioned above in the GDPR guideline discussion. While it is obvious to list the data that is intended for collection in the first place, metadata sets that are created by and from the collected data are often harder to pin down on paper. This is because such data (e.g., back up files) remain invisible unless they are searched for. Not all research projects set in stone how the data will be handled after the initial collection. Interviews can take the form of transcripts, using a speech recognition software that learns from the transcription to produce other transcriptions. These types of data might be worked into the speech recognition software as metadata that sits outside the researchers' control. Consequently, organisations should take measures to avoid potential unintended misuse of the research data by providing approved transcription tools that have gone through quality control. Therefore, a Data Management Platform (DMP) is required to explain how the data is collected.
3. Another way of keeping control of the data flow and of what happens to the data, is through secure storage. Universities have access to cloud space or servers that students and staff must use to secure and save data. It might not provide total security, but it is often the best and most secure option. In turn, the organisation takes on some of the responsibility if researchers store the data in the space provided. Data security extends to the way data is structured and explains how the data is stored (e.g., as named files, applying a coding system using pseudonyms instead of names, and cleaning the data of personal information). Finally, as part of the research design it is important to determine who has access to the data and in what form.
4. A section about ownership and intellectual property referring to any ethical implication sets out who will own the data and who has what kind of rights to the data. Are there any ethical, legal, or commercial considerations relating to the data that will impact the data flow? Questions must be asked, such as whether the data being used by a third party for a purpose that has not been originally stated (e.g., using filmed interview statements for commercial advertising or other purposes must be declared in advance and cannot be added retrospectively).

5. Data preservation and sharing must follow legal obligations. In the UK this is the GDPR UK and Data Protection Act from 2018. Data should only be kept as long as needed (i.e., for the shortest time possible, which should be defined in advance). It is possible to store data for archiving purposes, but this must be mentioned in the DMP. Sharing data is the second concern that should be addressed in advance. Smaller data sets (e. g., those collected for degree purposes) are usually not shared and remain property of the researcher, including students, but for larger sets organisational archiving policies need to be followed. I suggest discussing the project design with the data protection officer if in any doubt about how to handle the data during and after the research project has finished.

6. Researcher responsibility and training requirements are covered under data implementation. This is to ensure that researchers are made aware a final time of the need to act responsible and according to the ethical principles relating to data handling. Organisations have training modules in place when new members join, while for students DMP training has been included in the ethical training linked to the research they undertake as part of their degree studies.

Referencing and Plagiarism

Research ethics covers the collecting and analysing of data, but good referencing and citations play an important role in applied ethics by making sure that those who have contributed to the study are fully credited. Citing correctly is an indicator of respect and acknowledgement for the authors you reference, demonstrating that you care about the relationship between yourself and the authors, through the discussion of common interests.

Therefore, respect extends to writing. Thinking about the authority of the author's position as the only person to be credited allows for establishing the writer's credibility, but it also raises doubts considering that most research is a collective effort. Some methodologies reference collective writing practices or have developed specific tools such as memo writing. In grounded theory, this acts as a helping hand in reflecting about writing behaviour, as part of the research process. Using self-reflective experience as "field text", as an additional participant, works well for methodologies relating to capturing and understanding experience. The remit of ethical conduct extends much further. Referencing includes taking care of the academic community, enabling readers to locate sources, helping to spread knowledge, and facilitate growth and critical discourses of verified information. As an academic obligation, referencing ensures that all research is conducted according to ethical principles of honesty, integrity, transparency, and reproducibility. Failing to cite, which means not giving credit to authors or plagiarising (i.e., directly copying) work is considered academic theft, because it infringes on the rights of authors. Presenting somebody's work as one's own without citation and referencing is considered a

Data Management Plan

INFORMATION		
Name:		Date:
School/department:		
Email:		
Project title:		

DESCRIPTION OF THE DATA				
2.1 Describe the data that you will use in your project.				
	Description	**Primary/Secondary**	**Format/ scale**	**Sensitive? (yes/no)**
1.				
2.				
3.				
4.	*(Add new rows as required.)*			
2.2 How will the data be collected/generated/acquired?				

STORAGE AND SECURITY
3.1 How will you structure your data?
3.2 Where will you store your data, and how will it be backed up?
3.3 Who will require access to your data, and how will this be managed?
3.4 Identify the main risks to your data security. If any of your data is "Sensitive" (see 2.1), mention the stage at which anonymisation will take place.

FIGURE 9.5 Template for a Data Management Plan for a Postgraduate Research Project (based on McElroy, Birkbeck, University of London D licensed under CC BY 4.0)

ETHICS AND IP (INTELLECTUAL PROPERTY)
4.1 Who will own and have rights to your data?
4.2 Are there any ethical, legal, or commercial considerations relating to your data?
4.3 How will these concerns be dealt with?
PRESERVATION AND SHARING
5.1 What data should be retained in the long-term? How and when will it be ready for archiving?
5.2 Is the data you propose to collect (or existing data you propose to use) in the study suitable for sharing? Briefly state why it is/is not suitable.
5.3 If the data can be shared, how will you share it?
IMPLEMENTATION
6.1 Who is responsible for the actions described in this Data Management Plan?
6.2 Will you require any additional support or training in order to carry out the actions described in this Data Management Plan?

FIGURE 9.5 (Cont.)

breach of academic conduct. This is enforced through academic conduct policies that higher education institutions, for instance, have in place. Integrity, as an academic value, acknowledges that knowledge is built on the work of others, and therefore failing to reference breaks the flow of information, while neglecting responsibility and care for the academic community and the field of exploration. When researchers are unable to track citations, ideas cannot be traced back to the original author, cannot be verified, and therefore misinterpretations cannot be rectified. Consequently, the work produced is compromised. Ethics applications demands the specifics of how the research is conducted, including the use of secondary resources for justification, such as citing and referencing when the findings and outcomes are presented and discussed.

In practical terms, citations and referencing requires initial work in the early stages of academic work and study. But when the mechanism is understood, citing and referencing quickly becomes second nature. One simple rule to remember is that when using the work of other people, they need to be acknowledged in the form of academic conventions, as defined through a variety of styles. Failure to do so, could be counted as plagiarism. This applies to quoting or paraphrasing from another author, when stating opinions or when someone else's ideas are discussed.

To cite correctly, style conventions give detailed instructions on how to acknowledge works used in the text. For example, the APA style of referencing cites parenthetically, as practiced in this book. The key citation details are given directly after the quote, idea, or the piece of information used. It gives the last name of the author, the year of the publication, and the page number (if relevant). In addition, a list of references at the end of the text provides the full details of the source. Often overlooked is that self-plagiarism can be an issue and is treated as an offence when it comes to assessments. In practice, this should prevent previously submitted work from being assessed again in a different assessment.

Software tools such as the *Turnitin* platform highlight potential concerns before submission and give students and researchers the opportunity to correct any questionable or false claims. In short, any work that is submitted or has been published, including your own, must be cited. Materials that have been submitted previously also require citations and referencing. Paraphrasing is the most usual form of engaging in a discussion or putting forward an argument, summarising what the author said or taking their thoughts as inspiration to develop the argument further to illustrate a point or to underline an idea. Direct quotations, where the exact wording of the original is repeated in the text, is usually presented in quotation marks or as indented text. It could support a point with a well-chosen line from the author if the words cannot be expressed in an analogous way. Overquoting or stringing a list of quotes together does not form a good argument, and in the case of assessed work may be seen as an academic offence, even if it is referenced, because it limits the input from the person who submitted the work.

References are provided in addition to the text and depending on the style can be placed in various locations. For example, they can be positioned at the bottom of the page in the form of a numbered note, using the Chicago Manual of Style form of referencing, or with the Harvard style, at the end of the document or chapter. Paying attention to the slightly different requirements of the reference styles is important for consistency. For example, in the case of the Harvard style the terminology is specified as follows: a bibliography is a list of all the works that were used in preparing and writing up research outcomes, which is usually long and extensive; whilst a list of works cited (i.e., list of references) contains only cited references from the text. Both the bibliography and the list of references are listed alphabetically, using the author's last name or the first part of the organisation's title (e.g., works by Arts Council England are listed using "Arts"). In most cases, only one is required, either a bibliography or a list of references, but not both for the same piece of writing. The Modern Humanities Research Association style uses superscript numbers linked to a sequence of notes positioned at the bottom of each page, containing the full reference. The Modern Language Association (MLA) applies a parenthetical system (using brackets to cite in the text) but refers to the list of references at the end of the work as a bibliography. To avoid further confusion, I recommend examining the styles one at a time. Universities or subject fields, as well as publishers, all have their own preferences. In short, it will not take long to become familiar with the style guidelines, but consistent use of the same style is key, unless a distinctive style is required, such as with a different assignment coming from a different department in a university setting. Reference management software such as *Mendeley* or *Zotero* that can be integrated into writing programmes, accommodate distinctive styles, which saves time. Using these options requires that every single resource be scanned into the software programme, as a reference at least once.

Artificial Intelligence Writing Programmes

Recently, artificial intelligence-driven large language models (LLMs), such as ChatGPT and Gemini, are being used to generate ideas and act as writing assistants in many areas, including when writing up research in CCI. Among the academic community, these models have generated a great deal of discussion when deployed in relation to student assignments. As a result, many universities have implemented an AI policy that regulates specific use. This ranges from recommendations to check grammar and spelling to being classified as an assessment offence when large proportions of text produced by the AI model is falsely claimed as original work, and when sources are not acknowledged. While the models demand that users verify the information and exercise critical thinking, the speed at which the model generates text is often overwhelming and can compromise the qualities that should be employed when interpreting the text. Users of AI models are encouraged to validate the information and knowledge, but this requires that those who use these models can make judgements. In recent years, AI writing software has been adopted to facilitate critical thinking in the classroom. While exposing noncritical and incorrect examples, opinions and results of the current LLMs, it enables researchers to demonstrate that advanced academic reading and discussion remain important skills, despite advancing technological capabilities of the LLMs. AI models can only access information they have been fed with and as a result they carry forward existing bad practices, such as inequalities and inequities. These are concerns that researchers must unpack and discuss by applying academic rigour and judgement. Understanding AI models as data but not as finished text might help with validation, but it also encourages researchers to investigate the AI model itself, both in terms of what it can achieve and what it has achieved in the first instance. A similar step such as employing discourse analysis would allow for sufficient critical interpretation.

Ethical questions have also been raised around the subject of copyright and the use of unattributed online material employed to train the model. The fact that AI models produced the text and that researchers including students claim it as their original text is highly problematic and might violate copyright in two ways: (1) AI models do not distinguish between authored or nonauthored, or appropriate or non-appropriate information when searching; and (2) the text has not been structured, thought through, and written by the person who is submitting the assignment as their own work. As a moral obligation, the idea of fairness needs to be considered. For example, students in compliance with plagiarism policies and not using AI models to generate work will have invested more resources and time to draft an essay. Consequently, using AI will provide an unfair advantage. In addition, the lack of transparency and accountability of the models prevents researchers from safeguarding information in relation to serious concerns about bias, fairness, rights, and care, as outlined in the ethics of care.

AI applications are designed so that they adapt and learn on the go. Consequently, over time, the models will advance their critical discussion skills, raising many interesting questions. Now AI models can assist because they are able to process large amount of data at speed. They automate and through cross-domain comparisons can generate interdisciplinary work, but the ethical concerns have not been alleviated and therefore the use of the models without critical interpretation will remain questionable and mostly unethical.

Conclusion

Ethics, understood as a way of thinking, enables researchers to link research behaviours and actions with the fundamental value of care that society, academia, and CCI sector address together. The paradigms explained in Chapter 2 connect similarly to values assigned to generating knowledge and experience. Ethics is defined through values such as integrity, academic rigour, transparency, accountability, and taking care, enabling discussions about the moral implications of research actions.

The research ethics application processes as practiced in higher education institutions guide researchers through the various aspects that require consideration. This ranges from the ethics application to appendices, such as written consent forms, information sheets, and data management plans, as well as how to reference while avoiding plagiarism and how to approach AI language models through an ethical lens.

In this chapter, I emphasised that applied ethics as practiced and expressed through formal ethics processes transcends the idea of an administrative formality. Thinking through ethics means thinking through the process and the application. It enables an understanding of how an ethics of care can be applied by incorporating the researcher's responsibility as part of research practice that cannot be seen as separate from the content of the research.

References

Alacovska, A. & Bissonnette, J. 2021. Care-ful work: An ethics of care approach to contingent labour in creative industries. *Journal of Business Ethics*, 169: 135–151.

Aristotle 1999. *Metaphysics*. (J. Sachs, Trans.). Green Lion Press.

Aristotle 2006. *Poetics*. (J. Sachs, Trans.). Pullins Press.

Beauchamp, T. L. 2001. *Philosophical Ethics: An Introduction to Moral Philosophy*. McGraw-Hill.

Belfiore, E. 2022. Who cares? At what price? The hidden costs of socially engaged arts labour and the moral failure of cultural policy. *European Journal of Cultural Studies*, 25(1): 61–78.

Birkbeck, University of Longdon2023. Birkbeck ethics guidelines. https://www.bbk.ac.uk/research/bgrs/research-ethics-and-integrity (10 October 2023).

Bloomfield, P. 2014. *The Virtues of Happiness: A Theory of the Good Life*. Oxford University Press.

Creswell, J. W. & Creswell, J. D. 2017. *Research Design: Qualitative, Quantitative, and Mixed Methods Approach*. Sage Publications.

Denscombe, M. 2009. *Ground Rules for Social Research: Guidelines for Good Practice*. McGraw-Hill Education.

ESRC(Economic and Social Research Council)2023. *Framework for research ethics.* https://www.ukri.org/councils/esrc/guidance-for-applicants/research-ethics-guidance/framework-for-research-ethics/our-core-principles/#contents-list (accessed 5 July 2023).

Fieser, J. 2014. Ethics. *The Internet Encyclopedia of Philosophy.* http://www.iep.utm.edu/ (20 November 2023).

Fieser, J. 2000. *Moral Philosophy Through the Ages*. Mayfield Publishing Company.

Graham, C. 2012. Anonymisation: Managing data protection risk code of practice. *Information Commissioner's Office.* https://ico.org.uk/media/1061/anonymisation-code.pdf (accessed 25 March 2024).

Gregor, M. & Timmermann, J. 2014. *Immanuel Kant: Groundwork of the Metaphysics of Morals*. Cambridge University Press.

Lee, F. 2014. Anonymisation is great, but don't undervalue pseudonymisation. *fieldfisher.com.* https://www.fieldfisher.com/en/services/privacy-security-and-information/privacy-security-and-information-law-blog/anonymisation-is-great-but-dont-undervalue-pseudonymisation (25 March 2024).

Lloyd, M. (Ed.) 2015. *Butler and Ethics*. Edinburgh University Press.

Ross, W. D. 1939. *Foundations of Ethics*. Oxford University Press.

Tong, R. 1998. The ethics of care: A feminist virtue ethics of care for healthcare practitioners, *The Journal of Medicine and Philosophy: A Forum for Bioethics and Philosophy of Medicine*, 23(2): 131–152. https://doi.org/10.1076/jmep.23.2.131.8921.

Tronto J. C. 2013. *Caring Democracy: Markets, Equality, and Justice*. New York: New York University Press.

Tronto, J. C. 1998. An ethic of care. *Generations: Journal of the American Society on Aging*, 22(3): 15–20.

Van Manen, M. & van Manen, M. 2021. Doing phenomenological research and writing. *Qualitative Health Research*, 31(6): 1069–1082.

Zagzebski, L. 1996. *Virtues of the Mind*. Cambridge University Press.

Zagzebski, L. 2017. *Exemplarist Moral Theory*. Oxford University Press.

10

PRESENTING RESEARCH

Introduction

Once the research design has been implemented and the findings have been analysed and evaluated, the last step of the research process is to consider how best to present the write up. This chapter addresses the challenges that thinking and writing about methodological processes brings. It discusses how best to outline and structure a methodology chapter for a dissertation, where best to place it within the content of the larger piece of writing, and what forms and styles of presentations work for the relevant design and process.

Writing up academic research takes many forms, but it is often guided by instructions that cover framework and parameters, in which the researcher is asked to present findings and discussions about the outcomes. Practices specific to each academic discipline provide formats that extend into how and when and what to write about the methodological journey. But overall, the writing up process remains flexible and often comes down to personal preference.

Writing practices vary, can change over time, and are dependent on the nature of the project. Individual preferences come into play during writing and there is no common practice, instead there are many styles and ways that lead to the complete final piece of writing. Experience matters in writing and at degree level, assessment practices take into consideration the level and length of written work, building up the word count over time to the final piece, with a dissertation or project being the longest. This gradual increase could be reflected in writing up research outcomes, including writing practices throughout the research process. Regular comments and thoughts, as expressed in a research diary, can help with the writing up of the research. Some scholars write every day, others set aside time for writing blocks, while yet others go on writing retreats to structure the process of writing. For newer researchers, I recommend

DOI: 10.4324/9781003161912-10

trying out what works best for you, with the aim of establishing a writing routine over time.

Academic writing is a creative process and "being in the zone" (Banks 2014, Wesner 2018) or the notion of "flow" (Csikszentmihalyi et al., 2005) can be applied. This refers to those moments in writing when the words effortless appear on the page with the writer not noticing that time has passed, and when thoughts come together on paper that had remained unspoken but have been thought through before. While the notion of flow relates to the structure of thoughts and ideas, it can also be linked to the flow of the narrative, to its coherence, and the way the different parts and results are discussed. It could refer to how paragraphs are connected and how transitions are presented between arguments, paragraphs, and chapters. Ideally, a text flows when the arguments are linked to produce a coherent style of writing that captures what the researcher wanted to say as an emotive and rational experience. Good writing plans have been seen to aid coherence and logic, but this will not be a one-size-fits all approach. The actual writing process could equally be used as a structuring tool and some researchers plan best when writing, while others cannot start without having developed a detailed structure in advance. Finding out what works for you by trying out and experimenting with writing practices will deliver results that will save time and effort in subsequent research projects.

Writing as a form of expression demands mental preparation. Many professional writers go through meticulous routines before settling down to write every day, preparing themselves mentally to go into writing mode. However, writers still have good and bad days for producing written work, so being aware and accepting the ups and downs of writing practice will have to be considered when setting time limits and working towards deadlines. Writer's block remains a common challenge for many researchers, and it can occur at any stage of the writing process (Smith, 2020), for example, when it becomes difficult to concentrate or when starting to write appears as a hurdle that seems impossible to overcome. Importantly, recognition of experiencing writer's block and asking for help should go hand in hand, but the problem is not always obvious. Searching for what might be preventing you from writing is the first step towards tackling the issue.

There can be multiple factors that hinder writing flow, ranging from information overload to lack of motivation. The pressure to strive for perfection can impact a writer's motivation while a lack of clarity and direction in the research design can impede the writing progress. Translating the issues into helpful strategies would be a second step. For example, trying freewriting, which involves writing without constraints regarding perfect grammar, coherent logic, or structures, can generate momentum and help bypass self-criticism. Writing techniques such as brainstorming, and mind mapping can help to organise thoughts. In addition, sharing work with friends, peers, supervisors, and learning support tutors in the case of university-based researcher can help break the ice, provide constructive feedback, and rekindle motivation. Instead of focussing on completing the whole research write up, break it down into more manageable parts and reward yourself for completing those small individual sections, that will eventually combine to form the single overall picture. Seeking further help from writing councillors is advisable when none of the strategies work. Finally, taking a break and stepping away from the work can provide a fresh perspective as I have personally discovered on many occasions. Faced with the pressure of deadlines this often seems impossible, but by building in a buffer of time, it will better help you to manage the stress and keep you motivated.

Writing About Methodology

Explaining the process of how the research was carried out and how the data was collected and analysed may seem challenging, but to some extent it is straightforward as it covers a how-to approach. It is one of the reasons why this part of the research write up is usually done retrospectively, using materials, notes, and research diaries to share the research process with the reader and support the integrity of the research. This, in return, provides the reader with the overall validity of the research.

Addressing the complexities of the research design, as well as weaving the philosophical underpinnings of the research methodology into a coherent and convincing part of the research outcome adds another dimension to writing about methodologies. Students have often viewed this as overwhelming because of the research complexities that come together and have not always been part of their previous experience and training. The trio is a sustainable frame to understand, carry out, and explain exactly what the research entails. As explained in previous chapters, the trio of research covers the three dimensions of (1) paradigm (i.e., the philosophical underpinning), (2) methodology (i.e., the research strategy), and (3) methods (i.e., tools employed to collect and analyse data). With the help of this trio, writing about methodologies can be simplified by breaking it up into three subheadings and discussing and connecting the three separately explained processes and dimensions in a final discussion that could sit, for example, at the end of the methodology chapter for a dissertation or a doctorate.

When discussing the validity and integrity of the research, the biases and limitations of the research outcomes and research process are questioned. It provides the researcher with the opportunity to present a robust reflection on the pitfalls and an acknowledgment of the unforeseen changes in direction that occur while researching. This could be used to demonstrate to the research community what needs to be improved and reassessed when this research is repeated in a different environment. Research is meant to inspire other researchers to take the findings further, opening new research directions for the future. Being open about mistakes can be difficult and, depending on the cultural context, it may not be suitable in all situations. Students can bring this attitude to the discussion, thinking that their mistakes will be considered a failure and therefore impact them (e.g., in the form of reduced dissertation marks). In fact, the opposite is often true, at least in a UK university context, where criticality and self-reflection are an integral part of the analytical assessment. Leaving out limitations and thinking about bias will be seen as uncritical, as omission, and it could result in a lower mark in the case of HE assessments such as dissertations. What counts is an awareness that research is flexible, adaptable, and carried out by humans who don't just seek research perfection, but satisfaction and enjoyment while advancing knowledge.

While having a separate methodology chapter will work for larger research write ups, such as dissertations, for shorter pieces, a section about methodology will be sufficient. It should contain the research questions and briefly discuss the applied paradigm, methodology, and methods that will allow readers to understand how researchers arrived at the outcomes and research findings. Empowering the reader through an explanation of how the research was conducted will set the scene. Therefore, I recommend having a methodology section for shorter pieces in the introduction, but a methodology chapter for larger and longer research reports, either after the introductory chapter or after the literature review. For example, in a dissertation the methodology chapter also may act as a pre-chapter before discussing research findings generated in the field. Furthermore, if placed after the literature review that discusses multiple theoretical lenses, it will provide the foundation for the discussion of the findings (see Table 10.1). Having the methodology chapter located towards the end of the write up detracts from the importance of the outcomes, which should take centre stage in the latter part of the research paper, such as with a dissertation.

Forms and Styles of Presenting Research

For dissertations, the parameters of the how-to format are predefined in the dissertation handbook. It will be highly detailed, including font size, margins,

TABLE 10.1 Table of contents for a dissertation (including word count suggestion for a 14,000-word dissertation)

Chapters	Subheadings
Introduction (2,000 words)	
Literature review (4,000)	
Methodology (2,000)	<ul><li>Research paradigm</li><li>Methodology</li><li>Methods for data collection and for data analysis</li><li>Limitation/Bias</li></ul>
Findings (2,000)	
Discussion/analysis (3,000)	
Conclusion (1,000)	

referencing, guidance on how to present tables, grids, graphs, and illustrations. A word count margin of +/- 10% of the stated word count is likely to be adopted by most universities. An abstract or a one-page summary are also common. Most dissertations are produced, submitted, and increasingly being read as electronic copies and this should be taken into consideration when formatting.

The finishing touches to a piece of work relate to readability and how the content is organised. A common question from students asks how much detail should be presented in the text and what should be presented as evidence in the appendix. The short answer is that everything needs to go in the main body of the text that is essential for the reader to follow and understand the points raised and discussed. Further explanations, including detailed evidence, can be placed in an appendix. This follows the same logic as footnotes or endnotes that are defined as places for additional information that are useful, but not essential, for understanding the text. For example, with dissertations the appendix can contain transcripts of field notes and interviews, research memos, ethics approval paperwork, and tutorial notes, if requested by the higher education institution. Acknowledgments of all the research participants including the interviewees are foregrounded at the beginning of the dissertation or the research write up. Expressing our gratitude to research participants extends beyond the cultural kindness of a research ecology, as it also covers *duty of care* as the core value of ethical research.

As an equivalent to the dissertation the project report is another way to write up research following a predefined format. In CCI research students learn to analyse research reports that present results to the sector but this should not be confused with research papers that are published in academic journals or books. Often commissioned, these sector reports publish results in a report format, but not all academic research follows this style. In fact, the distinction between a research report and an academic paper might be determined by the research design. Reports tend to open with an executive summary of the findings, and this includes a brief note about the methodology, which is elaborated on later in a dedicated methodology section.

Not all publications that are termed research reports contain academic research. Instead, the common use of the term *research*, for example, when looking up information on the internet, can cause confusion. But after reading this book, you will be aware of the difference, and you can now distinguish between what is simply called research and the research that applies academic rigour and follows academic standards.

Storytelling

Presenting research practice in a meaningful way requires you to intertwine complex processes that cover communication, analysis, and lived experiences. The report format provides a logical structure that separates the research results from the research process, but it tends to leave out the insights that demonstrate the connection between the process and results. Narrative and story-telling embrace the holistic capacity of research, capturing the complexities of lived experiences. Therefore, presenting research as a story or in narrated form allows you to capture nuances and those previously unheard voices. As a format, narratives are accessible to a wider audience and this links to the dissemination aspect of research results. We live in a narrated world in which news, marketing, and business ideas are presented as stories to guide our understanding of the world. Utilising this when discussing research methodologies, I suggest that employing narrative tools will enhance the reader's attentiveness. I am not advocating that research write ups should be presented as novels, short stories, or film scripts, but storytelling should be a factor in the way information is presented.

Collins (2021) recalls Gabriel's six factors of storytelling practice: framing, focusing, filtering and fading, fusing, and fitting as helpful tools to engage the organisational cultures of CCI organisations. I argue these can be equally helpful activities to help propel the research write up.

1. In **framing**, characters are arranged according to their importance, thereby determining the role they play in moving the story forward. Research participants require role descriptions and explanations of who is doing what to provide a good starting point for showcasing the research process
2. For playwrights, **focusing** allows them to place special emphasis upon clusters of events at the expense of other movements and actors. Presenting methodology by focussing on one specific research result that follows through from design to implementation can be an effective example, thereby illustrating the research process in detail
3. **Filtering and fading** are activities that help to focus. In storytelling, filtering and fading occur when characters or events are removed to secure the integrity of the plot line. Likewise, researching includes filtering as an ongoing process. Materials and data are disregarded at every stage of the process, but when presenting the results thinking of a plotline equivalent that unites process thinking with focusing on results could be helpful. Asking the question of what kind of story data can tell involves two more activities: fusing and fitting
4. **Fusing** means aiding understanding through the merging of multiple events into singularities and could be read as a form of streamlining or cleaning of the plot to avoid confusion. In research, data is fused into themes that can be expressed, for example, in the form of headings while writing up. For methodologies, keeping information simple helps to ensure that the research results gain all the attention. Remember the focus will be on the results, but those need justification and validation and that is provided with the written-up research process including the methodologies
5. **Fitting** allows for the adjusting of characters and events to meet the overall requirements of the story. In research, we would adjust the writing so that it fits into the main argument. It should, but does not by default, include paying attention to the question of who will be reading the write up

In CCI, research audiences, cocreation, and participation are common topics of investigation (Bilton, 2023). I would argue that we can make beneficial use of subject-specific participation awareness not just when presenting results, but also when writing about methodologies. Being mindful of who will read the write up sets the tone and language in addition to the formal requirements of format and presentation styles. Given the popularity of storytelling beyond the art form itself, it is not surprising that some of the narrative tools work for writing up research. The relational character building that happens during the research process between the different activities goes beyond their common starting letter *F*. They are repeated in the write up, but the focus shifts from analysis as the highlight of the research process to presentation and dissemination.

Choosing narrative or storytelling presentation designs comes with the expectation that plots and characters are embedded in the write up and this can take multiple forms. While researching we encounter anecdotes, use metaphors for explanation, and create explanatory stories. When research results are presented as narratives, they can act as a reference point, for example, at the beginning and at the very end of a research paper. It might be a personal encounter or a self-reflective story that highlights the human side of research, which we tend to write out when having to conform to normative frames.

In this book, the house and associated activities that happen in the house, such as the build, the move, and living in the house have all been referenced. The house acts as a metaphor, telling the story of the research process in the different chapters and symbolising meaning, actions, and behaviours that make carrying out research worthwhile. It completes, enriches, and anchors research as an embedded activity.

Conclusion

As the final activity in the research process, writing up and presenting research not only takes many forms and practices, but it also changes over time, aided by experience. It provides the space to showcase the relationship between academic integrity and the creative writing process. It accumulates challenges that range from being in the zone to writer's block, and mental preparations provide helpful tools for navigating this process. Writing about methodology includes addressing how the research was designed, implemented, and evaluated. I suggest focussing on paradigms as the philosophical underpinning, methodologies as research strategies, and methods as tools to aid potential replication of the research process as a requirement of research integrity. Research practices develop over time and discussing research limitations can cover personal, collective, and/or societal dimensions. Research is flexible, adaptable, and can be satisfactory as a learning process, but it will never be perfect.

Where to place a methodology chapter within a longer piece of writing, such as a dissertation, depends on the frame of reference and on the methodology. Personally, I would place it in the first half of the work to avoid distracting from the analysis and the discussion of the results. Depending on the forms and style of the presentation, the weighting, and the level of detail of the research process differs. For example, many reports provide a short summary at the beginning and then additional detail later. In contrast, dissertation work utilises a separate chapter, while research papers cover the research process in a methodology section or paragraph.

Readability remains an important condition for any write up and in presenting research. Therefore, the role of participants and audiences must be considered, including their familiarity with academic writing. The use of narratives and storytelling practices can be helpful in providing a common ground of understanding, while metaphors, introductory narratives, and explanatory stories help capture the complexities of research, while simultaneously including the relational aspects.

Returning to the concept of the activities around the house as a symbol or metaphor for the content, I envisage that you have been living in the house for a while, using paradigms, methodologies, and methods comfortably. As a result, you are now familiar with the surroundings, and have explored the neighbourhood, in this case the adjacent literature. The house has become a home. Even though, you will have a few maintenance projects lined up, for example, exploring new emerging methodologies or paradigms, in the future you may move and start building once again.

References

Banks, M. 2014. 'Being in the Zone' of Cultural Work. *Culture Unbound*, 6(1): 241–262.

Bilton, C. 2023. *Cultural Management: A Research Overview*. Routledge.

Collins, D. 2021. *Rethinking Organizational Culture: Redeeming Culture Through Stories*. Routledge.

Elliot, Andrew. J., & Dweck, Carol. S. (Eds.) 2012. *Handbook of Competence and Motivation*. Guilford Publications.

Smith, H. 2020. *The Writing Experiment: Strategies for Innovative Creative Writing*. Routledge.

Wesner, S. 2018. Artists' professionalisation and careers in the cultural policy landscape. In S. Wesner, *Artists' Voices in Cultural Policy: Careers, Myths and the Creative Profession after German Unification* (pp. 145–176). Springer.

INDEX

Printed in the United States
by Baker & Taylor Publisher Services